Enter the Rest

Lessons from the epistle to the Hebrews

By
Israel Harel

PRESS

This book was originally written as a series of sermons I taught in Sha'ar HaEmeq Congregation. It was not my intention to delve deeply into all the issues discussed in the epistle to the Hebrews. If I had tried to do that, a room full of books would not have sufficed.

Jewish thought has always been varied and multi-directional, which is why the saying "provide yourself with a teacher"[1] is considered an important principle in Judaism. It means, in fact, that you should find yourself a teacher who shares your own worldview. From the days of the Second Temple there have been varying, even contradictory, schools of thought in Judaism. For example, until recently, the mainstream Orthodox Jews have regarded the Chassidic Jewish movement, and the Chassidic veneration of their Rebbe as Messiah, as both idol worship and a deviation from true Judaism. Nevertheless, in general Jewish belief, both schools of thoughts are a part Orthodox Judaism.

Many of the seeds of modern Jewish thought already existed two thousand years ago, in some form or other. The epistle to the Hebrews in the New Testament was written as part of an ongoing dialogue within the Jewish world. Its purpose was to respond to certain claims based on concepts that existed in the Jewish world at that time. Those same concepts are found, at least in part, in modern Judaism.

In this series of sermons I sought to single out the scarlet thread that passes through the epistle and to follow it through. I attempted to understand why the epistle was written, and for what purpose. What need among the Jews of his day was the author addressing in his epistle?

Work on this book has been a great blessing for me. It goes without saying that the book could never have been written without the support of all those who encouraged me to write down my sermons. My thanks to my wife who has always been there for me and has always made sure I lacked for nothing while I was working. Without you, Shlomit, I am lacking! Thanks to Hila, who laboriously transcribed the recorded sermons; to Jonathan who encouraged me; to Wiert Douglas of CGI in Holland, who motivated me to write; to Maya Rechnitzer who edited the text and asked all the right questions; to James Priest and Stephen Lowe who worked on the English manuscript; and to others around the world who have supported and encouraged me. And above all my thanks to Jesus, without whom I would either have been dead long ago or a homeless drug addict lost on the streets.

– Israel Harel

---

[1] Mishnah- Masechet Avot, 1:6

Table of Contents:

CHAPTER 1

Introduction:
The Uniqueness and Significance
of the Epistle

I think that when we read this epistle, we tend to miss its purpose, and whom it was intended for. As a Messianic Jew I understand that the letter was addressed to us in particular. As such, it would be a mistake for Jewish believers in Jesus to regard it as just another epistle written for all believers, and thus miss the relevance of the epistle to us. It was written specifically for Jewish believers as a whole. If the epistle had been written today it would probably have been called "The Letter to the Jews," for it speaks to the history, culture, and religious beliefs of the Jewish people, and how we tend to neglect or misunderstand the incredible and wonderful truth behind the Sabbath.

It is true, of course that the epistle was generally written for all believers, both Jews and Gentiles alike. It is a part of the Holy Scriptures. It was written by the inspiration of the Spirit of God. It is the Word of God, divine truth, and relevant to every person, whoever he may be. At the same time it was written specifically to Jewish believers who were suffering for their faith in

Jesus. We see at various places in the epistle (especially Chapter 12:1-7) that the Jewish believers were undergoing persecution and hardship:

> Therefore, since we have so great a cloud of witnesses surrounding us, let us also lay aside every encumbrance and the sin which so easily entangles us, and let us run with endurance the race that is set before us, fixing our eyes on Jesus, the author and perfecter of faith, who for the joy set before Him endured the cross, despising the shame, and has sat down at the right hand of the throne of God. For consider Him who has endured such hostility by sinners against Himself, so that you will not grow weary and lose heart. You have not yet resisted to the point of shedding blood in your striving against sin; and you have forgotten the exhortation which is addressed to you as sons, 'My son, do not regard lightly the discipline of the Lord, nor faint when you are reproved by Him; for those whom the Lord loves he disciplines, and he scourges every son whom He receives.' It is for discipline that you endure; God deals with you as with sons; for what son is there whom his father does not discipline?

These were Jews suffering persecution. In fact, this may be true of all first-generation Jewish followers of Jesus.

A Time of Transition

The epistle addressed the people of Israel at a time and age when the nation was experiencing tremendous transition. Any change in our lives is difficult. We need a great deal of time to adapt our way of thinking, to free ourselves from earlier habits and conceptions, to comprehend the freedom, and to take in the changes. I remember, for example, that after my marriage it took me almost a year to be able to say "my wife" without that sounding strange to me. When people move to a new house it can take over a year before they begin to feel "at home" in the new place.

This transition takes time. If an individual's transition takes so long, how much more difficult must it be for an entire nation? Think of the people of Israel in the exodus from Egypt. It took the span of a generation – forty years – for their way of thinking to be changed from that of slaves to that of a free people on their way to conquer the Promised Land. Only then were they ready to enter the land. It is said that it took God one night to get the people of Israel out of Egypt, but forty years to get Egypt out of the people of Israel.

When we first come to faith in Jesus Christ, it takes us quite some time to understand the Scriptures in depth, to internalize them, to be freed of old habits, and to begin to walk in the new life more and more. For us as individuals, it is a very difficult process to change our ways of thinking and understanding. As a nation, the process is even more complex and difficult. At least one generation is necessary to effect a change in a nation's way of thinking. The letter to the Hebrews was written in order to help the Jewish disciples of Jesus, as a group and as individuals, to internalize the necessary changes to their ways of thinking.

The Date, Author and Aims of the Letter

The epistle was written between 55-65 AD. We know that it was written before the destruction of the Second Temple because chapter 9:8-9 says, "The Holy Spirit

11

is signifying this, that the way into the Holy Place has not yet been disclosed while the outer Tabernacle is still standing, which is a symbol for the present time. Accordingly both gifts and sacrifices are offered which cannot make the worshiper perfect in conscience." The author mentions that "the outer Tabernacle is still standing." This would suggest that the epistle was written at a time when the Second Temple was still standing.

Jesus was crucified between the years AD 30-33, and the temple was destroyed in AD 70. Approximately forty years passed between the crucifixion of Messiah and the destruction of the temple. This is the span of a generation, the same time it took the people of Israel to move from Egypt to the Promised Land.

During these years when the Temple was still standing, the Jewish believers in Jesus needed to change their understanding and perception of the worship of God. Eventually they did come to the understanding that the Temple in Jerusalem had ceased to be the focus of worship to God on Earth. They saw that the center of worship had moved from the Temple in Jerusalem to the Heavenly Temple, and to the place within that is indwelt by the Spirit of God. Because the Jewish Believers in Jesus had made this mental change, the destruction of the Temple was not the mortal blow that it was to those who had rejected Jesus as the Messiah.

So even here there is a process that lasts the span of a generation, from the crucifixion of Jesus to the destruction of the Temple. This is not just a coincidence. God commands the times. He is the One who gave these forty years to move away from Temple-centered worship to the worship that centered in the Heavenly Temple: on Jesus. God knows exactly when events must take place, when the right moment has come, and when people are ready; as it is written, "But when the fullness of the time came, God sent forth His Son, born of a woman, born under the Law" (Gal. 4:4).

The epistle was written in order to help the Jewish disciples of Jesus, who were in the process of changing their understanding regarding the manner in which they worshipped. Their former understanding was rooted in their hearts and minds, because that particular manner had been practiced by Israel for hundreds of years. They had worshipped God by working to keep the Law, and now the time had come for them to rely on the work of Christ.

We are familiar with the debate among the Jewish believers in the first century: some demanded that Gentiles who started to follow the Jewish Messiah convert to Judaism and be circumcised (see Acts 15). This is a testimony to the process they were going through in an attempt to answer such questions as, "What does it mean to be a believer in Jesus?" "What actual consequences are there to faith in Jesus?" And, "How do we, as disciples of Jesus express this new relationship with God?" In the years between the crucifixion and the destruction of the second Temple, the believers struggled even more over these issues, as the old way of worship, the Temple, was still standing. As mentioned earlier, this epistle was written to help Jewish believers to internalize the required changes and to find an answer to these burning questions.

The epistle doesn't specify where it was written, but judging by the quote from chapter 13:24 that says, "… Those from Italy greet you…" we can infer that it was written in Italy. The author's identity is not known, neither is his name mentioned even once. One of the most accepted theories today, which was held by the Church

Fathers, is that Paul the Apostle wrote the epistle. Paul was imprisoned in Rome until his execution in AD 55. It could be that he wrote the epistle from prison, perhaps by means of Timothy who had been imprisoned with him for some of the time. But the problem with this theory is the total lack of the Paul's usual identifying marks. It is obvious that the author is deeply knowledgeable about the Temple worship; that he thinks as a Jew; and that he is well acquainted with the Old Testament. But in Paul's other epistles, he tended to add personal remarks such as "I write with my own hand," or used typical phrases such as: "Grace be unto you and peace from God our Father," or "The salutation by the hand of me Paul". Paul usually mentioned himself in his epistles. Yet none of these identifying marks are found in this letter to the Hebrews.

Another theory is that Silas is the author. Others assert that it was Apollos, of whom we are told that he was "mighty in the Scriptures" (Acts 18:24). We actually have no way of knowing exactly who wrote the epistle. In any case, when the New Testament writings were collated, this epistle was unquestioningly accepted as part of the canon. Everyone acknowledged the authority of its writer.

The main aims of the epistle are as follows:

- To explain more exactly who Jesus is and what He has done.
- To refute and correct common errors in Judaism – errors that still exist today in both Judaism and among believers in Jesus. For example, the issue of whether the Mosaic Law is still binding on Jewish believers in Jesus, and whether its authority is forever. The epistle touches on questions (still relevant in Israel today) such as: Is

Jesus God? Is He all man, or just in part? Usually the epistles to the Galatians and the Corinthians are quoted in such debates, but it is in fact the epistle to the Hebrews that presents the most powerful proofs to respond to the questions of who Jesus really is, whether believers are obliged to observe the Law, and if so, which Law.

The letter was composed in order to encourage, to give hope, and to strengthen the believers who were facing hardship and persecution. The epistle is principally addressed to Jewish believers but of course the purpose it serves is relevant to all believers, as we read in chapter 2:1: "For this reason we must pay much closer attention to what we have heard, so that we do not drift away from it."

We have been told that the purpose of the letter is to focus our hearts on the truth of God concerning the identity of Christ, and to correct mistaken thinking so that we stay on the true path. We really do need that! The main focus of the epistle is to address the identity of Christ, and how we can finally enter the Sabbath rest of God through His perfect works.

Who Is Jesus?

The author of the epistle begins with the claim that Jesus is God. The entire epistle is based on this central, opening declaration:

God, who at various times and in various ways spoke in time past to the fathers by the prophets, has in these last days spoken to us by His Son, whom He has appointed heir of all things, through whom also He made the worlds; who being the brightness of His glory and the

15

express image of His person, and upholding all things by the word of His power, when He had by Himself purged our sins, sat down at the right hand of the Majesty on high, having become so much better than the angels, as He has by inheritance obtained a more excellent name than they. (Heb.1:1-4 NKJV)

He opens with an earth-shattering statement, one that is hard to take in, especially in those days: Jesus is God. He is not half-God, or a little lower than God, as the Jehovah's Witnesses claim. He is God. He made the heavens and the earth. He is the brightness of God's glory, the express image of the invisible God; He carries all things by His mighty word of power.

If we ask a nuclear scientist what holds the atoms together so that the material of the universe does not fall apart and disperse, his answer (if he is forthright) would be that he doesn't know what holds the world together, or what causes the atom particles to stick together. He may speak of the electromagnetic field and positives and negatives, but in truth the magnetic field is not enough in itself to hold the atomic particles together. The distance between the protons and the electrons and the neutrons is immense. In fact, scientists do not know exactly what this mysterious power is that binds them together. We, on the other hand, know that God is the One who holds all things by His power and His mighty word.

Jesus sits on the right hand side of glory. We do not believe in three Gods. We believe that one God has revealed Himself to us in three ways. This one God has three persons. Jesus is God. That is the first statement.

The second assertion made is that Jesus is greater than the prophets. God spoke many times and in various ways to the fathers by the prophets, and He has spoken to us in these last days. Jesus is not the last of the prophets; He is the One who fulfills everything. The Muslims believe that Muhammad was the last and greatest of all the prophets, but it is Jesus who is greater and more important than all the rest of the prophets. His word is the last word. He fulfills everything they said. He is the ultimate authority.

The next assertion is that Jesus is greater than the angels. Chapter one speaks of this, particularly in verse four: "Being made so much better than the angels, as he hath by inheritance obtained a more excellent name than they". Judaism, and the Kabbalah in particular, speaks of three "shades" (*gvanim*), that are God: God, the Holy Spirit, and Metatron[1] - the angel of God's presence.[2] This angel is known in Jewish thought as a special angel who represents God. He speaks in the name of God and bears the name of God, but he is an angel. The Scriptures say that Jesus is much more than that, because the name he has inherited is far greater, far more exalted than that of the angels.

The following assertion made is that Jesus is greater than Moses. In chapter 3:1-6 we read:

> Therefore, holy brethren, partakers of a heavenly calling, consider Jesus, the Apostle and High Priest of our confession; He was faithful to Him who appointed Him, as Moses also was in all His house. For He has been counted worthy of more glory than Moses, by just so much as the builder of the house has more honor than the house. For every house is built by someone, but the builder of all things is God. Now Moses was faithful in all His house as a servant, for a testimony of those things which were to be spoken later; but Christ

was faithful as a Son over His house—whose house we are, if we hold fast our confidence and the boast of our hope firm until the end.

We must understand Jesus' supremacy today after two thousand years of Christian faith have passed. Believers in Jesus have been around for a long time, and have come to understand and comprehend many things that were not yet so clear in those days. For a Jew in the first century AD, in the era of the Second Temple, the thought of Jesus being greater than Moses was a drastic change, something immense.

The next assertion is that Jesus is even greater than Abraham, Father of the Nation:

> Now observe how great this man was to whom Abraham, the patriarch, gave a tenth of the choicest spoils. And those indeed of the sons of Levi who receive the priest's office have com- mandment in the Law to collect a tenth from the people, that is, from their brethren, although these are descended from Abraham. But the one whose genealogy is not traced from them collected a tenth from Abraham and blessed the one who had the promises. But without any dispute the lesser is blessed by the greater (Heb. 7:4-7).

The greater blesses the lesser. Here, Jesus blesses Abraham. The same priest, who arose on the order of Melchizedek rather than the order of Aaron, is Jesus. It is He who received the tithe from Abraham, He who blessed Abraham, as it is written that the lesser is blessed by the one greater than he, and as we see in the Sabbath blessing, when the father blesses his children. The greater blesses the lesser; Abraham was

18

blessed by the Messiah.

Jesus is greater than the priests and the High Priests:

> For it was fitting for us to have such a High Priest, holy, innocent, undefiled, separated from sinners and exalted above the heavens; who does not need daily, like those High Priests, to offer up sacrifices, first for His own sins and then for the sins of the people, because this He did once for all when He offered up Himself. For the Law appoints men as High Priests who are weak, but the word of the oath, which came after the Law, appoints a Son, made perfect forever (Heb. 7:26-28).

Chapter eight continues to develop the claim that Jesus is higher than the High Priests.

The central claims of the Epistle to the Hebrews are that Jesus is God (something that demands a fundamental change of thought); Jesus is the purpose – He is the end, the final word of the prophets; Jesus is higher than the angels; Jesus is greater than Moses; Jesus is greater than Abraham; Jesus is higher than the High Priests.

What Did Jesus Do?

Of all of the most important claims regarding what He did, the first thing – and perhaps the most surprising – is in chapter 7:12, "For when the priesthood is changed, of necessity there takes place a change of law also". Jesus changed the Law. Judaism today, as well as many believers in Jesus, teaches that the Law existed before the creation of the world. Jewish sources teach that the Law never changes and is eternal. Many followers of Jesus have adopted this view. These people are confused between what Law is, and include in the Law all the rabbinic teachings, legends and various conjectures.

Here we read clearly that the Law does change – Jesus has changed the Law. How He changed it and what He did – this is what we will study more carefully in the next chapters. But the main point concerning change in the Law is stated in chapter 9 verse 10, "since they relate only to food and drink and various washings, regulations for the body imposed until a time of reformation." The word "reformation" in Hebrew is *tikun*. Chassidism brought the term *tikun* into the Hebrew language as a commonly used word, but the Breslau or Chabad Chassidim mean something different by *tikun* than what we read here. They speak of rectification, or mending the world. They say we are broken, damaged, and that the world is damaged. By keeping the Law and observing the commandments we help to mend and restore the world. It is true that we are damaged and the world is damaged. But it is not man's observance of the Law that restores it. It is God Himself who will make a new creation, as He has already done in the lives of those who believe in Jesus.

It is written that Jesus changed the Law and the outward observances that were given until the time of reformation or restoration. Furthermore, it is Jesus who made the restoration. It follows that the outward observances of the commandments do not restore anything, but are themselves restored or mended by Jesus. Jesus is the restorer. Jesus changed the law when the priesthood was changed. We will enlarge upon this further on.

In chapter 9:11-12 it is written, "[b]ut when Christ appeared as a High Priest of the good things to come, He entered through the greater and more perfect Tabernacle, not made with hands, that is to say, not of this creation; and not through the blood of goats and calves, but through His own blood, He entered the Holy Place once for all, having obtained eternal redemption".

It is written here that He came into a more real Tabernacle, a greater Tabernacle, a more perfect Tabernacle that is not made by hands. Jesus serves in the Holy Place there. There he made His sacrifice, the true sacrifice that once and for all obtained redemption and the cleansing from sin. In verse 12 we see that there is a Holy of Holies there, and that Jesus has entered into it.

In Hebrews 8:6 we read, "[b]ut now He has obtained a more excellent ministry, by as much as He is also the mediator of a better covenant, which has been enacted on better promises." In other words, Jesus brings a better covenant than the one God made with the people of Israel when He brought them out of Egypt. He is the mediator of a more exalted covenant.

If you are a student in school, you get grades A, B, C, D, or F. These verses tell us that the covenant that Jesus brings is not only a better covenant, it is an A+ covenant! It is more excellent. In the same verse we read that Jesus is the mediator of a more excellent covenant, and also that Jesus gave us better promises. Jesus is a better priest, more exalted, and the mediator of a more excellent covenant that is based on better promises. That is, the promises that were given to those who have a part in the more excellent covenant are much better than the promises given to the people of Israel. It is not only that the promises He gave are better, but also He gives a greater hope, as we read in 7:19, "(for the law made nothing perfect), on the other hand, there is the bringing in of a better hope, through which we draw near to God".

He is also a better sacrifice:

> But when Christ appeared as a high priest of the good things to come, He entered through the greater and more perfect tabernacle, not made with hands, that is to say, not of this creation; and not through the blood of goats and calves, but through His own blood, He entered the Holy Place once for all, having obtained eternal redemption. For if the blood of goats and bulls and the ashes of a heifer sprinkling those who have been defiled sanctify for the cleansing of the flesh, how much more will the blood of Christ, who through the eternal Spirit offered Himself without blemish to God, cleanse your conscience from dead works to serve the living God? (9:11-14).

Again, here we read of the greater and more perfect Tabernacle that does not belong to this creation.

His sacrifice is also much more effective, as we read in chapter 10:11-14:

> Every priest stands daily ministering and offering time after time the same sacrifices, which can never take away sins; but He, having offered one sacrifice for sins for all time, sat down at the right hand of God, waiting from that time onward until His enemies be made a footstool for his feet. For by one offering He has perfected for all time those who are sanctified.

His sacrifice has perfected the saints.

The final and most important point is that Jesus has prepared something much better for us. "And all these, having gained approval through their faith, did not receive what was promised, because God had provided something better for us, so that apart from us they would not be made perfect" (11:39-40). In chapter 11 the writer of the Epistle speaks of the heroes of the faith, both those who did wonderful things and those who suffered. At the end of the chapter he says: "With all the things they did and with all they waited for in expectation, God has prepared something better for us".

---

[1] Babylonian Talmud, Hagiga 15a, Sanhedrin 38b, Avoda Zara 3b
[2] "The angel of His presence" is mentioned specifically in Isaiah 63:9 and referred to elsewhere.

CHAPTER 2

God Expresses Himself through His Son

The key sentence summarizing the theme of this epistle is found in chapter 1:1-4:

> God, after He spoke long ago to the fathers in the prophets in many portions and in many ways, in these last days has spoken to us in His Son, whom He appointed heir of all things, through whom also He made the world. And He is the radiance of His glory and the exact representation of His nature, and upholds all things by the word of His power. When He had made purification of sins, He sat down at the right hand of the Majesty on high, having become as much better than the angels, as He has inherited a more excellent name than they.

The author of the Epistle doesn't waste his readers' time. He doesn't ask "How are you doing?" or tell them "From me… to the saints that…" or "to the beloved of God" as we see in the other epistles. He gets straight to the point and opens with something that sounded bold then– and still seems very hard to swallow for many people today – Jesus is God[1].

God Wants Us to Know Him

The first thing he says is, "God has spoken again and again." He spoke so that we would listen to Him, so that we would know Him. When someone speaks, he speaks in order to express himself so that those around him will get to know who and what he is. And, they learn things about him such as, "What does he think about this or that? "Does he have a sense of humor?" "Does he have a hot temper?" "Is he frivolous?" "What is his character like?" "Who is he really?" All these can be learned from what a person says or speaks about. If someone keeps silent you cannot find out who he really is, just as it is written, "Even a fool, when he keeps silent, is considered wise; when he closes his lips, he is considered prudent" (Prov. 17:28). That is, when even a foolish man keeps quiet, he is thought to be wise because no one knows who he really is. They don't see what is in his heart, as is written, "A good man out of the good treasure of his heart brings forth good; and an evil man out of the evil treasure of his heart brings forth evil. For out of the abundance of the heart his mouth speaks" (Luke 6:45).

So it is through speech that the inner qualities of a man are revealed. Without communication it is impossible to hold a true relationship. It is not necessary to always speak, and sometimes it is good to be quiet altogether; but if we did not have times when we spoke and opened our hearts to each other, we wouldn't have a relationship. The more we open our heart, the closer we get to each other. Communication makes the development of relationship possible. Speech is an exposure of one's self. When someone wants others to get to know him he speaks up and introduces himself. We read in verse 1 that God is the One who spoke. While it is true that God is a God who hides, as is written in Isaiah 44:15, He is also a God who chooses to reveal Himself to us because He wants us to know Him. God doesn't just want us to know Him by demanding that we take all the steps necessary on our part, He is the one who takes the initiative! He is the God who speaks. He takes practical steps for us to get to know Him.

There are those who say, "Your God is not a good God. You claim that your God is a God of love and a God of judgment. If He is a good and loving God, how can He bring judgment on the earth? Judgment and punishment are the opposite of love. So all that you say about God judging the world and sending people to hell just goes to show that He is not good and loving. He is either a good God, who loves everyone and doesn't send anyone to hell, or He is bad and sends people to hell." They do not listen to what God says through the prophets, that He is a God of love and that His judgment comes out of love. Through His judgment we come to know God. They try to fit God into their way of thinking, so it is quite impossible to get them to see their error. The only way to know God is by paying attention to what He says, that is, to what He reveals of Himself, not what we want Him to be.

God spoke "by the prophets". The prophets were the ones who actually spoke the words of God, but they were a tool and a means, like the glass that lets in the light. The message was filtered through them, and therefore the character of the prophet was revealed in the way in which he spoke. For instance, Jeremiah is known as the lamenting prophet. The prophecies of Ezekiel have a different character, as do the prophecies of Isaiah and the other prophets. The style and manner of expression of each prophet is different even if the content is similar. But what they reveal to us about God and His character is the same. The way in which God spoke through Jesus was clearer, just as light that comes straight to us without going through glass first is clearer than light through glass. God's character was revealed in Jesus. Jesus Himself said, "He who has seen Me has seen the Father" (John 14:9). This is something no prophet ever claimed, nor ever could claim. The same God "spoke long ago to the fathers in the prophets in many portions and in many ways, in these last days has spoken to us in His Son" (Heb. 1:1-2). In these days He has spoken and speaks to us in the most perfect and direct way, by the Son.

Logos-The Word of God

The Son is called "the Word" in the Gospel of John chapter 1:1, "In the beginning was the Word, and the Word was with God, and the Word was God." In Greek the word translated as "word" is *logos*. What does this word mean? In Greek this concept of "the word that is God" is very strange, but if I were a Jew living in the days of the Second Temple this concept would have been absolutely clear to me. At that time the Jews were familiar with the term *mimra*. *Mimra de-ya* in Aramaic means the "word of God." This phrase takes several forms in the sources – *mimra de-ya, mimraya, mimra-yah, mimra dyyy*".

Psalms 33:6 says, "By the word of the Lord the heavens were made, And by the breath of His mouth all their host". In the first or second century Neophyte translation of the Torah into Aramaic, the term *mimra de-ya* is used over and over. For example in Genesis 1:3 we read, "and *the word of God (mimra de-ya)* said let there be light and there was light as the word of God commanded." This shows us that the concept *mimra de-ya* or *mimraya* or *mimra dyyy*, which means the word of God as the essence of God, was an understood concept, acceptable and familiar in the Judaism of the Second Temple period. Even today if we speak with orthodox Jews who are well acquainted with the Jewish sources, and use the term *mimra de-ya*, they will know what we mean.

Therefore, the author of the epistle is telling us that God spoke in the past in different ways and means to our forefathers through *mimra de-ya*, the word of God. The Greek word *logos* is actually a translation of a Jewish concept familiar in that day. This was not a concept that would have been familiar to the Greeks. There are many such terms in the New Testament that did not exist in Greek, but were coined in order to try to convey the meaning of the Hebrew terms that spoke of God.

Daniel Gruber speaks extensively on this subject in "Copernicus and the Jews."[2] One example he brings in his book are the words of love the Christian world loves to teach about– *philia, agape, and eros*. The common explanation in the Christian world is that *philia* is friendship or the love of companionship, *eros* is sexual love, and *agape* is the love that God gives generously and unconditionally.

There is a big problem with this kind of understanding of the word *agape*, because in effect these understandings were strange to the Greeks. Which of the Greek gods showed generous and unconditional love (*agape*)? Zeus? Hermes? Venus? None of them! In their culture, and in their mythology, nothing demonstrated or spoke of a divine unconditional love. What has happened is that these terms are actually "Greek-Hebrew;" that is, an attempt to convey Hebrew-Jewish concepts into Greek in such a way that could make these concept understood in a language that had no comparable concept. When one language is translated into another, one seeks a similar term that will convey the same picture. In Greek, the concept of a God who loves unconditionally did not exist until the Jewish God of love was introduced to them. In the Greek New Testament the words *agape* and *philia* are used again and again interchangeably in an attempt to convey the meaning of love into Greek. I recommend this very interesting book by Daniel Gruber.

The process of translating Hebrew concepts into Greek was common in those days as a result of the process of translating the Hebrew Bible into Greek (the Septuagint), the use of which was widespread by the beginning of the first century AD. In the process of translation, the translators had to cope with the difficulty of translating Hebrew words and concepts that lacked similar terms in Greek. The term *logos* went through the same process. It is an attempt to translate a Jewish concept that was familiar to the Judaism of the days before and after the destruction of the Second Temple: *mimra de-ya*.

The same God who wished to reveal Himself to mankind sent His word to represent Him in the purest form: not by various manners, not in many ways, but in the way that was most clear – Jesus as the Word of God, *Mimra De-Ya*. This same Word of God became man, "And the Word became flesh, and dwelt among us, and we saw His glory, glory as of the only begotten from the Father, full of grace and truth" (John 1:14).

God spoke to the world through Jesus, who is the Word of God, to reveal Himself to the world. That is why, when the disciples of Jesus asked Him to "show us the Father", he asked "What for?" He then explained, "He who has seen me has seen the Father…[because]…I and the Father are one (John14:9; 10:30).

We read of Jesus in Hebrews 1:3, "And He is the radiance of His glory and the exact representation of His nature, and upholds all things by the word of His power". What does this mean? Glory is the radiation and diffusion of light. When we say His face radiated, we mean that His face produced light. We can see that because of the glow of the light beams that bring the light to our eyes. When a lamp shines it diffuses light. The beams carry the light from the lamp to our eyes so that we can see it. When Jesus is called "the radiance of His glory", it means that He carries the glory of God to us in a way that enables us to see it. The same Word of God who put on flesh, who is the express image of God, who reflects Him, is the one who came to earth so that we may know God. He put on flesh. It is He who brought the glory of God to us so that we can see Him and know Him. Jesus said that whoever has seen Him has seen the Father.

It is written of Jesus that He is the express image of His person. The word "image" (*tselem*) in Hebrew is taken from the word *tsel*: a shadow. The Modern Hebrew word for 'photography', *tsilum,* is also based on the word *tassel.* In Greek the word for image has the connotation of "character". Jesus is the character of God, it is He who radiates the glory of God and brings it to our eyes so that we can see Him. He shows us the divine glory. He is the personality, the character of the invisible God – He came to dwell among us that we may see Him, know Him, and rest in Him. Immanuel!

---

[1] In the Kabala, when speaking of Ps. 89:38, there is a discussion of the term "*hitabarta im meshichecha*" (translated as: You have

been full of wrath against Your anointed) which could be translated as: You got pregnant with your anointed, your Messiah. The
Lubavitch say it speaks of their Rabbi. Taken from "The commandment is a candle and the Torah is a light by the middle
Rabbi of the Lubavitch" as was published in an ad in Maariv daily
newspaper 27.March.2011 page 9 in Hebrew.

[2] The Separation of Church & Faith, Vol. 1. Copernicus and the
Jews. Daniel Gruber, 2005. Elijah Publishing.

CHAPTER 3

Jesus Is Greater than the Angels

"Having become as much better than the angels, as He has inherited a more excellent name than they," (Heb. 1:4). Almost everything we read in chapters one and two of this epistle argues that Jesus is greater than the angels. Why was it so important to the author to make this statement at the very beginning of his letter? Because Judaism placed great emphasis on angels, both before the destruction of the second temple and after.

Judaism's Doctrine of Angels

In order to see how this understanding developed we have to understand what happened in the exile. The captivity of Babylon, which began at about 590BC, was understood to have come as punishment for idol worship, so the rabbis in Babylon made great efforts to distance themselves from any kind of personification of God. The Old Testament speaks of God bringing the people of Israel out of Egypt with a mighty hand and outstretched arm; of God sitting on His throne; and so on. All these are examples of anthropomorphism: the attribution of human form or behavior to something without human form or behavior. They help us to understand and to relate to God on one hand, but they also brought about idol worship and the creation of statues to represent the invisible and incomprehensible God – just as the statues and icons are venerated today in the Orthodox and Catholic churches. But even this attempt to avoid idol worship by eschewing any form of anthropomorphism has its dangers. The rabbis avoided anything even remotely resembling an attempt to personify God by attributing an image to Him, or portraying Him – even in thought. However, their reaction increasingly led to a conception of a distant God who was detached from man's daily life. Their policy exalted and glorified God, but it also alienated Him, making Him to be a God who cannot relate to us personally. Angels, who were believed to be closer to man, filled the resulting vacuum.

This way of thinking in Judaism of that day is reflected in the *targumim* (lit. "translations, interpretations"), the Aramaic translations of the Hebrew Bible for the Jews who lived in the Diaspora around the time of Jesus and after. The *targumim* were basically interpretations of the Bible. For instance, in Genesis 3:5 Satan is tempting Adam and Eve to eat from the fruit of the tree of the knowledge of good and evil, "and you will be like God, knowing good and evil." The Aramaic translation replaces the word "God" with "angels."[1] The angels take God's place, or at least, become partners in the act of Creation. This is still so in Judaism today.

In Genesis 1:26 we read, "Then God said, "Let Us make man in Our image, according to Our likeness", the *targum* say that He spoke to the angels, when He said "let us make man in our image."[2] According to rabbinical understanding, the angels shared in the work of creation. They were partners with God. They were the mediators between Him and man because God was too exalted to have a personal relationship with us. The angels fill the vacuum created by a God made distant.

Judaism speaks of various levels of angels. The four angels closest to God are Michael and Gabriel who are mentioned in the Bible, and Uriel and Raphael who appear in the Jewish sources. In addition, there are other angels of lesser standing. God is distant from man, but the angels are close to mankind, and are the mediators. It seems that in part this is true, as the New Testament bears witness to this kind of thinking and understanding.

In Acts 7:53 we read, "you who received the law as ordained by angels, and yet did not keep it." Stephen is speaking here to the Sanhedrin and addresses them in their own language. The Old Testament does not say that angels gave the Law. We read that God gave it to Moses. But this was the understanding of the day, and possibly the angels really were involved in the process. The epistle to the Galatians also says that the Law was given by the angels, "The law was given through angels and entrusted to a mediator" (Gal. 3:19, NIV).

The New Testament also mentions various levels of angels, though in a different manner from that of the rabbinical sources and the Apocrypha. In the epistle to the Romans we read, "For I am convinced that neither death, nor life, nor angels, nor principalities, nor things present, nor things to come, nor powers, nor height, nor depth, nor any other created thing, will be able to separate us from the love of God, which is in Christ Jesus our Lord" (Rom. 8:38-39). Here the author speaks of angels, powers, principalities, height and depth, and he defines them as creatures.

1 Peter says Jesus "is at the right hand of God, having gone into heaven, after angels and authorities and powers had been subjected to Him" (I Pet. 3:22). In

Ephesians we read "For our struggle is not against flesh and blood, but against the rulers, against the powers, against the world forces of this darkness, against the spiritual forces of wickedness in the heavenly places" (Eph. 6:12). Here again the apostle speaks of principalities and powers in heaven.

The epistle to the Hebrews was written to help the Jewish followers of Jesus change the way of thinking that was widespread in the days before Jesus came to deliver the believers from bondage. There was a transition in the way of thinking as free men in Messiah. It is important that we understand the Jewish way of thinking still evident today, according to which the angels are the mediators between God and man.

He Has Inherited a More Excellent Name than the Angels

So then, why and how is Jesus greater than the angels? First of all, we read in Hebrews 1:4 that He has inherited a more excellent name than they. When we think today of the word "inherit", the first thing that pops into our mind is that inheritance is obtained after someone near to us has died and bequeathed his property to us. But in the Bible, the word "inherit" also means to take by force something that is ours by right, which is being held from us. For instance, it is written that God commanded the people of Israel to inherit the Land, and that Joshua brought them to inherit the Land. The people of Israel were entitled to the Land. God gave it to Abraham, Isaac and Jacob, and by His vow the Land belonged to the people of Israel. But they had to conquer it and rid it of its inhabitants. They had to take possession of it.

So then, "inherit" means to be entitled to something. It is sometimes received with no effort, but at other times much effort must be applied to assert the authority of the heir. The name Jesus inherited gives Him authority over even the angels. A name is not just first name, or family name. The name reflects the authority and nature of the One who bears it. Jesus is more exalted than the angels.

Who is greater than the angels? Who is Jesus? Jesus is God. The statement here is that in fact, Jesus is God. He has inherited this name, and His authority is greater than the angels because He is the Son.

In Hebrews 1:5-6 we read, "For to which of the angels did He ever say, 'You are my son, today I have begotten you?' And again, 'I will be a father to him and he shall be a son to me?" And when He again brings the firstborn into the world, He says, 'and let all the angels of God worship Him.'"

Verse five is a quote from Psalms 2:7 and 2 Samuel 7:17. We read here that He is the first-born son. Does the fact that He is the Son mean that He was born? The answer is no. We do not have the time to delve deeply into this here, so we shall just note that the Messiah, Son of God, is part of the godhead, of the one, triune God. We know that in the Old Testament God revealed Himself in three forms. Genesis 1:1-2 says, "In the beginning God created the heavens and the earth. The earth was formless and void, and darkness was over the surface of the deep, and the Spirit of God was moving over the surface of the waters." Here both God and the Spirit of God are mentioned. In Proverbs 30:4 Jesus is revealed as the Son of God, "Who has ascended into heaven and descended? Who has gathered the wind in His fists? Who has wrapped the waters in His garment? Who has established all the ends of the earth? What is His name or His son's name? Surely you know!"

The understanding in Judaism is that the angel of

God's presence (Isa. 63:9) is not just any angel. Judaism speaks of Metatron, the angel of God's presence who bears the name of God, speaks in the name of God, and represents Him. In fact, he is spoken to as to God.[3] The angel of God's presence is the one with whom, some say, Abraham bargained over Sodom (Gen. 18:1-33).

Verses 8-13 of the first chapter of Hebrews (with quotes from Ps. 45, 102 and 110) tell us:

> But of the Son He says, "your throne, O God, is forever and ever, and the righteous scepter is the scepter of His kingdom. You have loved righteousness and hated lawlessness; therefore God, your God, has anointed you with the oil of gladness aboveyour companions." And "You, Lord, in the beginning laid the foundation of the earth, and the heavens are the works of Your hands; they will perish, but You remain; and they all will become old like a garment, and like a mantle You will roll them up; like a garmentthey will also be changed. But You are the same, and your years will not come to an end." But to which of the angels has He ever said, "Sit at My right hand, until I make your enemies a footstool for your feet"?

Messiah, Immanuel, the Mediator

It is written that the Messiah is the mediator between God and man, not the angels. We are told that in fact, God Himself came to meet us. True, God is great and exalted, high and lifted up but He is also a God that is close. God doesn't stay up there on His throne, far away from us; He is not a God who does not know us or feel for us, a God who does not understand us. No, He Himself took on flesh and blood. He drew near to us.

He Himself is the mediator between us and Himself. At Passover we say, "The Lord took us out of Egypt,"[4] not through an angel, not through a seraph and not through a messenger. The Holy One, blessed be He, did it in His glory by Himself!"

And so it is. God Himself came to save us. He didn't send someone else to be the mediator between us. In Ezekiel 34:12 we read, "As a shepherd cares for his herd in the day when he is among his scattered sheep, so I will care for My sheep and will deliver them." Just as a shepherd stays among his sheep, God came to be with us, to dwell among us: Immanuel. That is part of the transition of thought that is necessary here. It is not the angels that mediate between God and man, it is God Himself. Jesus the Son of God is the mediator. Moreover, in Heb. 2:14 we read, "Therefore, since the children share in flesh and blood, He Himself likewise also partook of the same, that through death He might render powerless him who had the power of death, that is, the devil." He partook of flesh and blood. Jesus is not only the mediator, He is not like an angel who stays in the spiritual dimension, and He is not only the exalted God. He came to earth and took on flesh and blood!

An understanding of this reality requires a complete change of thinking. God became one of us – that is a tremendous message! God became man. He didn't become an angel, or a ruler, or a principality or some other creation. He became man. Try to imagine the universe and all the creatures God created, some of which we are not even familiar with (and I am not referring to aliens from outer space). Then think of us sinners, who have sinfully damaged and destroyed God's perfect creation. Instead of God wiping us out and destroying us, He came to join with us and to be one of us. His love and mercy are astonishing! Instead of wiping us out and starting all over, He who was without sin, without pain, without suffering (all of which did not exist before Adam sinned because these are all a consequence of sin), who had never tasted death, came to share Himself with us! What a tremendous privilege we sons of Adam have, that God came to live among us as a man!

We read that God put all things under Jesus' feet. Jesus sits on the right hand of the Father. That is to say, that at this moment there is a man sitting at the right hand of the Father, the perfect man, Jesus Christ. He was raised from the death and rose to heaven in the flesh. These are hard things to comprehend, but that is what He has told us. He was raised from the dead. He has a new body. He told His disciples "touch me," and they touched Him (Luke 24:43). He said, "I am going to my Father to prepare a place for you" (John 14:3), and God the Father said, "Sit at my right hand until I make your enemies a footstool for your feet." A man is now sitting at the right hand of God, not because we are worthy. Oh, this wonderful grace!

Verses 10-11 in chapter two are difficult to understand: "For it was fitting for Him, for whom are all things, and through whom are all things, in bringing many sons to glory, to perfect the author of their salvation through sufferings. For both He who sanctifies and those who are sanctified are all from one Father; for which reason He is not ashamed to call them brethren".

What does it mean, "perfect through suffering?" Isn't God perfect? The key is in verse 11, where He calls them "brethren" and in verse 14, "Therefore, since the children share in flesh and blood, He Himself likewise also partook of the same, that through death He might render powerless him who had the power of death, that is, the devil". In chapter 2:9 we read, "But we do see Him who was made for a little while lower than the angels, namely, Jesus, because of the suffering of death crowned with glory and honor, so that by the grace of God He might taste death for everyone". According to the Scriptures, God did not taste death until Jesus tasted death. God never experienced physical pain, suffering, hunger, tiredness, sorrow, scorn, or being spit upon. God never actually suffered these things in the way we have, until Jesus came and suffered them. If Jesus had not come to earth and had not died, or had not suffered, each one of us would have been able to say to God, "I want You to help me, but You do not really understand what I am going through. I am having a hard time, but You cannot really relate to my troubles. I know You are God but I also know that unless someone has gone through something and felt the same pain, he cannot really understand my pain."

When my father died, I began to see things differently and relate differently to people who had lost their parents. During my time of mourning, people with good intentions came to visit me who had not experienced such loss, and had all kinds of pretty things to say to me, like, "Be strong, God is with you." It was all rather superficial. But when a friend came who had already experienced the loss of a parent or someone else close to him, and just hugged me without saying anything, the hug said, "I am with you. I am hurting too." The strength I received from those people was much more significant. I felt they understood what I was going through more than all those who gave me verses or said pretty words.

If God had not experienced life as man; if he had not Himself been tempted; if He had not suffered pain, injury, sorrow, death, scorn, spitting, and rejection – He would not have really been able to comfort and encourage us. He would not have been a true brother. He would not have been a perfect brother who shares with his brethren, and we could not find true rest in our relationship with Him.

In chapter 5 there is another passage that seems difficult, which says, "In the days of His flesh, He offered up both prayers and supplications with loud crying and tears to the One able to save Him from death, and He was heard because of His piety. Although He was a Son, He learned obedience from the things which He suffered. And having been made perfect, He became to all those who obey Him the source of eternal salvation" (vs. 7-9).

Jesus became the perfect Savior, the perfect High Priest, through suffering. It is hard for us to grasp this concept, even after 2000 years. Try to understand how difficult this was for the Jews at the time when the second temple was still standing: God taking on flesh, and being tempted; God suffering in order to become the perfect Savior; God calling us brothers, and rising back to heaven, sitting in the Highest Heavens. This is the One who calls us brothers, sits at the Father's right hand, and whose enemies are made His footstool.

Philippians 2:6-8 says of Jesus, "who, although He existed in the form of God, did not regard equality with God a thing to be grasped, but emptied Himself, taking the form of a bond-servant, and being made in the likeness of men. Being found in appearance as a man, He humbled Himself by becoming obedient to the point of death, even death on a cross."

The One who was higher than the angels, who existed in the form of God, was equal to God, and who was God, did not think it beneath Him to become like us. He emptied Himself and took on flesh and blood to be as a man. Not only that, as a man he took the form of a servant. He went down to the very depths, to death, but death could not hold Him. As He was going

41

through all that, He experienced things that God on His holy exalted throne could not have. He experienced all these things without sin, without giving in to temptation, without self-pity, without lying, without committing adultery, and, without stealing or cheating. He lived as a pure man in complete holiness. He reached the place of death, and then He was raised from the dead. When He was raised from the dead He became the source of salvation to man, and now He sits at the right hand of the Father. Having gone through all that, all things were put under His feet.

In effect, Jesus left the most exalted place in the Universe for the lowest place in the Universe, and then returned. But now we can "hitch a ride" with Him! He came to us and said, "You are stuck in the mud, your sin is destroying you, but I choose to call you brothers, to make you my brothers, and so I will make you partners." That is what He is saying in Hebrews chapter 3:1, "Therefore, holy brethren, partakers of a heavenly calling…" We have a part in the heavenly calling.

He is more exalted than the angels. Angels cannot experience pain as we do, they cannot die. But He could! That is why it is so significant that He is greater than the angels. We can all suffer, and we do suffer. We have no choice about it. We were born in sin, and we live in this sinful body. But God, who did have a choice, chose to suffer with us and for us. He chose this because He is a God of love. He did not have to. He chose to be good and do good to us! He chose to come and serve us; to descend from His exalted position where there is no pain or suffering, in order to suffer with us so that He could truly deliver us – not just encourage us with pretty words, nice verses, a pat on the shoulder and well-wishes.

When I first believed in Jesus, I was in a psychiatric hospital and had been diagnosed as a paranoid schizophrenic. I tried many times to commit suicide. A year after I had come to faith and God had healed me, I went back to the psychiatrist who had treated me. He was amazed at the great change in me and I told him, "I was drowning in a pool, and you stood next to the pool and with great intentions, advised me to 'try to do this,' or 'do that.' But Jesus jumped into the pool to get me out. That's the difference between what you and what Jesus did!"

Jesus jumps into the water with us. He also suffered from the waves, the cold, the current, the sharks, the tigers, the snakes, the scorpions, and the thorns. There is no suffering or difficulty we go through that He is not familiar with. We cannot condescendingly tell God that He does not understand what we are going through. He does understand. He himself partook of flesh and blood. And not only did He become as one of us in the abyss of our lives, He raised us up to live with Him on high.

1 Cor. 6:3 say, "Do you not know that we will judge angels?" Before the death and resurrection of Jesus the order of authority was, first God, after Him the various kinds of angels, and after them mankind. Today, thanks to what Jesus did when He went down from heaven to the depths of earth, he has taken us and set us up with Him on high (see Eph. 1, "we are in Christ"), and our authority is now greater than the authority of angels. Who judges another? Whoever has authority over him. Jesus took on flesh and blood. He bore our griefs and carried our sorrows, though we esteemed him stricken, smitten of God, and afflicted (Isa 53:4). Yet He has set us up on high and we will judge the angels.

That is why the author of the epistle considers it so important to make clear right from the beginning that Jesus is greater, more exalted, than the angels. This explains what He did for us and what the result of His work is for us in Him, both now and in the future. By His love he changed the order of authority in the Universe by giving us authority to judge the angels. God took on flesh and blood and suffered so that He would be perfected and would be the perfect Savior. And we, with all our sins, receive this gift in grace – not by any works on our part. He has become the perfect Savior of all who believe in His name and obey Him.

We are in Christ, in the Highest, and that is where we are supposed to be. This is what we need to understand, and to live our lives by. The letter to the Hebrews was given us to help us change, and to change our understanding so that we may find rest in everything God has prepared for us.

---

[1] "[Y]ou will be as the great angels, who are wise to know between good and evil", the Targum of Palestine, commonly entitled the Targum of Jonathan ben Uzziel on the Book of Genesis. (targum.info/pj/pjgen1-6.htm), first century AD.

[2] For example, "And the Lord said to the angels who ministered before Him, who had been created in the second day of the creation of the world, Let us make man in Our image, in Our likeness; and let them rule over the fish of the sea, and over the fowl which are in the atmosphere of heaven, and over the cattle, and over all the earth, and over every reptile creeping upon the earth. And the Lord created man in His Likeness." The Targum of Palestine, commonly entitled the Targum of Jonathan Ben Uzziel.

[3] **Metatron,** greatest of angels in Jewish myths and legends, variously identified as the Prince (or Angel) of the Presence, as Michael the archangel, or as Enoch after his ascent into heaven. He is likewise described as a celestial scribe recording the sins and merits of men, as a guardian of heavenly secrets, as God's mediator with men, as the "lesser Yahweh," as the archetype of man, and as one "whose name is like that of his master." The latter appellation is based on Hebrew numerology; *i.e.,* when the consonants that comprise the names Metatron and Shaddai (Almighty)

are analyzed according to preassigned numerical values, each name totals 314. From:http://www.britannica.com/EBchecked/topic/378043/Metatron

[4] Chabbad.org English Haggadah: http://www.chabad.org/holidays/passover/pesach_cdo/aid/1737/jewish/Maggid.htm

CHAPTER 4

Jesus Is Greater than Abraham

Now observe how great this man was to whom Abraham, the patriarch, gave a tenth of the choicest spoils. And those indeed of the sons of Levi who receive the priest's office have commandment in the Law to collect a tenth from the people, that is, from their brethren, although these are descended from Abraham. But the one whose genealogy is not traced from them collected a tenth from Abraham and blessed the one who had the promises. But without any dispute the lesser is blessed by the greater (Heb. 7:4-7).

Another point raised in this epistle to explain the identity of Jesus is that Jesus is greater than Abraham.

Abraham – Faith and Obedience to God

Abraham is honored not only in Jewish thought, but also in Islam, and of course in Christianity, which developed later. In fact, Abraham is one of the most admired characters in the history of mankind. All religions that believe in one God see Abraham as the

46

father of their faith.

Abraham has a very honored place in Jewish thought. Judaism glorifies him even in a physical way[1]. Just as Moses is always referred to as "Moses our Teacher," Abraham is always called "Abraham our father." The biblical narrative about Abraham begins when he is already about 75 years old. Jewish tradition has many tales and legends about Abraham attempting to understand where he came from, how he came to faith in God, and why God chose him.

According to Jewish legend, Abraham was the first to believe in the one God. He grew up in a home of idol worshippers who sold idols in their shop.[2] It is said that once he realized that the idols were not real, he smashed them to pieces and left his stick in the hand of one of them. When he was confronted, he claimed that there had been a big fight between the idols over who would eat first. When he was told that they couldn't possibly do that, he replied, "Do your ears not hear what your lips are saying?"

Nimrod, the king of Babylon, condemned him to be burned but God delivered him. That is why, according to tradition, Abraham forsook all and fled. There are high points and low points in Abraham's life but several things stand out as milestones. The first is mentioned in Genesis 12:1-3 when God commands him, "Go forth from your country, And from your relatives and from your father's house, To the land which I will show you; And I will make you a great nation, And I will bless you, And make your name great; And so you shall be a blessing; And I will bless those who bless you, And the one who curses you I will curse. And in you all the families of the earth will be blessed."

In Abraham's day, people did not leave their home to wander to other places unless they were trying to escape from something or someone. This is why Jewish tradition tried to explain Abraham's story as a flight from King Nimrod of Babylon. The Bible tells us that God commanded Abraham to do something that was not socially acceptable, and Abraham obeyed. Wherever he wandered, people distrusted him because wandering was normally the result of breaking the law. Anyone who has wandered away from his home must be cursed, so they thought. So God's promise to him was all the more amazing, "I will make of thee a great nation . . . I will bless them that bless them . . . in thee shall all families of the earth be blessed".

It is said of Abraham, "Then he believed in the Lord; and He reckoned it to him as righteousness" (Gen.15:6), after God promised him that his descendants would be as the stars in the heavens. This is the first time the word "righteousness" is mentioned in the Bible, and it comes right after Abraham's meeting with Melchizedek in chapter 14. From the first time this word is mentioned, it is connected with faith. Righteousness is not the outcome of works, but of faith. Abraham received righteousness from God because he believed the God who promised, without seeing anything.

Abraham lived by faith, and God accounted this to him as righteousness. For almost his entire life he lived in the land God had promised him as a "stranger in a strange country."[3] He believed the promises of God even though he only saw a tiny bit of them come true in his lifetime. The ability to obey God without seeing the results gave him the title "the Father of the believers" (Rom. 4:11), because obedience comes from faith.

Another significant event in Abraham's life is recorded in Genesis 22 – the sacrifice of Isaac. Isaac, the child God had promised them, was born to Abraham and Sarah after many years of expectation. Abraham loved him more than his own soul. God commanded Abraham, "Take now your son, your only son, whom you love, Isaac, and go to the land of Moriah, and offer him there as a burnt offering on one of the mountains of which I will tell you" (Gen. 22:2). "Your son, your only son Isaac, whom you love." Abraham had other sons, but this was the special son whom he loved with all his soul. God commanded him to do something inexplicable, which becomes clear only in the mirror of history, but Abraham obeyed. He is prepared to do all God commands him, even if he doesn't understand it.

All the Families of the Earth Will Be Blessed

What is special about Abraham is not only what he did through his faith in God, but also the role that God has appointed him to. God appointed Abraham to a very special position in the history of mankind, and therefore demanded a special faith of him.

The first role God appointed Abraham to was "in you all the families of the earth will be blessed" (Gen. 12:3). God chose Abraham so that through him all the families of the earth would be blessed. The seed of Abraham is found first of all in Israel, through whom the Holy Scriptures came to all mankind, the prophets who were all Jews, and through the many other revelations and inventions that have come through Jews, and have been a blessing to all the families of earth. And of course, the seed is found in the Messiah, who came through the people of Israel to bring obedience and faith to all the nations of the earth. So, in Abraham, indeed all the families of the earth have been blessed.

The Father of Many Nations

The second position God appointed Abraham to was the "father of many nations[4]." On the human level, Abraham did father many nations and powers. Everyone knows the nation of Israel, who descended from Abraham through Isaac and Jacob, but Ishmael also fathered many nations. In Genesis 25:13 we read that he had twelve sons, or "rulers"; that is to say, twelve tribes or twelve nations. Edom was the descendant of Esau, as we read in Genesis 36. Many nations descended from Abraham through his concubines, so that there is a great number of nations and tribes that came down from Abraham. We, the people of Israel, are very proud of being the descendants of Abraham[5]. The Arab nations also came to be his sons through Ishmael, so that God did keep His promise to Abraham that he would be the father of many nations.

Abraham is not only the physical father of many nations; he is also the father of all the believers. "For this reason it is by faith, in order that it may be in accordance with grace, so that the promise will be guaranteed to all the descendants, not only to those who are of the Law, but also to those who are of the faith of Abraham, who is the father of us all" (Rom. 4:16). Abraham became the father of all those who believe, and live in faith as he did. In John 8:39 Jesus told the leaders of the people, "If you are Abraham's children, do the deeds of Abraham." The true sons of Abraham from all the nations do the works of Abraham. They leave their homeland in order to follow God. They live in faith even if they do not always see the promises of God being fulfilled before their eyes. And, they sacrifice that which is most precious to them because God is more important to them than any other thing in their life.

Jesus and Abraham

The epistle to the Hebrews claims that Jesus is greater than Abraham. Jesus' opponents disagreed:

"Surely You are not greater than our father Abraham, who died? The prophets died too; whom do You make Yourself out to be?" Jesus answered, "If I glorify Myself, My glory is nothing; it is My Father who glorifies Me, of whom you say, 'He is our God'; and you have not come to know Him, but I know Him; and if I say that I do not know Him, I will be a liar like you, but I do know Him and keep His word. Your father Abraham rejoiced to see My day and he saw it and was glad." So the Jews said to Him, "You are not yet fifty years old, and have You seen Abraham?" Jesus said to them, "Truly, truly, I say to you, before Abraham was born, I am" (John 8:53-58).

Jesus claims, "Before Abraham was . . . I am." His hearers understand very well what He means, and pick up rocks to stone Him for heresy. He compares himself to God, and that is also why they sentenced him to death later. Indeed, Jesus is God who took on flesh and blood and dwelt among us. He was greater than Abraham who lived and died. But Jesus was also greater than Abraham in His works and role.

The first thing Abraham did was to leave his home and native land. Compared to Abraham, Jesus left much more. "[W]ho, although He existed in the form of God, did not regard equality with God a thing to be grasped, but emptied Himself, taking the form of a bond-servant, and being made in the likeness of men. Being found in appearance as a man, He humbled Himself by becoming obedient to the point of death, even death on a cross" (Phil. 2:6-8). He who was equal to God, who was in the most perfect place in the universe, left everything out of His love for us, and came to a world spoiled by sin in order to defeat Satan, to banish him from the inheritance of God, and to restore man to the Kingdom of God. Abraham may have left his home and country to live as a stranger in the land of promise that was in the hands of idol worshippers, but Jesus left much more. He lived in the world He had created, and the world did not recognize Him. He obeyed unto death on the cross in order to obtain the keys of Sheol and death, and to bring man to salvation under His authority. Our inheritance is in Him[6] and we are His inheritance[7] – not by anything we have done, but by His grace.

Abraham lived a life of faith, and thus received the righteousness that is based on faith, even though he stumbled a few times in various sins. Jesus, who was always righteous and pure, lived a perfect life of faith without sin. Faith is expressed in obedience, and Jesus said, "Truly, truly, I say to you, the Son can do nothing of Himself, unless it is something He sees the Father doing; for whatever the Father does, these things the Son also does in like manner" (John 5:19). Jesus did nothing of Himself, He did not lie in order to get out of dangerous situations like Abraham did, nor did he sin in any other kind of way. When He stood before the people He said, "Which of you convinces me of any sin?" (John 8:46)

Jesus did not need to receive righteousness because He always was righteous; and we are justified in His righteousness. "You know that He appeared in order to take away sins; and in Him there is no sin. No one who abides in Him sins; no one who sins has seen Him or knows Him. Little children, make sure no one deceives you; the one who practices righteousness is righteous, just as He is righteous" (1 John 3:5-7).

Jesus gave Himself up as a sacrifice. He sacrificed first his status as God because of his love for us, and then He gave up His life for us. He said: "I lay down my life for the sheep" (John 10:15).

But the free gift is not like the transgression. For if by the transgression of the one the many died, much more did the grace of God and the gift by the grace of the one Man, Jesus Christ, abound to the many. The gift is not like that which came through the one who sinned; for on the one hand the judgment arose from one transgression resulting in condemnation, but on the other hand the free gift arose from many transgressions resulting in justification. For if by the transgression of the one, death reigned through the one, much more those who receive the abundance of grace and of the gift of righteousness will reign in life through the One, Jesus Christ. So then as through one transgression there resulted condemnation to all men, even so through one act of righteousness there resulted justification of life to all men. For as through the one man's disobedience the many were made sinners, even so through the obedience of the One the many will be made righteous (Rom. 5:15-19).

By His sacrifice, by His faith and obedience, we have all received His righteousness.

Abraham influenced the entire world, and in him all the families of the world have been blessed, but the influence of Jesus was and still is much greater. In Him people from all over the world, from every tribe and language and nation are blessed. He was not only an example of a man living by faith, He brought forgiveness of sins to all those who believe, regardless of gender, nationality or age. Abraham rejected Ishmael and disinherited him, but Jesus rejects no one. In Jesus the divine blessing has come to all men and by means of the atonement and forgiveness they can all be a part of His Kingdom and His inheritance. In Jesus every believer is a son of Abraham.

> ...in order that in Christ Jesus the blessing of Abraham might come to the Gentiles, so that we would receive the promise of the Spirit through faith. Brethren, I speak in terms of human relations: even though it is only a man's covenant, yet when it has been ratified, no one sets it aside or adds conditions to it. Now the promises were spoken to Abraham and to his seed. He does not say, "And to seeds," as referring to many, but rather to one, "And to your seed," that is, Christ. What I am saying is this: the Law, which came four hundred and thirty years later, does not invalidate a covenant previously ratified by God, so as to nullify the promise (Gal. 3:14-17).

True, Abraham is considered to be the father of all believers and is a perfect example of a life of faith, but Jesus is the true father of all believers. Through Jesus, all believers have become the sons of Abraham worthy of the inheritance, and therefore inheritors of the promises given to Abraham.

> For you are all sons of God through faith in Christ Jesus. For all of you who were baptized into Christ have clothed yourselves with Christ. There is neither Jew nor Greek, there is neither slave nor free man, there is neither male nor female; for you are all one in Christ Jesus. And if you belong to Christ, then you are Abraham's descendants, heirs according to promise (Galatians 3:26-29).

Abraham was promised that he would be the father of many nations. Jesus became the father of the nations. Through Him all the nations can draw near to God, to be acceptable before Him and to be his sons.

And I saw between the throne (with the four living creatures) and the elders a Lamb standing, as if slain, having seven horns and seven eyes, which are the seven Spirits of God, sent out into all the earth. And He came and took the book out of the right hand of Him who sat on the throne. When He had taken the book, the four living creatures and the twenty-four elders fell down before the Lamb, each one holding a harp and golden bowls full of incense, which are the prayers of the saints. And they sang a new song, saying, "Worthy are You to take the book and to break its seals; for You were slain, and purchased for God with Your blood men from every tribe and tongue and people and nation. You have made them to be a kingdom and priests to our God; and they will reign upon the earth." Then I looked, and I heard the voice of many angels around the throne and the living creatures and the elders; and the number of them was myriads of myriads, and thousands of thousands, saying with a loud voice, "Worthy is the Lamb that was slain to receive power and riches and wisdom and might and honor and glory and blessing". And every created thing which is in heaven and on the earth and under the earth and on the sea, and all things in them, I heard saying, "To Him who sits on the throne, and to the Lamb, be blessing and honor and glory and dominion forever and ever". And the four living creatures kept saying, "Amen". And the elders fell down and worshiped (Rev. 5:6-14).

Abraham was a great man, but Jesus is much greater. Abraham knew that and rejoiced to see the day of Messiah. In giving tithes to Melchizedek (Hebrews 7) he acknowledged Messiah's authority over him. Abraham was, more or less, good person who believed in the promises of God, but we cannot find rest in him or his faith.

---

[1] Massechet Sofrim 21:9 "The greatest among the giants was our forefather Abraham, whose height was equal to seventy-four men (over four hundred feet), and whose eating and drinking was that of seventy-four men, and whose strength was likewise…"

[2] Midrash Bereishit 38:18

[3] Hebrews 11:9

[4] Genesis 17:4

[5] One example of such pride is found in John 8:33, when the leaders of the people said to Jesus: "We be Abraham's seed, and were never in bondage to any man. How sayest thou, 'Ye shall be made free?'" –completely ignoring the fact that they were under Roman rule.

[6] Ephesians 1:11 "In whom also we have obtained an inheritance".

[7] Ephesians 1:18: "And what the riches of his inheritance in the saints"

CHAPTER 5

Jesus Is Greater than Moses

Therefore, holy brethren, partakers of a heavenly calling, consider Jesus, the Apostle and High Priest of our confession; He was faithful to Him who appointed Him, as Moses also was in all His house. For He has been counted worthy of more glory than Moses, by just so much as the builder of the house has more honor than the house. For every house is built by someone, but the builder of all things is God. Now Moses was faithful in all His house as a servant, for a testimony of those things which were to be spoken later; but Christ was faithful as a Son over His house—whose house we are, if we hold fast our confidence and the boast of our hope firm until the end (Heb. 3:1-6).

Moses in Judaism

In order to understand why it is so important that Jesus is greater than Moses, we have to first understand the Jewish point of view on Moses in the days of the New Testament during the time of the second temple. What did they think of Moses in those days? For this we will have a look at Deuteronomy 18:15-19:

The Lord your God will raise up for you a prophet like me from among you, from your countrymen, you shall listen to him. This is according to all that you asked of the LORD your God in Horeb on the day of the assembly, saying, "Let me not hear again the voice of the LORD my God, let me not see this great fire anymore, or I will die." The LORD said to me, "They have spoken well. I will raise up a prophet from among their countrymen like you, and I will put My words in his mouth, and he shall speak to them all that I command him. It shall come about that whoever will not listen to My words which he shall speak in My name, I Myself will require it of him".

In the eyes of the Jewish people in the days of the second temple, Moses was the most important man – the ultimate authority. He gave us the Law. He was the first of the prophets, the most humble of men, and the only man God spoke to face to face.

When Jesus healed the blind man, and his opposers brought the man before the Sanhedrin (John chapter 9), he told them what Jesus had done and asked, "Will you also be his disciples?" (verse 27). The Pharisees reviled him, and said, "No, we are Moses' disciples!" That is, they walked the path of Moses. The Jewish people and their rabbis see themselves as disciples of Moses. The Mosaic covenant, or the Sinai covenant, was the only event in history where an entire nation stood before God and God spoke to them with thunder and lightning from the mountain. The one who led them there was Moses; therefore, Moses is the most important Jew. He must be heard and obeyed. Rabbinical understanding in Jesus' day was not yet developed to what it is today, and they did not consider themselves to be above Moses (something that is true today even if they won't admit it). Moses was the superior.[1] The book of Deuteronomy concluded with a special declaration, "Since that time no prophet has risen in Israel like Moses, whom the LORD knew face to face, for all the signs and wonders which the LORD sent him to perform in the land of Egypt against Pharaoh, all his servants, and all his land, and for all the mighty power and for all the great terror which Moses performed in the sight of all Israel" (34:10-12).

The Expectation for a "Prophet Like Moses"

The people lived in the expectation that another special person would come. Moses himself had promised that a prophet like him would come. God, who spoke through Moses, had promised another prophet who would be like Moses (Deut. 18:15-19). So we see that when Moses died, it was said "there arose not a prophet since in Israel like unto Moses, whom the Lord knew face to face".

Testimony of this emotional expectation is evident in John 1:19-23, particularly in verse 21:

This is the testimony of John, when the Jews sent to him priests and Levites from Jerusalem to ask him, "Who are you?" And he confessed and did not deny, but confessed, "I am not the Christ." They asked him, "What then? Are you Elijah?" And he said, "I am not." "Are you the Prophet?" And he answered, "No." Then they said to him, "Who are you, so that we may give an answer to those who sent us? What do you say about yourself?" He said, "I am a voice of one crying in the wilderness, 'make straight the way of the Lord', as Isaiah the prophet said".

The expectation for a prophet like Moses was so powerful that any person who fulfilled the conditions even partially was considered to possibly be the prophet Moses had spoken of. John the Baptist was baptizing in the desert, and the leaders in Jerusalem sent messengers to him to ask who he was. Why did they ask him if he was Elijah? Because Malachi 4:5 tells us "Behold, I am going to send you Elijah the prophet before the coming of the great and terrible day of the LORD." The people and their leaders knew this. This is why to this day we place an extra chair at the Passover table for Elijah. The rabbis believed he would come at Passover. Opening the door for Elijah to come in is an expression of a hope that the promise will be fulfilled this year. So the first thing the leaders asked John was, "Are you Elijah? Are you the one who is to come before Messiah?" He replied in the negative. Their next question was, "Are you that prophet?" What prophet were they speaking about? The same prophet that Moses had promised them would come.

When John told them that he was not that same prophet, they asked him, "Who are you? What do you say about yourself?" He answered, "I am a voice crying out in the wilderness, as the prophet Isaiah said." He claims that he is not Elijah. Elijah is to come before Messiah's second coming – as prophesied by Malachi, "before the great and terrible day of the LORD". This was not clear to the leaders of the people in those days, and it is still not clear to the rabbis today. But John knew the difference. John is also not the prophet like Moses (who is the Messiah Himself). From these questions, we can see the expectation beating in the hearts and minds of the people. So much so that when this eccentric prophet appeared in the desert – John the Baptist – the priests and Levites in Jerusalem wondered, "Maybe it is him?" and sent messengers to check him out.

Was Rabbi Akiva Greater than Moses?

Later on, Jewish thought developed and changed. Rabbi Akiva altered the face of Judaism when he placed rabbinical teaching between the Bible and the people; between the writings of Moses and the people. The Talmudists called the process of making the rabbis the authority on interpretation, between the people and the Bible, *aspaklaria*, or "mirror" in Aramaic. The *aspaklaria* is the glass that reflects what is seen through it, but whose quality also affects what is seen or not seen. Rabbi Akiva accorded the rabbinical teaching – the *Halacha* - greater authority than that of Moses or even of God (see "The Oven of Aknai", Talmud Bavli, Baba Metsi'a 59b). The Jewish sources[2] tell a story of Moses who comes to the study hall of Rabbi Akiva where the rabbi is expounding the mysteries of the Law of Moses. In the study hall the students sit around their teacher in eight circles. In the farthest circle are those students who understood the least of what Rabbi Akiva was teaching. The closer the circle to the rabbi, the better the student understood. Moses has to sit in the last row because he cannot understand the halachic discussions. When he hears the rabbi teaching, he says, "Wow, I didn't know that's what I said!" According to this legend, Rabbi Akiva was considered greater and wiser than Moses.

The trend to accord rabbis the ultimate authority is clear here. They place themselves on Moses' seat. In the days of the second temple this was called *katedra demoshe* – the seat of Moses. The ruler of the synagogue sat on the seat of Moses, which symbolized the authority passed on to him from Moses. What first began as a veneration of Moses as the supreme authority developed more and more in the direction of considering themselves as more authoritative than Moses – and this remains the religious view today.

The rabbis have the authority to change everything, which is why it is so important that people understand that Jesus alone, not the teachers, is greater than Moses. Jesus is that prophet "like unto Moses." He is the one the leaders were expecting when they sent messengers to John asking who he was. Remember that this is a change in thought, a change in mindset of an entire people who for generations had revered Moses. The epistle to the Hebrews was written to help the believers then, and us now, to make the transition of thought.

Jesus – the Prophet Like Moses

What does "a prophet like Moses" mean exactly? Derek Prince once wrote a booklet in which he described the similarities between Jesus and Moses. He found 27 points of similarity. I will mention a few of them here. Moses was for a time rejected by the people, and so was Jesus. The people of Israel told Moses, "Who made you to rule over us?" That is what they still say about Jesus. Both Jesus and Moses were almost killed as babies by the decree of a cruel king. Both fasted for 40 days. Moses was used by God to deliver the people of Israel from slavery into liberty; to mediate between the people and God; to establish a covenant between God and His people; to bring them through the desert; to help the people to change; and to create a nation that could conquer and inherit the Promised Land from a nation of slaves. He did not complete his role because of sin, and Joshua inherited his work. We read in Deuteronomy 12:9-10 that his task was to bring the people of Israel into their rest and their inheritance. There is no need to dig far to see the parallels to Jesus.

Jesus came to deliver us from a much greater slavery than that of Egypt – the slavery to sin. We must understand that it is possible to be enslaved while free. We can also be slaves just like our forefathers in Egypt, but in our hearts, our spirits, our souls and our minds, we can be free. Viktor Frankl, a psychologist captured by the Nazis and deported first to Theresienstadt and then to Auschwitz, suffered terrible things; but one thing he understood very well. He writes in his book, "Man's Search for Meaning," that he understood that the Nazis could destroy everything; they could change everything through destruction and plunder, but they could never change his will or his inner freedom. No matter what they did to him, they could not take from him his freedom of choice. They could not force him to react the way they wanted him to react. He realized that they can beat him, but he does not have to be filled with hate. They can hurt him but he does not have to wish revenge. He could choose to forgive, choose to love. He was not a believer in Jesus but he discovered this secret of free choice – the liberty we each have within ourselves – and wrote books about it. In fact, many books have been written about his books.

We may be slaves but if we exercise our freedom to choose, then even as slaves we are free. The opposite is true also. We may be free men, slaves to no one, but instead of owning our own free wills we are bound in our reactions to what people do to us. If someone hurts me, than I have to be hurt and I am filled with bitterness, and keep a distance from him. Or I repay evil with evil. If you ask most people who have done bad things, they will say that they have only done that in response to someone else wronging them. Ask any child, "Why did you hit your sister?" and he will answer, "Because she hit me first!" But just because she did something to you does not allow you to react in the way you reacted. At some point in time, between what she did to you and what you did to her, you made the choice to react this way. That split second when a man chooses how to react and behave is a crossroads that can affect the direction of his life. That is why it is so important that we use our free will to decide to do what is right, not just react because of our feelings.

In the past we could see this liberty, but we did not always have the power to live by it. Jesus delivered us from slavery to sin, and gave us the power to live in this liberty; so that, if someone hurts us or treats us badly, we do not have to react the way we are used to. We can stop and ask, "God, how do you want me to react in this situation? What do you want me to do?" And then our reaction rests in God's will. This is true liberty.

Jesus delivered us from the deepest slavery to sin, and made it possible to live in the greatest liberty. Jesus placed us before God to make a covenant with Him, even when we tried to avoid it and walk away from the light of God. The thunder and lightning are not outside on the mountain. They echo within our hearts. What is being broken are not the stone tablets of the Law, but our hearts.

When I stand before God, I am seeing myself in His light. I see myself with all my shortcomings, and all the dirt and imperfections. Then I know that God chose to make a covenant with me, not because I am special or good or wise, but because of His grace. Many of us still find it hard to get rid of the thought that, "God chose me because I am special". When we try to understand why God chose us, still, in some deep place within us, we think that God chose us because He found something special in us. When God speaks of choosing the nation of Israel, He doesn't say He found something special in them. On the contrary! God says, "You were the dirtiest, most sinful, and the weakest, and that's why I chose you: to reveal my glory". In Ezekiel 16:6 we read: "When I passed by you and saw you squirming in your blood, I said to you while you were in your blood, 'Live!' Yes, I said to you while you were in your blood, 'Live!'" Here God tells them, "I passed by you when you were lying there in your blood, dirty. You weren't wise, wonderful seekers of God".

God chose us not because we are special and good, but because we were the very worst. Through us He would be able to reveal His majesty. Knowing this, there is less likelihood that we would take the glory for ourselves and hide His. Jesus placed us before God who speaks in our hearts through thunders and lightning; changes us from the inside out; and writes His law on our hearts. This is why He is greater than Moses.

Moses' task was to take us through the desert. The desert is a beautiful place; impressive, and wonderful. I love it very much, but it is not an easy place to be. Jesus takes us through life in this world. This life is like the desert – beautiful but difficult. I find it hard to understand how people make it through life without Jesus. One wonders why the psychiatric hospitals are not more crowded.

Jesus takes us by the hand and guides as like the pillar of cloud or of fire. He provides us with manna, with strength, and with water. He takes us through the desert. We do not go through the desert all at once – there are places of oasis and rest in our lives. Some of us wonder, "Will I have the strength to get through this life? I see the difficulties and the problems. I am fighting against the Amalekites. I feel the heat. I am thirsty when I don't have water, and hungry when there is no food. How will I manage to get through?"

The answer is, "If God be for us, who can be against us?" (Rom. 8:31). "For I am confident of this very thing, that He who began a good work in you will perfect it until the day of Christ Jesus." (Phil. 1:6). Jesus takes us through the desert. It may be that some of us walk through the desert for 40 years. Perhaps others take 80 years. The desert of our lives is more difficult than the Sinai desert. Snakes and scorpions abound, the thorns and difficulties come when we least expect. We are all experienced in battle, but Jesus walks before us. He brings us through the desert in a much better way than Moses.

Moses had the task of transforming a nation of slaves into a nation of conquerors. We are all familiar with this process. Each one of us has come out of slavery, and some of us still carry remnants of this slavery with us. Jesus delivers us and renews our minds. That is why we study the Scriptures. They help us to renew our minds, and change the way we see the world and ourselves.

A Rest and an Inheritance

Moses was meant to bring the people to the Promised Land. Jesus actually has, and will, brought us in to the Promised Land. Did Moses succeed in bringing us to our inheritance and rest? Is there such a rest here in Israel? This is a land that has known constant war since we first entered in to it. This is not the place of rest. We have not yet entered into our eternal Sabbath rest. "For if Joshua had given them rest, He would not have spoken of God" (Heb. 4:8-9). It says here that Jesus will give us a better rest. What does this involve?

Judaism says, "You have to do this, or do that. Work hard and make the effort so that, in the end, God will have mercy on you." For us also, who believe in Jesus, there is a long list of things we think believers should do.

And if they do not do them, we doubt whether they are in fact true believers. I usually measure my spirituality and my closeness to Jesus by how I am fulfilling these things. Do I forgive people? Do I read the Scriptures? Do I pray? All these things are good, right and necessary; and, they make me feel good with myself. I feel that I truly am walking in God's ways. But if I am angry, uptight, or speak rudely, then I feel bad because the things I do are wrong. True, it's just as well to feel guilty for such things, but there are people who focus on their guilt and even use it. Modern Hebrew has a term that is taken from the Yiddish for this behavior: "Yiddisher Mama," or, a mother who keeps her children in line by playing on their guilt.

In short, we measure spirituality by works. We say of others, "He is very spiritual – he does this, and he does that. I could be more spiritual if I would only do this, or do that". We judge others and ourselves by works. We accuse others and suffer guilt because, despite our best efforts, we do not live according to the standards we have set for ourselves. But the Sabbath day is described as the day when God rested from all His works. He rested from the work of creation. According to what is written in Heb. 4:10, "For the one who has entered His rest has himself also rested from his works, as God did from His". Whoever has entered the true rest, the true Sabbath, has also rested from his works as God rested from His works and His efforts. True, we are told that we must make the effort, but not an effort to be more spiritual by changing ourselves – because we have no power to change ourselves. Only God can do that. It is written, "Therefore let us be diligent to enter that rest" (4:11). To be diligent means to make the effort. Make the effort to enter into the rest. It may sound like a contradiction, but it is what we are called to do. If we are honest we will admit that we are always pressured and stressed, trying to make an effort to be spiritual. We strive to work with God; we strive to be the way God wants us to be. And when we fail to reach these goals, we feel guilty.

Hebrews 4:10-11 tells us: "For the one who has entered His rest has himself also rested from his works, as God did from His. Therefore let us be diligent to enter that rest, so that no one will fall, through following the same example of disobedience." The Scriptures tell us that this kind of effort comes from rebellion, or disobedience. Whoever strives, instead of resting, is rebelling. We depend on our own efforts and ourselves more than we depend on God. Otherwise we would strive less! This is the kind of attitude that is rooted in rebellion, pride and unbelief. Our own efforts come from the fact that we have no peace or rest from God. We fail to understand that we have been saved by grace, and are living each day by grace.

Chapter 3:14 say, "For we have become partakers of Christ, if we hold fast the beginning of our assurance firm until the end." When we came to the Lord, what was the first confidence we began with? What was our assurance? The confidence was that he had saved me. Did He save me because I kept all the commandments? Because I prayed three times a day facing Jerusalem? Because I witnessed of Him to others? Because I read and studied the Scriptures? All these things are important, and we need them, but are they the basis of the confidence we have held from the beginning? What is the assurance we began with?

There is a song entitled "Just As I Am" that is commonly sung in Billy Graham's crusades: Take me just as I am. You took me just as I am, with the dirt, with the anger, with the unforgiveness; just as I am. That is our confidence right from the start. Have we been saved by a different confidence? When Jesus saved me, he told me, "Come to me as you are." We came to Him as we are. He received us as we are. That is the basis of our confidence. He did not say, "I love you now conditionally, until you grow up." He did not say, "Later on, when you study the Scriptures, or when you have learned how to pray, or when you witness of me to others, then I will love you more." We know that Jesus loved us with an unconditional love to the end .[3] Our confidence in our relationship with Him and His love never came from our works. That is how it was at the beginning, and then we began to grow in the Lord. We began to learn the Scriptures, but then regretfully we also began to compare ourselves with others. If I saw I was more familiar with the Scriptures than my brother, 15 points! If I prayed beautifully in the congregational prayer meetings, that must mean I get to move another three places closer to God. When I tell my friends of the Gospel I get to move another 15 places up. Now I am very close to God, and I am sure He will love me more now. So what has happened? We have turned from our first confidence, which was based on the fact that He received us as we were, into a false confidence based on our efforts to draw near to God by works. We have turned grace into works.

In the Western world many people base their faith and their closeness to God on works. Not by laws that dictate, for instance, that we have to pray three times a day facing Jerusalem; rather, by keeping other com- mandments such as studying the Scriptures, witnessing, or praying and fasting. If you do not do enough you are not considered spiritual enough. That is pretty much the attitude of the Pharisees that Jesus condemned. Each one of us makes this mistake, especially those of us who are Jewish. That is why we have been called to hold fast the declaration of our faith, "Therefore, since we have a great High Priest who has passed through the heavens, Jesus the Son of God, let us hold fast our confession" (Heb. 4:14). This means to hold fast our confession of faith, not the declaration of our works.

We began with this confidence, but then we abandoned it. We began to depend on our own spirituality, which is why we were told, "For the one who has entered His rest has himself also rested from his works, as God did from His. Therefore let us be diligent to enter that rest, so that no one will fall, through following the same example of disobedience" (4:10-11). How will he fall? By not entering the rest! We are called to be careful, lest we fall into unbelief and disobedience. We are not to live contrary to what God has said, by laboring to become more of what we think He wants us to be, but rather labor to enter into His rest. Our efforts should not be directed toward attempting to change ourselves. This is what we must let God do. He does a much better job than we do. We have to labor to be closer to Jesus. Always resting in Him, and realizing that He has done it all. It does not depend on me.

In the Gospel of Mark chapter 2 we read about the four friends of a sick man who brought him to Jesus. They did not try to heal the sick man, but they did make the effort to bring him to the feet of Jesus. They made a hole in the roof; not to heal the man, but to let him down through the roof to Jesus.

Jesus brings us in to the true rest, the true Sabbath, to the place or situation where we do not only enjoy a Sabbath or a sabbatical year, but where we live our lives day after day in peace and rest; knowing that God has accepted us and will not throw us out. God saved me, but not because of my works. Now he continues to receive me – again, not because of my works. He is the One who changes me if I allow Him, or do not oppose Him.

Opposition is also a kind of work. It is written of the people of Israel that they walked by stubbornness of their heart (Ps. 81:12). In Hebrew the word for "stubbornness" is *shrirut*, which comes from *shrir* or "muscle." We flex the muscle in our own attempts to do the will of God in our own strength, instead of coming before Him in rest and saying, "God, you created me. You must change me. Please let me be near you. Let me always trust in You to live in your Sabbath, even when I am attacked. Even when things are hard. Even when the past whispers in my ear saying, "Until now you have behaved in certain way. Keep doing whatever you have been doing; do not change." Let me live in your Sabbath. Live through me, and help me not to hinder You from living through me."

Jesus calls us into the Sabbath rest, and then brings us into it. Because of this, and because of all the other things Jesus did, He is worthy of a far greater honor than that of Moses. He did much more than deliver us from slavery in Egypt and across the desert. At Passover we sing, "If you had brought us out of Egypt and not judged them – *dayenu*, it would have sufficed us; if you had taken us through the desert – *dayenu*, it would have sufficed us." As believers we not only sing "*dayenu*". For all that Jesus has done for us we sing "*ashreynu* –we are blessed!" Blessed are the poor in Spirit for they shall inherit the Kingdom of God. The poor in Spirit do not look at themselves thinking how rich they are in knowledge and in good works. Knowledge is good and important, but is not the goal. Good works and "spirituality" are important, but they are not the goal. The goal is to live every moment of our lives close to Him. The danger that accompanies knowledge, or good works, is pride. The story of Miriam and Martha shows us this point clearly. Martha was working hard. She did wonderful things: she served food, she washed feet, and she washed the dishes. She did all the things a true believer should do. Miriam, on the other hand, came and sat at the feet of Jesus. Jesus did not tell her, "Mary, what are you doing here? Go be a good believer and help Martha. Prepare food, serve the guests, and clean up! That is how a true believer should act!" He said instead, "Mary has chosen the better way, the most important thing." The better and more important thing is to stop all those efforts, and instead, sit at the feet of Jesus.

The moment I live in this rest, the life of Jesus flows through me and from me. If He tells me to do certain things and I resist Him, I do not enjoy his rest. When He tells me to forgive and I resist; or when He tells me to love and turn the other cheek, and I resists, then I am rebelling against God. I am hardening my heart. We have been called to a life of obedience in rest. We have not been called to change ourselves, or to know the Scriptures well, as an aim in and of itself. Nowhere is it written that one of the entry requirements to heaven will be to check our knowledge of the Scriptures. The Scriptures are the basis for our life – our roadmap. I personally know the Scriptures, and love to study and delve deeper into them. That is important, but it is not what saves us. This is not our goal. The study of the Scriptures is a tool given us to learn more about Jesus. It is a tool that teaches us how to grow closer to Him, how to follow Him, how to place all things at His feet, how to live in the rest and the inheritance He desires to give us, and how to allow His life to flow through us.

Moses was like a servant, but Jesus is the Son over His own house. He is the builder of the house. We are the members of His household! He builds us as a house that brings glory to His name. It may be difficult for some believers who come from different backgrounds to read what I am writing here, and they may see it as slightly heretical – opposed to the word of God. So many teachers pressure us to live like Jesus, and to strive to work in His footsteps. But the Scriptures tell us to strive not to be like Him, but instead to rest in Him and in the confidence we first began with. The Scriptures instruct us not to strive, but to rest. That is a great difference. The true rest comes from holding on, to the end, to the same confidence we began with. This is what we have been called to. This must be our life. Do not stray from the focus of living in God's Sabbath. Moses did not bring us into the rest, but Jesus has brought us out of slavery into liberty. He stands with us in the presence of God. He walks us through the desert of our lives while providing all our needs. And then, He helps us to enter into the inheritance and the rest, and to live our lives there. This is why Jesus is greater than Moses.

---

[1] Midrash on Devarim 33:1 Moses being called "man of God" - "From his waist down-a man; from his waist up-Elohim (God)" see also discussion in Devarim Rabba 11:14 (http://www. eretzhemdah.org/newsletterArticle.asp?lang=en&pageid=48&c at=7&newsletter=98&article=306)

[2] Menachot 29:b Rab Judah said in the name of Rab, "When Moses ascended on high he found the Holy One, blessed be He, engaged in affixing coronets to the letters.5 Said Moses, 'Lord of the Universe, Who stays Thy hand?'6 He answered, 'There will arise a man, at the end of many generations, Akiba b. Joseph by name, who will expound upon each tittle heaps and heaps of laws'. 'Lord of the Universe', said Moses; 'permit me to see him'. He replied, 'Turn thee round'. Moses went and sat down behind eight rows7 [and listened to the discourses upon the

law]. Not being able to follow their arguments he was ill at ease, but when they came to a certain subject and the disciples said to the master 'Whence do you know it?' and the latter replied 'It is a law given unto Moses at Sinai' he was comforted. Thereupon he returned to the Holy One, blessed be He, and said, 'Lord of the Universe, Thou hast such a man and Thou givest the Torah by me!' He replied, 'Be silent, for such is My decree'.8 Then said Moses, 'Lord of the Universe, Thou hast shown me his Torah, show me his reward'. 'Turn thee round', said He; and Moses turned round and saw them weighing out his flesh at the market-stalls.9 'Lord of the Universe', cried Moses, 'such Torah, and such a reward!' He replied, 'Be silent, for such is My decree'."

³ John 13:1

CHAPTER 6

Jesus Is Greater than the High Priest

The central passage of the epistle to the Hebrews is chapter 4:14 through 5:6. This passage speaks of the High Priest, and of his position appointment. Everything said so far leads to this. All the comparisons that pointed to the superiority of Jesus lead to this point. The author gives a comprehensive explanation to show that it was God who made Jesus a "priest for ever after the order of Melchizedek", and not according to the order of Aaron.

The Priesthood

What is the duty of the High Priest? Why is Jesus more excellent than he? It is very important to understand why the author expands on this point. The spiritual authority of the people of Israel – the same authority the rabbis of today claim to have, as well as the same authority that the Pharisees of Jesus' day began to demand for themselves – belonged in biblical times to the High Priest. The author of the epistle to the Hebrews claims that Jesus alone has the authority of the High Priest. We must keep in mind that the letter to the Hebrews was written before the destruction of the Second Temple. In this time, although the power was officially in the hands of the Romans, in fact it was the High Priests who were the ruling party. It was they who made decisions regarding the people's daily life. Now then, whoever claims that Jesus is greater than the High Priest is claiming that Jesus' authority is greater than the authority in the hands of the ruling party of those days. That is why the passage before us is so comprehensive and vital.

When God made a nation of the people of Israel at the Mount Sinai, he did not form a kingdom with a king at its head, nor did He create a democracy. He formed a kingdom of priests.[1] In Exodus 19:5-6 we read, "'Now then, if you will indeed obey My voice and keep My covenant, then you shall be My own possession among all the peoples, for all the earth is Mine; and you shall be to Me a kingdom of priests and a holy nation.' These are the words that you shall speak to the sons of Israel." God calls the people of Israel at Mount Sinai to be a Kingdom of Priests. The entire kingdom, all the people of Israel, were called to be priests. In this kingdom of priests, the priests rule.

It is they who represent God, and they who determine what to do and what not to do. They are the judges, the teachers, and the guides of the people. The form of government of the people of Israel was to be entirely different from those of other nations, since God chose the people of Israel to represent Him in the eyes of the other nations. The people of Israel were to make it possible to catch a glimpse of the kingdom of God as it existed – His spiritual kingdom invading earth. This form of government was to be a kind of bridgehead of the kingdom of heaven on earth. The priest was called to stand at the head of this kingdom, representing the spiritual that ruled over the material. When the people of Israel demanded a king, God told Samuel – who functioned as the High Priest in those days, and was therefore the leader of the people – that it was not Samuel they were tired of as priest. It was not Samuel they wished to replace for a king; it was God himself. They wanted to change the ruling system and be like the other nations. They wanted to create an authority that is rooted in the king and comes from the king. As a result, God changed the form of government of the people, and created two kingdoms, or two forms of government, in the people of Israel. He made a compromise with the people – or rather, the people compromised and God agreed to the compromise. God changed the system to one where the priests and the king existed side by side, but the higher authority still belonged to the priests. The king was anointed by the priest, not the priest by the king. When the king tried to appoint his own priests this caused confusion and rebellion, as happened when Jeroboam presented the golden calves in Bethel and Dan, and appointed his own priests.[2] The priests were always called to obey higher laws than those of the king. When Athalia killed all the sons of the king, the High Priest took one of them, Joash, and hid him until he turned seven years old, when crowned him king.[3] The High Priest rebelled against Athalia because Athalia was not supposed to be the queen.

Despite the deterioration in the government God had ordained, and the compromise with the people, the formation of a monarchy went in the right direction at first. God was the one who chose first Saul, then David. Later we see how things went downhill when the kings killed each other in an effort to obtain the kingdom for themselves. The authority flowed from God through the king, and to the people. But the priests were always called to obey God's laws, which are different from the laws of the king. As long as there was no contradiction between the laws of the king and the laws of God – and the laws of the king were subject to the laws of God – the priests were called to obey the laws of the king. But when the king demanded that they worship false gods, they had to obey the higher law of God.

It is interesting that chapter 5:4-5 tells us that every priest was appointed by God. Please note: these things were written before the destruction of the Second Temple. The priests in those days were appointed by the Romans and not by God. Every priest with connections to the ruling families, and who was ambitious to rule, tried to carry favor with the Roman governor by paying huge amounts of money in hopes of being appointed High Priest. They were eager to rule, and the question whether God wanted them to did not concern them. Were they really the representatives of God? No. They ruled for the Romans. When the author of the epistle to the Hebrews states that every priest is appointed by God, he is actually criticizing the day's system of priesthood and the readers of his day understood it as such.

The people of Israel could have functioned as a kingdom of priests under Roman rule. They had returned to a situation where they did not have their own king. True, there had been a period of time of integration between priest and king during the reign of Judah Maccabee and the Hasmoneans. The Hasmoneans were priests who ruled over the land, but they did not take advantage of the opportunity to put themselves under God's rule once again. The priest was to have been God's representative because his position was appointed by God for the sake of the people. Instead, we see that the kingdom of priests submitted to the will of the Romans. Because of jealousy, and struggle for power and ascendancy, the system of priestly rule submitted to Roman rule.

The Rabbis Take the Place of the Priests

We must understand that whoever wrote these things knew very well what he was doing, and his readers understood exactly what he was saying. He called the people to understand and return to the priesthood that originates with God, because the existing priesthood, the one currently ruling, was not of God. When he wrote the epistle he knew the temple would be destroyed.

> The Holy Spirit is signifying this, that the way into the Holy Place has not yet been disclosed while the outer Tabernacle is still standing, which is a symbol for the present time. Accordingly both gifts and sacrifices are offered which cannot make the worshiper perfect in conscience, since they relate only to food and drink and various washings, regulations for the body imposed until a time of reformation (Heb. 9:8-10).

In these verses he makes the point that the temple was still standing, and that the things he is mentioning exist until they are reformed. When he says "while the Tabernacle was standing," he indicates that he knows there will be a time when the Tabernacle will no longer stand. Because of his knowledge and understanding, he proclaims that Jesus is the High Priest. Jesus is the true ruler of the people of Israel, and the one who represents the kingdom of God. He is the one we need to submit and listen to.

When the temple was destroyed in AD 70, a vacuum in leadership was created, especially among those who did not receive Jesus. The rabbis filled this vacuum.

They set themselves up to be the leaders of the people and placed themselves in the place God had determined for the priests as representatives of the spiritual kingdom. That process had begun many years earlier. Because the priests were corrupt, they did not represent God in a worthy manner. They represented themselves and the Romans. As a result, a rabbinical system of rule developed, which in those days was in the hands of the Pharisees, and served as a parallel system to the priesthood. When the Romans got rid of the priests (when the temple was destroyed), the rabbis took their place. Since the positions they filled had originally belonged to the priests who were the highest religious authority, religious people today consider the word of the rabbis to be more binding than the law of their country.

For instance, when the government of Israel ruled that Ashkenazi and Sephardi children should study together in the same schools, and the rabbis refused, many of the parents obeyed the rabbis, even at the price of going to prison. If only we also, who believe in Jesus, would behave likewise – not that we would heed our rabbis, but that we would heed our High Priest and not be afraid to pay the price of incarceration for acting differently from what the state or others tell us. In the end it is we who choose for ourselves which authority we live under. Do we live under the authority of the worlds' rulers, or under heavenly authority? There are those who say, "I am not prepared to obey the governmental authorities, only to heavenly authority." But we have to obey the government as long as they do not require us to oppose the laws of God. If we disobey the law we must be prepared to go through with it to the end. Not in war, but in submission. When Daniel chose not to obey the laws of the King of Babylon,[4] he did so humbly, not arrogantly.

The Roles of the Priests

Who and what is the High Priest, and what role did he fulfill? The first thing he was called to be was a leader of the priests. He was the head priest who guided, led, and instructed the priests in their work. He was also called to be holy to God and to proclaim that through his life. In Exodus 28:36-38 it is written:

> You shall also make a plate of pure gold and shall engrave on it, like the engravings of a seal, "Holy to the LORD." You shall fasten it on a blue cord, and it shall be on the turban; it shall be at the front of the turban. It shall be on Aaron's forehead, and Aaron shall take away the iniquity of the holy things which the sons of Israel consecrate, with regard to all their holy gifts; and it shall always be on his forehead, that they may be accepted before the LORD.

The priestly garments are described here. The High Priest had a turban with the words "Holy to the Lord" on it in gold. Some explain that holiness means to be set apart, detached from the world. But holiness is much more than just being set apart. The emphasis on this word means exactly the opposite – not set apart, but total belonging. When a man says to his wife, "You are consecrated to me" (In Hebrew: You are holy unto me), he is not saying, "You are separate from the others, set apart from the world," even though this could be the outcome of consecration to him, or part of the process. No, he tells her, "You belong to me absolutely; exclusively one flesh with me." The emphasis is on the bond between the two, the belonging together, and not the separation from others. When the High Priest wore his garments, he carried a plate on his forehead that read

"Holy to the Lord." That is, I belong completely to God. He is everything for me. I represent Him, not myself. I belong to Him, not to you. This was his declaration. Everywhere he went, the first thing people saw was his turban and the plate attached to it that announced: "I belong completely to God."

Another detail in the garments of the High Priest were the two stones on the shoulders of the ephod, one for each side. The names of six tribes were engraved on each stone, as written in Exodus 28:9-12:

> You shall take two onyx stones and engrave on them the names of the sons of Israel, six of their names on the one stone and the names of the remaining six on the other stone, according to their birth. As a jeweler engraves a signet, you shall engrave the two stones according to the names of the sons of Israel; you shall set them in filigree settings of gold. You shall put the two stones on the shoulder pieces of the ephod, as stones of memorial for the sons of Israel, and Aaron shall bear their names before the LORD on his two shoulders for a memorial.

The High Priest bore the names of the people of Israel on his shoulders as a memorial to the Lord. This was a reminder, not only to God, but also to the sons of Israel. They were to remember that the priest was bearing spiritual responsibility for them before God.

The High Priest also carried the people of Israel on his heart:

> The stones shall be according to the names of the sons of Israel: twelve, according to their names; they shall be like the engravings of a

seal, each according to his name for the twelve tribes . . . Aaron shall carry the names of the sons of Israel in the breastpiece of judgment over his heart when he enters the Holy Place, for a memorial before the LORD continually. You shall put in the breastpiece of judgment the Urim and the Thummim, and they shall be over Aaron's heart when he goes in before the LORD; and Aaron shall carry the judgment of the sons of Israel over his heart before the LORD (Ex. 28:21, 29-30).

Every precious stone represented a tribe, so that he was carrying the people of Israel on his heart. We read above that God appointed the High Priest for the people. It is vital that we understand that this appointment was for the people. He carried the sons of Israel on his shoulders and on his heart before God.

One of the duties of the High Priest was to offer the most important sacrifice of atonement on the Day of Atonement. The High Priest first made a sacrifice for himself, and then for the sons of Israel. He was the only man to enter the Holy of Holies, into the presence of the Spirit of God. This detail also reflects Jesus, who as a man entered the heavenly Tabernacle and opened the way for men to draw near to God.

As we have seen, the duty of the High Priest was to make sacrifices and offerings for sins on our behalf, for our sins, just as Jesus our High Priest gave up Himself for us. It is interesting that even in the Old Testament, the death of the High Priest atoned for the people. In Joshua 20:1-9, and in Deuteronomy 19, we read that when someone murdered another person unintentionally[5] he fled from the avengers of blood to a safe city. There were six such cities: Hebron, Shechem, Kadesh, and Naphtali to the west of the Jordan River; Batsar, Rama, and Golan on the east of the Jordan. The murderer had to remain in the city until the death of the High Priest. When the High Priest died he was able to return to his city, safe from the fear of vengeance. If he had left the city during the lifetime of the High Priest, the avenger was allowed to kill him. That means that the death of the High Priest made atonement for the murder he had committed. He fulfilled this function for the sake of the people in both his lifetime, and in his death. He entered the Holy of Holies, made the atoning sacrifice, and led the priests and the people – all that he did in the fulfillment of his duties was for the people of Israel.

Another area the priests were responsible for was justice. Deuteronomy 17:8-12 says:

If any case is too difficult for you to decide, between one kind of homicide or another, between one kind of lawsuit or another, and between one kind of assault or another, being cases of dispute in your courts, then you shall arise and go up to the place which the LORD your God chooses. So you shall come to the Levitical priest or the judge who is in office in those days, and you shall inquire of them and they will declare to you the verdict in the case. You shall do according to the terms of the verdict which they declare to you from that place which the LORD chooses; and you shall be careful to observe according to all that they teach you. According to the terms of the law which they teach you, and according to the verdict which they tell you, you shall do; you shall not turn aside from the word which they declare to you, to the right or the left. The man who acts presumptuously by not listening to the priest who stands there to serve the LORD your God, nor to the judge, that man shall die; thus you shall purge the evil from Israel.

The authority attributed to the rabbis is based on these verses. They take these verses for themselves and say, "This is talking about us, so whoever doesn't pay heed to us is wicked and must be destroyed. The Torah tells you to heed us." But these verses are speaking of the priests, not the rabbis. We are told to go to the place determined by God, the temple in Jerusalem! There the priests, the Levites and the judges will judge between good and evil. Any dispute that arises and has need of arbitration must be taken to them. Today we have a legal system. If we have a dispute, we take it to the court appointed by the state. The judge will determine what is right to do. In certain matters, and at certain times the High Priest functioned as a king – as in the days of Samuel. In other matters the High Priest fulfilled the function of a Supreme Court judge.

The task of the priests, which further on we shall see is relevant to us, was to assist the High Priest in teaching the word of God to the people. The Levites lived in cities scattered throughout the land. They taught the word of God to the people and arbitrated in lesser matters. They also served in the temple in worship, sacrifice, cleaning, renovations and whatever else needed to be taken care of in the temple. That is why they worked in shifts, going up to Jerusalem for their time of service. We also as a kingdom of priests must live among the people to serve in holy ministry, which means teaching the word of God and taking care of the practical helps.

Jesus the Messiah – a Better High Priest

Why is Jesus a better High Priest? What are the claims of the epistle to the Hebrews that establish Jesus as a greater priest than the one presently ruling over the people? "Now the main point in what has been said is this: we have such a High Priest, who has taken His seat at the right hand of the throne of the Majesty in the heavens, a minister in the sanctuary and in the true Tabernacle, which the Lord pitched, not man" (Heb.8:1-2). First of all, Jesus the Messiah, our High Priest, serves in the highest places with the highest authority. The people of Israel, who were called to be a kingdom of priests, were destined to be the bridgehead of the Kingdom of Heaven on earth. That did not happen. That is why the High Priest, Jesus the Messiah-God, came to dwell among us and in us. He brought to us, within us, the bridgehead of the Kingdom of God on earth. Jesus was first and foremost the High Priest in heaven, in the true Tabernacle after which Moses was instructed to build a pattern on earth.[6] Jesus passed through heaven, through the real Tabernacle. He is the priest who represents the highest possible authority, not the authority of the Roman Empire or any other human authority.

The second point is that Jesus can feel our weaknesses. In chapter 4:15 we read, "For we do not have a High Priest who cannot sympathize with our weaknesses, but One who has been tempted in all things as we are, yet without sin." Jesus not only sympathizes with our weaknesses and sorrows, since he lives within those who believe in Him, he also feels them with us. Jesus, who is God, feels our weaknesses. Every time we sin, every time we fail, every time we are weak – He feels the pain because we hurt the Holy Spirit. Even with my wife, whom I feel the closest to, when she feels pain, all I can say is, "Oh, honey, that hurts, I know. I am with you, we will go through this together." I empathize with her pain, but I cannot feel it. Jesus, on the other hand, not only empathizes with our pain from without, He feels our weakness from within us. He hurts with us; He feels every lack, weakness and inability.

Our High Priest is not an ordinary, sinful and weak person. He felt and feels what we feel, but He went through it all without sin. We cannot say to God, "You are God, not man, so you cannot know exactly what I am going through." That is why He came and took on flesh and blood, living among us. Before that we may have been able to say, "You never experienced pain, death, sin, separation, loneliness." Now we cannot claim that, because He did experience all that. He felt everything with us. That means that when things are rough for us, they are not difficult only for us. It is hard for Him with us, though we must remember that as it is written of Him, "One who has been tempted in all things as we are, yet without sin" (Heb. 4:15). The pain did not cause Him to sin.

The third point is that Jesus not only carries our names on His shoulders symbolically, He actually does carry us on His shoulders. Isaiah 53:4 tells us, "Surely our griefs He Himself bore, And our sorrows He carried; Yet we ourselves esteemed Him stricken, Smitten of God, and afflicted." He carried our griefs on Himself. He carried our sins on the cross – not just symbolically. In His blood we have forgiveness of sins. The apostle Peter declares, "And He Himself bore our sins in His body on the cross, so that we might die to sin and live to righteousness; for by His wounds you were healed" (1Pet. 2:24). The apostle Paul asks, "Who is the one who condemns? Christ Jesus is He who died, yes, rather who was raised, who is at the right hand of God, who also intercedes for us" (Rom. 8:34). He carries us in prayer constantly, even now. When things are hard for you, when you are sick, even when no one else is praying for you, Jesus prays for you. Jesus makes intercession for you in the best place possible – in the Holy of Holies. The High Priest entered in to the Holy of Holies just once a year.

Jesus, however, is present all the time on the right hand of power. He does not go just once a year to sprinkle the blood of the atoning sacrifice, He is there for eternity. He always feels our pain, and prays immediately for us at the right hand of the Father. He went in once and for all to the Holy of Holies. He carried us on His heart, in His love. John 13:1[7] tell us that Jesus loved His disciples to the end. That was just a short time before He washed their feet and went to the cross. He also said that as He has loved us, we should love one another.[8] The commandment given us is to love others, as He has loved, to the end.

A High Priest Forever According to the Order of Melchizedek

Our High Priest carries us on His heart. He doesn't just make a yearly sacrifice for atonement (because the sacrifice in the temple was not enough, it had to be sacrificed again, year by year). He Himself is the source of salvation for all who obey him.[9] He took on this role of Aaron's not because He was flesh and blood, not because He belonged to the priestly tribe of Levi – but according to the order of Melchizedek (Heb. 6:20).

What does "after the order of Melchizedek" mean? In the Psalms King David breaks out in a song of praise to God (Ps. 110, particularly verse 4), "The LORD has sworn and will not change His mind, 'You are a priest forever according to the order of Melchizedek.'" Jesus, many years later, asks the Pharisees a question that at the time they had no answer for: if the Messiah were the Son of David, how can it be that David calls Him Lord? The logic of the question is simple, because if David is his forefather, then he should call David "Lord." With this question he tried to show the Pharisees that the Messiah is more than the son of David, he is also the Son of God. David continues to say, "You are a priest forever according to the order of Melchizedek." The author of the epistle to the Hebrews, in quoting Psalm 110, asks, "Who on earth is he talking about?" (7:11). In David's day the priests were from the line of Aaron. Why is it that out of the blue David talks here of the one who sits at the right hand of God, being according to the order of Melchizedek and not Aaron? And then the writer starts speaking of Melchizedek and asks who it is that, as David wrote, will establish a new order of priest-hood, different from the Aaronic priesthood.

In his answer he refers to the sudden appearance of Melchizedek in history. He continues to detail in chapter 7 that Melchizedek was a priest to the Most High God, with no father, no mother, and no genealogy. We do not know who he was or where he came from. He is a picture of the Messiah. Verse 3 tells us that he was a priest forever.[10] Melchizedek made a sudden appear-ance in human history in his encounter with Abraham our father. Abraham gave him tithes. The author of Hebrews emphasizes that Levi, the father of the priests, gave tithes to Melchizedek while "in the loins" of Abraham. The one of highest authority receives the tithes from those who acknowledge his authority and mastery. From this we can infer that Abraham acknowledged the authority of Melchizedek. Melchizedek was a priest of the Most High God even though he was not of the tribe of Levi. More than that, his authority was higher than Abraham and the tribe of Levi. The author of the epistle tells us that it is the same with the Messiah: He is eternal.

We know who Jesus was when He lived on earth. We have his human genealogy. The author mentions this here when he tells us that the Messiah was of the tribe of Judah,[11] that is, not from the priestly tribe. But we have no genealogy to describe the true, eternal identity of the Son of God. From this aspect, he appeared suddenly in history, He is eternal, He was and is and always will be, and He was never created. In this He is like Melchizedek, who appeared suddenly in history and then disappeared. Abraham accepted him as a superior authority. He was a priest to the Most High God who was not descended from the tribe of Levi – and so is the Messiah. But the Messiah is "forever." "[B]ut Jesus, on the other hand, because He continues forever, holds His priesthood permanently. Therefore He is able also to save forever those who draw near to God through Him, since He always lives to make intercession for them" (Heb. 7:24-25). There is no need now to replace the High Priest every time he dies. Our High Priest died once for all time, rose from the dead and lives forever.

The Messiah also changed the priesthood. The priesthood is no longer from the tribe of Levi, or of the seed of Aaron. It no longer belongs to the ruling party as in the days the epistle was written. Today the priesthood is different. Jesus is not only like the High Priest, He has greater authority than the High Priest. He not only changed the priesthood, He changed the Torah (we will expand on this further on). He sits at the right hand of power; He serves in the true Holy of Holies. Jesus is a greater High Priest because He is not just a symbol; He is the true High Priest who fulfills the symbol. Jesus is the true High Priest, and this is why His authority is the highest of all.

A Kingdom of Priests

In his first epistle, chapter 2:9, Peter refers to Exodus 19:6, "But you are a chosen race, a royal priesthood, a holy nation, a people for God's own possession, so that you may proclaim the excellencies of Him who has called you out of darkness into His marvelous light." The verse in Exodus speaks only of the people of Israel, but here in the New Testament, Peter, quoting Exodus, is speaking not only of the people of Israel but of all those who believe in Jesus. If Jesus is the High Priest, then you do not need to be of the tribe of Levi. Your name does not have to be "Cohen" or "Levi" in order to be a priest. You can have any name– Leibovitz, Buskila, Harel, Jones, McDonald or Chan. It doesn't matter. We are all a kingdom of priests!

If we are a kingdom of priests, it follows that first and foremost we live under the authority of the High Priest. We live in a kingdom that is parallel, yet more authoritative, to the kingdom we live in today. We must obey the laws of this government as long as they do not oppose God's laws, which are the laws of the Kingdom we belong to and represent. But we have no right to say, "The government doesn't represent God's Kingdom, so we won't obey it." We are called to obey the laws of the land as long as they do not contradict the Scriptures. And to the same degree, we must not make people, whether rabbis or Christian pastors, our ultimate authority. Our highest authority is from our High Priest. This is why it is vital that each one of us be well versed in the Scriptures. This is why it is important to study and learn to know God, and to draw nearer in intimacy with God. He created us for this. The same intimacy we seek in all kinds of other places but cannot find – it is in this relationship with Him.

We, as a kingdom of priests, have been called to

be the representatives of God to mankind, just as the priests were. We must not withdraw ourselves, because that is contradictory to our role. We were not called to create a ghetto, or to stay behind protective walls and never step out into the world lest they hurt us. We were called to represent God to man. That means we need to be with the people, touching them, helping them. Our duty is to serve the people by making sacrifices – not sacrifices of lambs and bulls, but first and foremost by giving ourselves to Him and to His service.

> Therefore I urge you, brethren, by the mercies of God, to present your bodies a livingand holy sacrifice, acceptable to God, which is your spiritual service of worship. And do not be conformed to this world, but be transformed by the renewing of your mind, so that you may prove what the will of God is, that which is good and acceptable and perfect (Rom. 12:1-2).

Our call to serve is, first and foremost, by the giving of ourselves: first to God, and then to others around us. We do so not from feelings of obligation or guilt, but from knowing God will give us what we need to serve (Phil. 4:13).

Do I give of my time and my strength? Is my giving like the offering of the rich men in the temple, who did not give sacrificially, but out of their surplus? Or am I giving like the widow who had only two mites and gave all she had? Do I give even when it hurts me? We are told that we have to sacrifice prayers and supplications.[12] That is part of the sacrifice we have to give for those around us – for the believers, the unbelievers, and the family. We have to sacrifice prayers and supplications, and, of course, also prayers of praise and thanksgiving, the sacrifice of praise. That is a part of our role. It isn't always pleasant or easy to do something sacrificially. None of us gets up every single morning with a song of praise on our lips and in our heart, and we don't always enjoy praying for those around us. Sometimes that happens, but not every day. Usually we sacrifice for ourselves, we pray for our own needs. This is like the High Priest only making a sacrifice for himself, and not for the people. If he had done that, he would not have been fulfilling his role. Usually when we get up in the morning our eyes are swollen and we have to make an effort to begin to praise God. It means making that choice. But as priests we are called to do that, in every situation, even when we don't feel like it. It is the same in a relationship between man and wife. Every morning when my wife gets up and sees my crumpled, wrinkly face, does she always think, "Oh, how I love that guy?" No! Very often she has to make a conscious decision to love me, and sometimes that's hard to do. But praise God, she chooses to make that decision!

Part of our role as believers is to serve others in practical ways. We have to look for a need, whether with believers or unbelievers. We have to serve the society we live in. When a believer takes a paramedics course and volunteers in the Red Cross, or serves in the police, or helps at the community center, he is fulfilling a calling to be a kingdom of priests. He serves his people sacrificially by giving practical help where it is needed. The practical help may not seem very spiritual, but it is an important part of the role we are called to fulfill. In biblical days there were priests and Levites who worked in cleaning, skinning, butchery, renovations and repairs in the temple, and more. And there were priests whose job was to teach the word of God to the people. These are our duties too.

Wherever we go, we are to proclaim that we are holy to the Lord. We have to wear the gold plate that says "Holy to the Lord," that is, belonging entirely to God, and to teach others about God and His ways. In all times and in all places. "For it was fitting for us to have such a High Priest, holy, innocent, undefiled, separated from sinners and exalted above the heavens; who does not need daily, like those High Priests, to offer up sacrifices, first for His own sins and then for the sins of the people, because this He did once for all when He offered up Himself" (Heb. 7:26-27).

What a glorious High Priest we have! His authority is the highest authority of all! He is holy, He is blameless, and He is pure! He is separate from the sinners and loves sinners! He is lifted up far above the heavens! He has made one sacrifice for all time!

"Therefore, since we have a great High Priest who has passed through the heavens, Jesus the Son of God, let us hold fast our confession. For we do not have a High Priest who cannot sympathize with our weaknesses, but One who has been tempted in all things as we are, yet without sin" (Heb. 4:14-16). So then we can draw near with boldness – not in fear and trembling – to the throne of grace, because we have a High Priest who died and rose again, who can feel for us and has experienced all things, and who came from heaven and once and for all paid the price of our sins and made us a nation of priests to our Lord. Let us draw near then with boldness to the throne of grace and receive mercy – and there is much mercy – and find grace to help in time of need.

---

[1] It is a common mistake in English to call this a "royal priesthood". It is simply a "kingdom of priests".

[2] 1 Kings 12:26-33

[3] 2 Kings 11

[4] Daniel 1:8-16

[5] In biblical days unintentional killing was still considered murder, not manslaughter as in modern law

[6] Exodus 25:40

[7] "Now before the feast of the Passover, when Jesus knew that his hour was come that he should depart out of this world unto the Father, having loved his own which were in the world, he loved them unto the end."

[8] John 13:34

[9] "And being made perfect, he became the author of eternal salvation unto all them that obey him" Heb. 5:9

[10] "Without father, without mother, without genealogy, having neither beginning of days nor end of life, but made like the Son of God, he remains a priest perpetually." Heb. 7:3

[11] Heb. 7:14

[12] "I exhort therefore that, first of all, supplications, prayers, intercessions, and giving of thanks, be made for all men" 1 Tim. 2:1. "Who in the days of his flesh, when he had offered up prayers and supplications with strong crying and tears unto him that was able to save him from death, and was heard in that he feared" Heb. 5:7

CHAPTER 7

Jesus Changed the Torah

Does Jewish Thought Allow for Changes in the Torah (Law)?

In Hebrews 7:12 it is written, "For when the priesthood is changed, of necessity there takes place a change of law also." This is a sensational announcement, which resounded in the Jewish ears as well as the ears of many believers in these days, as well as then. We have seen that the author of the epistle speaks about the priesthood changing, and here he continues that thought and says that when the priesthood changed, so did the Law!

Every religious Jew who is asked, "Has the Law changed? Does it change? Will it ever change?" will answer as a matter of course; "Of course not, the Law existed before the creation of the universe, together with the Messiah, together with God, and will exist for eternity. As it is written in Mishne Torah, Yesodei HaTorah 9:1, 'It is clear and explicit in the Torah that God's commandment remains forever without change, addition, or diminishment . . . we are commanded to fulfill all the Torah's directives forever.'" Even if we ask many believers if the Law has changed, they will answer, "No! The Law of God is eternal." Many believers accept the claim that the Law is eternal and does not change as the Gospel truth.

So Then, Is the Law Eternal or Does It change?

The ninth principle of the Thirteen Principles of Faith compiled by Maimonides, one of the most respected Rabbis in history, says, "I believe with perfect faith that this Torah will not be changed, and that there will never be another given by G-d." God will never give another law. It will not be changed. There will never be another law. Yet, the Babylonian Talmud in Masechet Nida 61b,[1] in discussing whether burial linen wrappings are ceremoniously clean or not, has a sentence that confuses our rabbinical brothers. It is written there, "[M]itzvos will be nullified in the future to come." That is, the commandments will cease in the future. What does this mean? What is this talking about? We have read or heard that the Law is eternal and will never be replaced. By the way, even the Maimonides claim that in the future the Law will be replaced. He supports the Babylonian Talmud in this statement. Even the "Shulchan Arouch"[2] supports the claim that the commandments will be changed in the future, as do the Tosafot (the annotations to the Talmud).

So even rabbinical writings clearly support, however incomprehensibly, the understanding that in the future the commandments will be annulled. This creates a problem for them. The rabbis argue amongst themselves, asking, "What will be annulled? How and when? Will it actually be annulled?" There are some who say that only the "thou shalt" laws will be replaced, and others argue that only the "thou shalt not" laws will be replaced, and others who say everything will be replaced.[3]

Through the generations the rabbis discussed the question of when this would happen. Some said in the days of the Messiah, others said after the resurrection from the dead. Shabtai Zvi, a false Messiah who rose up in the 17th century and carried many of his contemporaries away with him, depended on these claims that the Law would be replaced in the days of the Messiah. He claimed that he was the Messiah, claimed to bring the days of Messiah, and that one of the things to happen in the days of Messiah would be that he would change the Law. His followers indulged in all kinds of activities that today would be called orgies, and other things that have nothing to do with a holy faith. Shabtai Zvi excused that with the claim that he, the Messiah, came to change the commandments.

The argument among the rabbis continued over many generations. Some believed the Law would change, others said perhaps it would, and others said, "No way." Could the answer be that these changes would occur at the resurrection from the dead? Many of the rabbis say that the commandments will be annulled at the resurrection, because the dead will be free from the Law. This explanation is especially interesting for us as disciples of Jesus the Messiah, and sounds familiar because that is the line of thought that we find in the New Testament:

> Or do you not know, brethren (for I am speaking to those who know the law), that the law has jurisdiction over a person as long as he lives? For the married woman is bound by law to her husband while he is living; but if her husband dies, she is released from the law concerning the husband. So then, if while her husband is living she is joined to another man, she shall be

called an adulteress; but if her husband dies, she is free from the law, so that she is not an adulteress though she is joined to another man. Therefore, my brethren, you also were made to die to the Law through the body of Christ, so that you might be joined to another, to Him who was raised from the dead, in order that we might bear fruit for God. For while we were in the flesh, the sinful passions, which were aroused by the Law, were at work in the members of our body to bear fruit for death. But now we have been released from the Law, having died to thatby which we were bound, so that we serve in newness of the Spirit and not in oldness of the letter (Rom. 7:1-6).

We are told here that the Messiah has freed us from the law because when He died, He died to the commandments of the law. We died with Him, and the dead are freed from the Law. The understanding that death frees us from the Law exists all along in Jewish thought, including in the understanding of Jewish disciples of Jesus.

Well then, does Jewish thought hold that the Law is replaced, or that it is eternal? Eternity includes the time that was before time existed, and continues forever and ever to when there is no time anymore. But if things will change, whether at the resurrection from the dead, or in the days of Messiah – and regardless of what exactly it is that changes – the Law cannot be eternal. Does not the Halacha (Jewish laws that adapt the Torah to present times) itself change the Law? Teachers in every religious school teach that the Halacha is the process in which the Torah is being adapted to our day and age. If the Halacha is changing and adapting the Torah (Law), then the Torah (Law) is changing and adapting, and therefore not eternal. [4]

I had a look at the Internet site "Moreshet"[5] to look into this subject, and see what modern rabbis say about it. I found a question someone had sent in to Rabbi Yuval Sherlo. I will quote the question and answer almost in their entirety. The question was:

> *"Shalom Honorable Rabbi, is it likely that in the future God will change some of the Laws to make them appropriate for today? Like the sacrifices that were offered by the nations, which God sanctified and that's what was appropriate back then . . . or the old fashioned death penalty. Could it be He will change everything just like before the flood eating animals was forbidden but it was allowed after the flood. Because there was a descent in the world . . . and we see that God gave new laws like for instance the unclean that could not make the Passover sacrifice in time, so He gave a new law because of that, or in the case of the daughters of Zalaphad where He gave a new law to match the occasion... so we see that there is a connection between the laws in the Torah that God gave them according to the spirit of the times and special instances. So why shouldn't that happen in the future?"*

His question is simple: throughout history, throughout the Bible, we see that laws were changed and adapted, so why shouldn't it happen in the future too? The answer from Rabbi Yuval Sherlo is a bit more complicated:

"Peace and blessings, we believe with total faith that the Law in our hands will never be replaced as long as earth shall stand as we live today. This is one of the thirteen principles of faith. What will happen in some future? We have no way to know. We must remember that there are opinions in the Jewish writings that the "commandments will be annulled in the future". We learn from prophecy that in the future a new covenant will be made (careful with that expression!) whose basis will not be the exodus from Egypt but the new redemption (although the exodus from Egypt will still have its place), and so on. So in fact: There are various sources that teach that a day will come when perhaps (not for certain!) the Almighty will reappear with a prophet like Moses our Teacher and command us different things."

So then, let's have a close look at the answer: "All of this is irrelevant to us. We live the life according to system of the law, and here the Law is eternal and we are committed to obey it." The rabbi says that as long as the world exists in the way we live today, the Law will not be changed. That is one of the thirteen principles of faith. He claims that we have no tools by which to know what is to come in the future, but then he immediately refers back to a very important prophecy from Jeremiah 31, "We learn from prophecy that in the future a new covenant will be made (careful with that expression!)." He warns against the expression "new covenant", naturally afraid that people will understand this to mean the new covenant of Jesus, but he cannot ignore the fact that the Bible tells of a new covenant that will apparently change the Law. This basis of the new covenant, according to the rabbi, is the new redemption. It is interesting that he understands correctly the new covenant but errs in placing it in the future and not in the past, two thousand years ago.

He goes on to say, "There are various sources that teach that a day will come when perhaps (not for certain!) The Almighty will reappear with a prophet like Moses our Teacher and command us different things." This is exactly what we learned earlier in the epistle to the Hebrews about the prophet like Moses who is greater than Moses. The rabbi is speaking here of the Messiah, who will be a prophet like Moses, and will give a different Law than the Law given by Moses. Moses himself spoke of him in Deuteronomy 18:18, "I will raise up a prophet from among their countrymen like you, and I will put My words in his mouth, and he shall speak to them all that I command him," just as we mentioned earlier. But in the same breath the rabbi tries to state the opposite. "All of this is irrelevant to us. We live our life according to the system of the law, and here the Law is eternal and we are committed to obey it." The use of words here is confusing. In actual fact his answer to the question whether the Law will be changed is: "yes-no" or "no-yes". His answer is, "The Law is eternal but it will change, or it will change but it's eternal" at the same time. He says, "A new covenant will come that will change the Law, another prophet like Moses will come and will give a different Law."

We answer him, "Dear brother Rabbi Yuval Sherlo, this won't be in the future, this happened two thousand years ago! The Messiah came and changed the Law. There has been a prophet like Moses who gave us a new covenant that is not based on the Sinai covenant, but on new redemption. It has already happened!"

So, is the Law eternal according to the rabbis? The

answer is: That depends who they are speaking with. If they speak with us, or with someone who is not religious, they say the Law will never change. It is for eternity. But if they are speaking with someone from their own circle, the answer is, "Yes, because the Halacha changes and adapts the Law to the day. Yes, because in the future a prophet like Moses will come and make a new covenant based on a new redemption and will change the Torah."

What Is the Torah?

After a look at the Jewish sources, let's look at what the Bible says about the changes in the Law. In order to understand this better, let us try and understand first what the Torah is. The word "Torah" is a misused word, and is connected to anything that we want to have some kind of authority. But what does the word actually mean?

Smith's Bible Dictionary Defines it as such, "The word is properly used . . . to express a definite commandment laid down by any recognized authority; but when the word is used with the article . . . it refers to the expressed will to God, and in nine cases out of ten to the Mosaic law, or to the Pentateuch of which it forms the chief portion. The Hebrew word *torah* (law) lays more stress on its moral authority, as teaching the truth and guiding in the right way; the Greek *nomos* (law), on its constraining power as imposed and enforced by a recognized authority."

Wiktionary gives these definitions for Torah:[6]

From Hebrew *TORAH* ("instruction, law or teaching").

1. The body of rules and standards issued by a government, or to be applied by courts and similar authorities.

2. The first five books of the Hebrew Scriptures, attributed to Moses and therefore also known as the Five Books of Moses. Tradition holds that the Torah was handed down to Moses on Mount Sinai.
3. The full body of written Jewish law, including the Tanakh, the Talmud, the Mishnah and the midrashic texts.
4. The whole of Jewish law, both written and unwritten.
5. The encompassing philiaophy of Judaism.

The word "law" comes from the word "Torah", which is derived from the same root as the Hebrew words for instruction, parent, teacher, and learning. The word Torah has many nuances of meaning, including study, doctrine, teaching, and law.

Generally the word is used as a name for the Pentateuch, which is the first five books of the Bible. Sometimes "Torah" is used for the Oral Law (Talmud, Mishnah etc.). Other times it refers to what the rabbis say at any given stage, and sometimes it is used to refer to the entire Old Testament, including the Law, the prophets and the writings. Many times the word "Torah" is used to represent different meanings in the same conversation according to what suits the speaker at the moment. The use in conversation can sway from "Torah" in the sense of the Mosaic Law, to the modern rabbinical laws, to the Oral Law and then back to the Mosaic Law. That is why it is so important that when someone begins speaking with you about "Torah", make sure you clarify what he means. Which Torah is it that will never change? When they say the Torah is the word of God, what Torah are they talking about? According to the rabbis, even the oral law was the word of God that Moses received on Mount Sinai. Does it never change?

We have already seen that Halacha changes. So which Torah are we talking about?

Different Covenants – Different Laws

Let's begin by defining the subject, and speak of the Laws of God gave in the Bible. These laws and commandments given in the Bible, do they change or have they always stayed the same? If they are eternal, that would mean that they always existed and will always exist without changing.

Just as our friend the yeshiva student asked the rabbi on the "Moreshet" website, we see many changes in the laws in the Bible. We see that before the flood people ate seeds, fruit and vegetables without meat. After the flood they were allowed to eat meat. The law that defined what was allowed and what was not allowed to eat had changed. The daughters of Zelophehad [7] mentioned by the yeshiva student were of the tribe of Menashe. Their father had no sons, and before they entered the Promised Land they asked Moses, "When we marry, what will happen to our father's inheritance? He has no sons and the inheritance will be taken by another tribe." Moses came before God and returned with a new law that said that when a man had only daughters, his inheritance would be passed on to his daughters, and they would be allowed to marry only with someone from the same tribe. This new law did not exist before – until then the inheritance had been given only to sons. The Law had changed.

Has there been a change in the sacrifice system? When God created man in the Garden of Eden, before sin, no mention was made of sacrifices. Later on Abel offered a sacrifice that was more acceptable than that of Cain. Later on the Mosaic Law gives a very long list of sacrifices, detailing when and how to bring different

sacrifices – a sacrifice of thanks, a sacrifice of consecration, a burnt sacrifice, etc.... - many kinds of sacrifices that hadn't existed before as part of the worship
of God, at least not in such detail. Is this addition a
change? The answer must be, "Yes!"

Let's continue along the history timeline and see
what happened with the sacrifices today according to
the rabbis. In order to resolve the dilemma that today
there is no temple and we cannot sacrifice, the sages
determined that prayers replace sacrifice, and based
their ruling on Hosea 14:2, "We will render the calves of
our lips" (KJV). In other words, with my lips, by means
of prayer, I am offering up the calf of the sacrifice. But
Psalms 141:2 says, "May my prayer be counted as
incense before You; The lifting up of my hands as the
evening offering." My prayer is like incense, and when
I lift up my hands it's like the *mincha*, or the evening
sacrifice. I have not yet heard a rabbi say, "Let's lift up
our hands, and that will be in place of the evening sacrifice." Again, there is selective interpretation here. I have
no idea why they took the first half of the verse, but not
the second. In any case the answer to the question, "Do
we see in the Bible changes in the Laws God gave?"
is, "Yes! We certainly do see changes in the commandments God gave."

A Significant Change

Since the Law has to do with how we are justified by
a covenant, when the covenant changes, the Laws of
the covenant change as well. But the Bible also speaks
of other changes. Jeremiah 31:31-33 says:

> "Behold, days are coming," declares the LORD,
> "when I will make a new covenant with the house
> of Israel and with the house of Judah, not like the

covenant which I made with their fathers in the day I took them by the hand to bring them out of the land of Egypt, My covenant which they broke, although I was a husband to them," declares the LORD. "But this is the covenant which I will make with the house of Israel after those days," declares the LORD, "I will put My law within them and on their heart I will write it; and I will be their God, and they shall be My people."

The prophet speaks in the name of God saying that the days are coming when God will make a new covenant that will be different from the covenant He made with the people of Israel when He brought them out of Egypt; the Mosaic Covenant that was sealed on Mount Sinai! The covenant will be different in that it will be written on the heart. God will put it within us.

A different covenant also means different laws. The Bible numbers several covenants God made with man and with every covenant we find different laws. When God created man He made a covenant with him. He gave Adam laws regarding what he was allowed to eat, and what was forbidden. Adam was only allowed to eat from all of the vegetation. After the flood, God made a covenant with Noah. Noah was allowed to eat meat. Things had changed. Later yet, God made a covenant with the people of Israel at Sinai, what we also call the Mosaic Covenant. This covenant came with a tremendous system of laws that detailed what was allowed to be eaten and what was forbidden.

Because the different covenants have different laws, it was understood that when a new covenant was made the Torah would be different, and the laws would be different, as we see in Rabbi Yuval Sherlo's response. Every covenant involves a change of law. The various covenants had different laws. Another important difference is that this new covenant is not written on tablets of stone. It is not written outside of man, but on the hearts of man, within the people God covenants with.

Psalms 110:1-4 says, "The LORD says to my LORD: 'Sit at My right hand until I make Your enemies a footstool for Your feet.' . . . The LORD has sworn and will not change His mind, 'You are a priest forever According to the order of Melchizedek.'" In these verses, quoted by Jesus in the famous question He posed to the leaders of the Jews,[8] David is speaking to his Lord. God says to the Lord of David, "Sit at my right hand until I make your enemies a footstool for your feet." Then He speaks to the Lord of David and tells him in verse four, that he will be a priest forever in the order of Melchizedek. When God says "forever," He means forever, for eternity.

The meaning of "According to the order of" is, by the word, by the promise, or like Melchizedek. Why does He speak of another priest that is like Melchizedek, when in those days there were priests descended from Aaron of the tribe of Levi and there was already priesthood in the order of Aaron? If so, why is a new priesthood necessary? The priesthood of the tribe of Levi was serving from the time God made the Mosaic covenant – the Sinai Covenant. Here He is speaking of a new priesthood that will exist for eternity. A new priesthood indicates a new covenant, a different covenant in which the laws are changed. As we are told in Hebrews 7:12, if the priesthood has changed then the Law has also changed.

Important and Less Important
Jeremiah 7:22-26 says:

> For I did not speak to your fathers, or command them in the day that I brought them out of the

land of Egypt, concerning burnt offerings and sacrifices. But this is what I commanded them, saying, "Obey My voice, and I will be your God, and you will be My people; and you will walk in all the way which I command you, that it may be well with you." Yet they did not obey or incline their ear, but walked in their own counsels and in the stubbornness of their evil heart, and went backward and not forward. Since the day that your fathers came out of the land of Egypt until this day, I have sent you all My servants the prophets, daily rising early and sending them. Yet they did not listen to Me or incline their ear, but stiffened their neck; they did more evil than their fathers.

God is saying here: I did not command you about burnt offerings and sacrifices. What does He mean? The Law instructs us on how to offer burnt sacrifices, sacrifices for sin, peace offerings, and so on. Is there a contradiction in the Bible? The answer, of course, is no. He tells them, "You placed the emphasis in the wrong place. Sacrifices and burnt offerings aren't the main thing. The main thing is to obey Me, to listen, and to walk in My ways so that there is a relationship between us, and you willingly obey Me. But you made all the other things, the less important things, into the most important."

The purpose of the covenant and its laws was to be justified by God. Here the prophet tells the people, you have tried so hard to do all these things to prove to Me how righteous you are, but instead of walking in My ways, you went in the evil way of your hearts. Just as a previous chapter explained, the word used here in Hebrew, *shrirut* (literally "arbitrariness"), comes from the word *shrir*, or "muscle." You are trying to achieve things in your own strength, by your own will. You do not listen to Me. You choose to depend on your own strength. You give the utmost authority to the desires of your own hearts, not to God. I send you My prophets again and again to tell you, "Return to me and I will return to you, turn back, tear your hearts and not your clothes! That is what I have cried out to you again and again from my broken heart. The main thing is your relationship with Me, not a law".

We have seen how the Law of God, the Torah, changed throughout history. The Bible describes different covenants that God made with man and with Israel. Every covenant had laws that were different from those of other covenants. The question remaining is, what has changed in the Law? Was it once forbidden to murder but now it's not? In the days of Adam and Eve was murder permitted? What about lying? Adultery?

What Has Changed in the New Covenant?

As was said earlier, we see that changes were made in the laws throughout history. For example, while Israel was under the authority of the Torah, it was forbidden to commit adultery. But since it was not forbidden to look on a woman with lust, doing that was not considered a sin, and therefore was allowed by the Torah given by Moses. Today, under the New Covenant, there is a law that forbids it, as a result of what Jesus said when he equated it to committing adultery. Under the Torah, committing adultery was forbidden, today even looking on a woman with lust is forbidden.

A mistake many have made, including many believers, is to think that the Law of Moses held all the absolute moral laws of God. This is not so. The Law of Moses is only a legal step to reaching the goal, which is righteousness before God in the Sinai covenant. The

Law came to define sin,[9] true, but it did not define all sins. It established a certain level of holiness, and a way to obtain justification. We see that Jesus himself said that the absolute moral laws of God did not allow for divorce, but in the Law of Moses divorce was allowed.[10] Job, who lived many years before the giving of the Law, and lived his life by God's moral law, said, "I have made a covenant with my eyes; How then could I gaze at a virgin?"(Job 31:1). That is to say, he understood God's moral law without the commandments of the Torah.

If so, have the moral laws changed? In one way, yes! The moral statutes have changed in that they have become much more stringent in the New Covenant than they were in the Sinai Covenant. Jesus has placed God's moral statues in a clearer light. And what happens with commandments that touch on our relationship with God? In the days of Adam and Eve mankind was required to love the Lord God with all their hearts, all their minds, and all their soul. In the days of the Mosaic Law we were commanded to love the Lord our God with all our hearts, all our soul, and all our might. In the days of the New Covenant we are also to love God with all our hearts, all our souls, and all our might. The commandments concerning the relationship between God and man have not changed. In fact we see in the Torah, and in other covenants, five areas that the laws and commandments pertain to:

1. Commandments regarding relationships between man and his fellow regulating the relationships between people, such as "Thou shall not murder."
2. Commandments between man and God – which detail man's duties towards God, such as "Love the Lord your God with all your heart."
3. Sacrificial laws – which regulate the various

sacrifices at different times.

4. Dietary laws – which regulate what is allowed and what is forbidden to eat.

5. Laws relating to various ceremonies such as the feasts, circumcision and so on.

In all of these we see changes, except for the ones that speak of our relationship with God. Regarding sacrifices, for instance, we see that in the framework of the New Covenant, Jesus fulfilled the prophetic and symbolic significance of all the sacrifices that have to do with sin. He was the final atoning sacrifice, once and for all, and the sacrifices of praise are fulfilled in our lives of praise and worship when we live our lives for Him.[11]

The Purpose of the Commandments – Justification Before God

"It does not, therefore, depend on human desire or effort, but on God's mercy" (Rom. 9:16, NIV). This Torah does not depend on the will of man or his works to obtain justification, but only on a merciful God. The Law we have in the New Covenant is at the same time different and the same. It is different from the Law of Moses while being similar to it. It is freer in certain things, and more stringent in others.

The New Covenant was not written on tablets of stone, it was not written outside of man. It was written within us; on our hearts. The moment we confess our sins and receive Jesus as Lord and Savior, he comes and dwells within us. He writes His Law on our hearts. In Jeremiah 7 he emphasizes the fact that the people walked in the strength of their own hearts. They depended on their own strength and their own efforts. Here we see that the Torah God gave in the New Covenant does not "depend on human desire or effort," but rather, God has mercy on whoever received the Law. We have to make note of this. It seems a small, unimportant difference, but it is one of the most important things there is. Man cannot gain righteousness through effort; it is in the hands of a merciful God.

> And He also told this parable to some people who trusted in themselves that they were righteous, and viewed others with contempt: "Two men went up into the temple to pray, one a Pharisee and the other a tax collector. The Pharisee stood and was praying this to himself: 'God, I thank You that I am not like other people: swindlers, unjust, adulterers, or even like this tax collector. I fast twice a week; I pay tithes of all that I get.' But the tax collector, standing some distance away, was even unwilling to lift up his eyes to heaven, but was beating his breast, saying, 'God, be merciful to me, the sinner!' I tell you, this man went to his house justified rather than the other; for everyone who exalts himself will be humbled, but he who humbles himself will be exalted" (Luke 18:9-14).

These two men who went up to the temple had similar intentions, as we read in verse 14 – to be justified before God. That is the aim of keeping the commandments of the Law. The aim of the Law was to obtain justification. It was intended to justify or to condemn, helping us discern what righteousness is in God's sight. In this parable we see two people who come to the temple with different attitudes. The Pharisee comes to God and says, "Here is proof that I am worthy of your righteousness: I fast twice a week, I am not like the others. I don't steal, I am not wicked, and I don't commit adultery. I give a tithe of everything I earn." It's clear that he does all these things in order to show God the seriousness of his intentions, and his desire to be found righteous before God. Today too, a religious Jew will tell you that he observes all the commandments in order to show God that his intentions are serious, that he really loves God, and wants His righteousness. He thinks that God will consider his efforts and strong will, and will justify him. That is the way the Pharisees thought – and many of us today mistakenly think the same thing – that we must work for God's acceptance.

The same Pharisee, in order to prove to God that he is worthy to be justified before Him, numbers all the things he does for God. One of the most important things he says is this, "I am not like that tax collected over there; I am better than him." In order to show God how good he was, he compared himself to others and concluded that he was more righteous than they. In his constant striving and judging of others to prove himself to God, he missed the whole point.

In contrast to him, the tax collector stands before God and says, "God, I am helpless. I have nothing to bring to you. Nothing. I don't read the Scriptures twice a day, I don't fast twice a week; I am sinful. Forgive me." He says simply, "God, have mercy on me, a sinful man." First and foremost the tax collector acknowledges that he is a sinner, and second, he confesses before God without caring whether people hear, "I am a sinner, and I have no right. I cannot prove to you that I deserve to be justified, because to be honest with You and with myself – I don't deserve anything. Please, have mercy on me."

Which of them will be justified? The one who proved his love to God? The one who proved how much he is willing to suffer and to do in order to show God that he is deserving of righteousness? No! It is the one who comes to God and says, "I am a sinner." A Pharisee lives by the Law (of Judaism or of any other religion), he tries with all his might, and compares himself to others. A tax collector lives by the principles of the New Covenant. He sees himself in all his weakness and confesses them before God and man. "I am a sinner, God, have mercy on me." Just one of them gets what he was looking for – righteousness! And it is not the one the world considered righteous, on the contrary.

I do not believe that God desired monks and nuns to live separate from the world. Their emphasis on physical separation from the world and self-flagellation is not based on the Scriptures. Saying that, there is a certain organization of Protestant nuns called "Sisters of Mary" (which originates in Germany and was founded by Sister Basilea Schlink) who do live by the Scriptures. They place placards in many places in Europe with verses from the Scriptures that praise God. They also are active in Israel, and try to bless the people of Israel, especially those who suffered in the Holocaust. Their aim in life is to repent constantly. They spend a great deal of time before God in repentance and contrition for their sins. They have discovered the secret that sin is not in actions, but is rooted in their hearts. It doesn't matter what works they do, they still have much to repent for. It is important that we also understand that sin is not what we do. Our actions are just a symptom, the result of sin. Sin is rooted within us. Each one of us sins day after day by placing himself at the center of the universe, instead of God. That is why we have much reason to repent before God. "He does not delight in the strength of the horse; He does not take pleasure in the legs of a man. The LORD favors those who fear Him, Those who wait for His loving-kindness" (Ps. 147:10-11).

The word that is translated here as loving kindness, and which other translations translate as mercy, is actually "grace" in the Hebrew. Nothing has changed. God never put emphasis on works in the Torah. That is what man has emphasized. And in emphasizing our works and walking after the strength of our hearts, we have sinned against God. God says here, "I don't desire the strength of the horse (which is a strong animal), I don't desire the legs of man (the leg muscles are the strongest in the body)." He does not desire your strength and efforts. If you want to make an effort, make an effort to cultivate a fear of God. Make an effort to desire and wait for His grace, and to receive what you do not deserve. Ask for mercy. Make an effort to come before Him, like the people who made a hole in the roof in order to bring their friend before Jesus.[12] They did not try to heal the sick man; they tried to bring him to Jesus.

We must not focus our efforts on works, or on seeking righteousness through our works. Instead, we must make an effort to go back again and again to where we began: I am a sinner in need of mercy. The Law is written on our hearts and we cannot escape it, because we always see our hearts and the Law written within us shows us our helplessness to live by it. It's scary, because God is perfect and we are sinners. Seeing the tremendous gap, the sin in us in light of His holiness, should drive us to repentance. We cannot change ourselves and be more righteous in our own efforts. On the contrary, we are then acting in the strength of our hearts and sinning even more. God is the only One who can change us and He does so by grace and mercy. It is written here that God seeks those who long for His grace. What should I yearn for? His grace! That is the only way to be justified by Him. "What shall we say then? That Gentiles, who did not pursue righteousness, attained righteousness, even the righteousness which is by faith; but Israel, pursuing a law of righteousness, did not arrive at that law. Why? Because they did not pursue it by faith, but as though it were by works. They stumbled over the stumbling stone" (Rom. 9:30-32).

So then, has the Law changed? Yes, absolutely! We are not talking here about laws or commandments that we must do, but rather about the yearning for His grace. The whole purpose of the Law was to be justified! The people of Israel desired the justification from God. We also desire it. We hope that when God looks at us he won't say "guilty," but "you are righteous before me." That is the heart's desire of everyone who seeks and desires God. That is what Paul is writing about here in the epistle to the Romans. He says that we have all sought it, we have all striven for the law of righteousness, but the people of Israel stumbled on the stumbling stone. The stumbling stone he talks about here is that they sought to achieve righteousness by works.

I see many believers failing at the same stumbling stone. Many think, "I came to faith, and now I need to do this and do that, because otherwise I am not a good believer. If I don't go to all the conferences, if I don't pray for others, if I do not evangelize, then I am not a good believer." I have news for you, in case you don't know it yet: You will never be a "good believer." Sorry.

I prefer to be in the place of that tax collector who said, "I am a sinner, forgive me," than to be a "believer" who says, "Look, God, how much I am doing for You." We are sons of the New Covenant. The Torah has been given to us and written on our hearts, and we believe. Our entire purpose is to attain righteousness, and such righteousness cannot be attained by deeds. This was true before we came to faith and it is still true after we began to believe in Jesus. Our righteousness is not a righteousness of works. It is a righteousness of grace. "[N]evertheless knowing that a man is not justified by the works of the Law but through faith in Christ Jesus, even we have believed in Christ Jesus, so that we may be justified by faith in Christ and not by the works of the Law; since by the works of the Law no flesh will be justified" (Gal. 2:16). No one can be justified by keeping the commandments of the Law. That is what the New Covenant tells us, and this is what we read in Jeremiah. Our righteousness is obtained by putting our faith in Jesus, by acknowledging that we are sinners. It is so simple, and yet so difficult, because we prefer to put in an effort and do things and then come and say to God, "Here, see how serious I am in my love for You!"

If I ask each of the readers, "Why does God love you? Why did He choose you and not someone else?" most, if not all, would reply, "Because He found something in me that another person didn't have. He found something in me He liked, and He wanted to use it", or "He has special plans for me, and I am the only one that can do it for Him." That answer simply isn't true.

He didn't choose us because of something special in us, or because He needed something from us, but rather out of love, grace, and mercy. He chose us because He wanted to. He chose us because He loved us.[13] It is hard for us to grasp that because we want to obtain our place by ourselves, we really want there to be something special in us that God couldn't resist. We want to think that God checked out all the people and when He got to me, some kind of diamond sparkled beneath all that dirt and He said to Himself, "I will take him and clean him up; I will make him into a beautiful, polished diamond." But that's not true! We are not a rough diamond in need of polishing; we are black and dirty coal. But the pressure He puts on us, and the fire He makes us pass through, turn that coal into a diamond. We have to get to the place where we are ready to accept the fact that we are, all the time, sinners in need of God's mercy to be saved. Not only that, we have to live day-by-day, moment-by-moment in this certainty. We live day by day in the heavenly temple saying, "God, I am a sinner and I need Your mercy!"

The Scriptures do not tell us to love ourselves; that is something the world tells us. I have heard many sermons that say, "Loving your neighbor as yourself means you have to first love yourself, and then you have to love others." That's the way the world thinks. But the Scriptures say exactly the opposite. We have to hate our flesh, crucify it and not love it. The Scriptures tell us that our problem is not that we don't love ourselves enough, but that we love ourselves too much. That is our problem.

Ephesians 5:29 tell us, "[F]or no one ever hated his own flesh, but nourishes and cherishes it, just as Christ also does the church." No one hates himself. Our problem is that we love ourselves too much, and we get angry when people don't love us the way we think we deserve. The Scriptures direct us to crucify our flesh, to oppose the flesh and to come to God for mercy. We don't just do that once, it has to be every day. And if we have the courage, we have to live our lives like that, while looking in the mirror every day. The mirror is the word of God, as we read in James 1:22-26:

But prove yourselves doers of the word, and not merely hearers who delude themselves. For if anyone is a hearer of the word and not a doer, he is like a man who looks at his natural face in a mirror; for once he has looked at himself and gone away, he has immediately forgotten what kind of person he was. But one who looks intently at the perfect law, the law of liberty, and abides by it, not having become a forgetful hearer but an effectual doer, this man will be blessed in what he does. If anyone thinks himself to be religious, and yet does not bridle his tongue but deceives his own heart, this man's religion is worthless.

Every time I examine my heart I see my sinfulness, because the Law is written on my heart. I see myself as I really am, with the lustful thoughts, the anger, and the "almost-lies." The "almost-sins" are always there. The "almost-adultery" is always there, and I have to fight against it. "Almost-anger", "almost-strike," and "almost-curse" are always there. Sometimes they get expressed when I am driving and someone cuts me off, but the thing that keeps us before God is only His grace. We must never forget that. The danger lurking for us believers is that we will forget. We have to approach God as sinners and ask for forgiveness, every moment, in every situation, and thank Him for his grace. The forgiveness and righteousness don't come thanks to my works, but despite my works. Not by the Torah but by grace, "([F]or the Law made nothing perfect), and on the other hand there is a bringing in of a better hope, through which we draw near to God" (Heb. 7:19).

So yes, Jesus changed the covenant, changed the priesthood and changed the Law. He put a focus on the main point – "His grace is great towards us" (Ps. 117), because His grace has conquered us and continues to conquer us day after day. He has given us a righteousness rooted not in what we do or don't do, but in His grace. Thanks be to God!

---

[1] Rabbi Yehuda Chayun in his book Treasures of the Last Days dedicates the entire twelfth chapter to this subject. Available on the internet (www.aharit.com/A-12.html)

[2] literally: "Set Table" also known as the Code of Jewish Law, is the most authoritative legal code of Judaism. It was authored in

Safed, Israel, by Yosef Karo in 1563 and published in Venice two years later

[3] Isaiah 51:4: "for a law shall proceed from me" is discussed in midrash Vayikra Rabba 13:3 "new Torah will emerge from Me", "In that time, the Holy One, blessed be He, will sit… and expound the new Torah that He will give through Moshaich" Yalkut Shimoni, Isaiah sec 429, "The Torah which a person learns in this world is vanity in comparison to the Torah of Messiah."Kohelet Rabba 11:8

[4] According to the testimony of a man who was present in a class in a religious school, one of the pupils asked the teacher, "What you taught in the lesson isn't exactly the Law," and the teacher answered, "It doesn't matter what the Law said because there have been changes, the Halacha changes the Law".

[5] http:www.moreshet.co.il/web/shut/shut2.asp?id=105244

[6] http://en.wiktionary.org/wiki/Torah

[7] Num. 26:33 – 27:7

[8] Matt. 22:42-46

[9] Rom. 5:13, 20

[10] Matt. 19:8

[11] Rom. 12:1-2

[12] Luke 5:17-26

[13] Jer. 31:3 "I have loved you with an everlasting love; *Therefore* I have drawn you with lovingkindness (grace).

CHAPTER 8

Jesus Served in a Greater and More Perfect Tabernacle

"**B**ut when Christ appeared as a High Priest of the good things to come, He entered through the greater and more perfect Tabernacle, not made with hands, that is to say, not of this creation" (Heb. 9:11).

Jesus served in the real Tabernacle, not the earthly Tabernacle that is a reflection of, and was built on, the pattern of the heavenly Tabernacle. We read here that Jesus served in a Tabernacle that is greater and more perfect; a Tabernacle that does not belong to this creation. We know that the temple of Solomon and the temple of Herod were wonderful, impressive buildings, but here we are told that Jesus entered through a greater and more perfect Tabernacle than they; the Tabernacle that does not belong to this creation.

Moses Erected the Tabernacle According to God's Instructions

"Now if He were on earth, He would not be a priest at all, since there are those who offer the gifts according to the Law; who serve a copy and shadow of the heavenly things, just as Moses was warned by God when he was about to erect the Tabernacle; for, 'See,' He says, 'that you make all things according to the pattern which was shown you on the mountain" (Heb. 8:4-5). This verse is a quote from Exodus 25:40 (similar verses appear also in other places) which reads, "See that you make them after the pattern for them, which was shown to you on the mountain." God instructed Moses to go up on Mount Sinai, and there He would show him the pattern (the form and structure) of the Tabernacle he was to build.

The Model and the Original

This subject raises many questions, not all of which we can answer. We are not capable of understanding everything and it's important to understand that God is much greater than our ability to understand. That's why there are things about God we just have to accept, even if we cannot understand. God speaks here of a "pattern," or a "model." What is this pattern?

The Greek word for "pattern" is *tupos*, from which the English words "type" and "prototype" come from. That is, it is a pattern that reflects the original. Actually, this can be compared with a map. It is a map, a blueprint that reflects the real thing.

> Then David gave to his son Solomon the plan of the porch of the temple, its buildings, its storehouses, its upper rooms, its inner rooms and the room for the mercy seat; and the plan of all that he had in mind, for the courts of the house of the Lord, and for all the surrounding rooms, for the storehouses of the house of God and for the storehouses of the dedicated things (1 Chron. 28:11-12).

The word that is translated as "plan" is the same word in Hebrew (*tavnit*) that was used for what God showed Moses on the mountain. David prepared for Solomon everything that was necessary to build the temple. He gave his son Solomon a plan for the courtyards and rooms; that is to say, he prepared detailed blueprints and measurements.

These blueprints, or patterns, that God showed Moses on Mount Sinai for the Tabernacle go into great detail. God gave instructions for the depth, the width and the height of the beams, what kind of fabric and what color, what is to be placed on what, how to put it all together, what to coat the wood with, and even what kind of wood to use. The pattern He gave Moses was not just of the details of the building. It specified the details of the worship and the sacrifices to be made in the Tabernacle: what kind of sacrifices, where to slaughter the animals, exactly how and where to pour out their blood, what the priest was to do with each kind of sacrifice, what clothes the priest was to wear in one area of the Tabernacle, and what he was to wear in another area. God gave Moses the smallest details and told him, "Make sure you do everything exactly according to the pattern I am showing you here on the mountain." We are told that Jesus entered through a greater and more perfect Tabernacle so we understand that the Tabernacle we had here on earth is a reflection of a greater and more perfect Tabernacle.

Jewish scholars understand it this way also. The Jewish philosopher Philo of Alexandria, who interpreted the Scriptures allegorically, said that the Tabernacle represented divine creation of the world. According to Philo[1] the entire world is a temple to God, and the Tabernacle is a smaller pattern of it. Cassuto[2] and Martin Buber[3] acknowledge that the Tabernacle represents something greater. In many Jewish sources we find that the Tabernacle signifies something of greater meaning. It is claimed that the earthly Tabernacle is patterned after the higher worlds, the invisible worlds, and reflects them all as a shadow or a miniature version[4].

Historically, a later version of the Tabernacle— the Temples which Solomon and Herod built—were counted among the wonders of the ancient world and people like the Queen of Sheba[5] came from a distance to see it. When Israel wandered in the wilderness, a pillar of cloud hovered over the Tabernacle by day and a pillar of fire hovered over it by night. Not only could the millions of Israelites see these signs, but also the story of the spies in Jericho shows us that all the nations around had heard of it. The people of Jericho, including Rahab, had already heard of Israel and spoke with fear of the nation whose God dwelt with them. Nothing like that had ever happened before – a people whose God tabernacled among them.

But this impressive, enormous structure was only a small model of something much greater and more perfect. It was a reflection of the real thing.

This pattern is not simple. It is a pattern with many layers, which signify various things. We will discuss three layers, but I am sure there are many more.

1. The physical pattern: God gave the details for the physical pattern
2. The idea's pattern: the idea the pattern expresses.
3. The pattern of procedures: the sacrifices, the priesthood, work laws

The pattern, and what is built by it, helps us understand the greater idea behind the pattern. We are made of physical substance. We see, measure, and feel physical or material things. It is easier for us to understand them. God is Spirit. Before the original sin we fellowshipped freely with Him in the Spirit, we understood the spiritual world just the same as we understand the physical world. When sin entered the world we died spiritually and became blind to the spiritual world. It's hard for us to see it. We cannot understand it, and it's hard for us to even think in a spiritual way. Many times we grasp something spiritual and then forget it.

More than once I have talked with people who said, "I know God loves me, but if He were a person and would give me a hug, then it would be easier for me to understand His love." The spiritual concept seems like something theoretical, an abstract. But the spiritual world is not just a theory. We live in a physical world that is just a small part compared to the spiritual world. Because of our sin we have been blinded, and the more we grow in faith the more aware we become of the spiritual world that surrounds us; we become able to live in the spiritual realm while in this physical world. This is why Jesus came to earth: to raise our spirits from the dead, and to help us understand that there is a realm beyond the physical. We need Jesus – God become man, God the Spirit who took on flesh and blood, a physical form – because otherwise we would be incapable of understanding His love. We need the physical Tabernacle in the physical world, in order to receive understanding, and to comprehend the spiritual realm. The physical structure is here on earth and reflects the spiritual Tabernacle. It helps us understand truths regarding the spiritual realm, and to live our lives in the spiritual world.

The Tabernacle Here and the Tabernacle in Heaven

Let us first look at the physical pattern: Is there really a heavenly temple or Tabernacle, in the spiritual realm? Is the earthly Tabernacle a copy that reflects the form and structure of a temple that is in heaven?

> In the year of King Uzziah's death I saw the Lord sitting on a throne, lofty and exalted, with the train of His robe filling the temple. Seraphim stood above Him, each having six wings: with two he covered his face, and with two he covered his feet, and with two he flew. And one called out to another and said, "Holy, Holy, Holy, is the Lord of hosts, The whole earth is full of His glory". And the foundations of the thresholds trembled at the voice of him who called out, while the temple was filling with smoke. Then I said, "Woe is me, for I am ruined! Because I am a man of unclean lips, And I live among a people of unclean lips; For my eyes have seen the King, the Lord of hosts". Then one of the seraphim flew to me with a burning coal in his hand, which he had taken from the altar with tongs. He touched my mouth with it and said, "Behold, this has touched your lips; and your iniquity is taken away and your sin is forgiven" (Isa. 6:1-7).

Isaiah sees several things. He sees God on His throne, he sees the train of His robe filling the temple, he sees seraphim standing in front of God, he sees the temple filled with smoke, he sees his own sin and he sees the altar of fire from which something is taken that gives him atonement. Does he see all this with his physical eyes? Were his spiritual eyes opened? The answer is not given and so we don't know. We are only told that it happened "in the year King Uzziah died." Uzziah reigned for 50 years and throughout his reign the land had quiet and stability. The death of the king brought uncertainty. Isaiah was evidently praying for the people because of the situation. While he was praying he suddenly saw God sitting on His throne high and lifted up. You may well ask: Does God sit? How does He sit? Does He have a body? But we won't spend time on these questions because we may not have exact answers for them. Here we have a throne on which God sits, and his edges (that is what the Hebrew says for what is translated as "train of His robe") fill the temple. What are those edges? Does God have edges? Like I said, this verse raises lots of questions since God has no beginning and no end, there is no limit to Him. But the important point is the existence of a temple that God fills.

What is this temple that Isaiah sees? Is it the entire Universe, as some commentators explain, and the train of God's robe fills the universe? Perhaps, but in any case, Isaiah is talking here of a temple, a Tabernacle. He also mentions seraphim that were standing over the throne of God. This picture is interesting because in the Holy of Holies the cherubim stood above the Ark of the Covenant (Ex. 37:1-9). Isaiah's vision is a bit similar to what was in the temple, even though there are some question marks that should be addressed, "the whole earth is full of His glory," and, "His train filled the temple." If the entire earth is full of His glory, then perhaps the earth is the temple. But if "the whole earth" is only the physical world, then why will God, who fills the physical world, replace it when He creates a new heaven and a new earth? When Isaiah says "the whole earth is full of His glory" he means much more than the physical world. The "whole earth" means the spiritual world too.

Another interesting point is that the temple Isaiah sees is full of smoke. The temple and the Tabernacle were filled with smoke several times, when the presence of God filled them – especially when they were dedicated. God filled the Tabernacle and the temple with a cloud that came down and the priests were unable to enter in (Ex. 40:34-35, 1Kings 8:10-11). We see the same cloud leading the people of Israel in the wilderness (Deut. 1:33). We see Jesus taken up to heaven in a cloud (Acts 1:9). We know that He will return in the clouds of heaven, and then every eye shall see Him (Rev 1:7), and we will be taken in the clouds to be with Him (1Thes. 4:17). So also the smoke of the sacrifices and the incense offerings in the earthly Tabernacle represent something much greater.

Isaiah sees that the temple in his vision also has an altar. The angel takes tongs to lift a hot coal from it, and touches the lips of Isaiah with it. When he touches Isaiah's lips, the coal from the altar atones for his sin. That which happens on the heavenly altar gives atonement to Isaiah. If so, we have seen that the Old Testament gives us a description of the heavenly temple. Let us now look at the New Testament:

When the Lamb broke the seventh seal, there was silence in heaven for about half an hour. And I saw the seven angels who stand before God, and seven trumpets were given to them. Another angel came and stood at the altar, holding a golden censer; and much incense was given to him, so that he might add it to the prayers of all the saints on the golden altar which was before the throne. And the smoke of the incense, with the prayers of the saints, went up before God out of the angel's hand. Then the angel took the censer and filled it with the fire of the altar, and threw it to the earth; and there followed peals of thunder and sounds and flashes of lightning and an earthquake (Rev. 8:1-5).

The book of Revelation describes what will happen in the last days and gives us a glimpse into what happens in heaven. John is "present in spirit," and sees many wonderful sights. Here we read that John sees an altar, and an angel comes to stand by it. The angel has a golden censer, like the censers the priests had to offer up incense in the Holy of Holies. The censer holds incense, which is mixed with the prayers of the saints; the believers. That means that prayers are like incense. Again we see a throne, a golden altar, and the burning incense. The smoke of the incense is the same as mentioned in Isaiah. The angel takes fire from the heavenly altar and throws it to earth. The heavens are filled with voices, thundering, lightning and earthquakes. Again we see the elements and activities in the temple of earth only mirror the temple in heaven.

Revelation 11:19 states, "And the temple of God which is in heaven was opened; and the Ark of His Covenant appeared in His temple, and there were flashes of lightning and sounds and peals of thunder and an earthquake and a great hailstorm." We are told that the temple of God is in heaven. It was opened and we see something in it we have never seen before, the Ark of the Covenant. This is very clearly the heavenly temple of God and it has very similar elements to the earthly temple: the seat of mercy in the Holy of Holies, cherubim or seraphim, the Ark of the Covenant, the altar of incense, a golden censer, the altar, and the priest who takes the censer and does the holy work.

If there is such a temple in heaven, this raises

additional questions: Who built it, when was it built, and for what purpose? Why is there a need for a Tabernacle in heaven? Are there places in heaven that God fills more than others? Doesn't God fill all of heaven? One of the main reasons the temple exists is to offer sacrifices for atonement. Why is there need for atonement in heaven?

Let us see who built it and when? The letter to the Hebrews offers clues, "Now the main point in what has been said is this: we have such a High Priest, who has taken His seat at the right hand of the throne of the Majesty in the heavens, a minister in the sanctuary and in the true Tabernacle, which the Lord pitched, not man" (Heb. 8:1-2). Here too we read that there is a throne and a Tabernacle in heaven, and that our High Priest is Jesus. Jesus, the High Priest "is set on the right hand of the throne of the Majesty in the heavens, a minister . . . in the true Tabernacle, which the Lord pitched, not man." The Tabernacle on earth was not the real Tabernacle. Jesus our High Priest ministers in the true temple made by God, not man.

Men built the Tabernacle and the temples on earth: Bezalel, Solomon and others. Here we read that God erected the heavenly Tabernacle. Did He set it up after He created the world? Was it created together with the world? We know that God is eternal. Is the temple in heaven also eternal?

"But when Christ appeared as a High Priest of the good things to come, He entered through the greater and more perfect Tabernacle, not made with hands, that is to say, not of this creation" (Heb. 9:11). The Bible says that the heavenly Tabernacle is not part of this creation. This creation is physical, made of material. God has always existed, and He made the Tabernacle. The word "pitched" in Heb. 8:2 means to build, and could also mean "prepared." So again the question is: Why was there a need for such a Tabernacle? That's a good question, and does not always have an answer. The Tabernacle is not part of creation. That is, it is spiritual, not physical. It is said that God "pitched" it, not that He created it. That is to say, it did not always exist. At some point God took some existing things and pitched the Tabernacle.

Heb. 9:24 continues, "For Christ did not enter a Holy Place made with hands, a mere copy of the true one, but into heaven itself, now to appear in the presence of God for us." So to review a few things: man did not make the heavenly Tabernacle. It was made by God and the Tabernacle that was built by human hands is the reflection of the real thing. Every time a person looks into the mirror he sees a reflection of himself. The reflection is not the person himself; it doesn't dream or do things on its own. The only thing the reflection does is reflecting exactly what the person does. It has fewer dimensions than the real thing. It only shows the person in a reflection that is not perfectly clear. You do not see his back, and, if he stands far enough away, you do not see his wrinkles. The reflection gives us only a partial picture, and is not always clear.

According to this verse, the Tabernacle on earth is just a partial picture of the heavenly Tabernacle. It is a reflection. The earthly Tabernacle was a three dimensional reflection. It's pretty clear that the heavenly Tabernacle has dimensions beyond our ability to understand. We find even the fourth dimension – time – difficult to understand. We see time in relative terms, as constantly changing. For example, to a seven year old the summer vacation of two months seems really long, almost an eternity, never ending; for an adult those two months go by so fast we hardly feel them. Three dimensions are easier for us to understand, but if there are other dimensions – and I am sure there are – we are incapable of comprehending them. The temple or earthly Tabernacle was a reflection of the reality. It is a three-dimensional reflection of something much greater.

Our Limited Understanding

We are told, in the verses above, that the Messiah served in the real temple, which was a greater temple. Here we read that He came "into heaven itself." What does heaven itself mean? It means that the temple Jesus served in was heaven itself, the core, and the essence of heaven. It is hard for us to completely understand that. When we talk about God, His character and His person, and try to understand who He is, there are things we can understand just a little and many other things we cannot understand at all. Many spiritual things are too lofty for us. The heavens are the real thing, and we comprehend the words that describe them, but what they actually say – we have no idea. I am not able to understand it.

It is important to realize that we are limited in understanding. In the days of the Emancipation when German philosophy took over Western thought (about 150 years ago), one of the problems was that they placed the power of the intellect above anything else. In effect, they made a god out of human understanding. Everything has to go through our understanding, and if you cannot understand it, it does not exist. This approach explains the development of liberal theology in the Christian faith in Europe and other places. Because the moment we limit God to our own understanding, that is exactly what happens – we limit Him. We have to realize that our understanding is human, earthly, and sinful, and therefore limited. Before sin came to the world we were able to understand more. If we try to shrink God to suit our understanding, we will never truly know Him or understand Him. I have been married for nearly thirty years and I have to say there are some things about my wife that I still don't understand. I love her. I accept her, enjoy her and like her. But there are some things about her that I just don't get. There are some things I do not get about myself. Why do I do certain things? Why do I react in such a certain way? There are many things my understanding is limited in but that doesn't limit my ability to love or to know.

There is a difference between knowing and understanding. I can know someone without understanding him. Knowing means personal relationship, an intimacy. Understanding means using our thoughts and minds, and our ability to analyze. We love to understand things and people. We love to put them in a box, catalogue them and organize them. We think that understanding things gives us control over them.

In "The Lion, The Witch, and The Wardrobe" by C.S. Lewis, one of the children who sees Aslan—a literary representation of Jesus—asks, "Is he tame?" The answer she gets is, "No! But he is good!" We feel more comfortable when someone or something is "tamed". If we could understand God, then He would be trained, and we would have tamed Him, put Him in a box, filed Him away, and thought that we know all about Him. We can understand more and more about Him, but we have to realize that our understanding of Him will always be limited. God is not tame. We will never manage to tame Him, to limit Him, and fit Him inside the box called our brain. But we can allow Him into our hearts. We can accept Him as Lord and as Savior. That is how we can know Him personally and have intimacy with Him.

One of things we have to know about our relationship

with God is that we have no control over Him and we never will. God is not a formula, or some button to press, that if only I do this thing or that thing, then this or that will happen to me. Or, if I do A, B, and C then the result will be D. God is God, and I have to let Him be God for me. He has total control, and no one can tame Him. He is the Sovereign Lord, not my assistant.

Our inability to completely understand God often puts us in an unclear place and that can make us feel insecure. I remember when I reached that stage in life, and God asked me, "Are you prepared to trust Me even if you don't understand Me?" It was really hard for me to trust God without understanding Him. But I had to take that step if I wanted to continue growing. I could also have decided not to trust Him as long as I did not understand Him. Our response to God always should be, "Yes, God, I trust You. I choose to trust You, even if I don't understand everything."

So, we do not understand everything that happens in heaven. We can ask questions and try to understand some of the things, but we have to understand that all we have is a reflection of the real thing; a shadow of it.

The Role of the Heavenly Temple

Why is there a temple in heaven? Is the temple for the angels or heavenly creatures God created, who are always in His presence, gazing on His face? If the temple is a place to meet God, why is there a need for it in heaven, where He is always seen? Perhaps the temple was built in heaven for God to meet man in heaven? The question may seem a bit strange, but we have to understand that man is a unique and strange creation. There is no other creature like him.

As Genesis 2:7 says, "Then the Lord God formed man from the dust of the ground and breathed into his nostrils the breath or spirit of life, and man became a living being" (AMP). God takes dust – a substance from the physical world – and creates man and breathes the spirit of life (as the Hebrew says) into him. Nothing else was created like that. The animals and trees also came out of the ground, but God did not breathe His Spirit into them. They were made only of earth. "Out of the ground the Lord God formed every beast of the field and every bird of the sky" (Gen. 2:19). The angels are spirits and have nothing physical in them, even if at times we are able to see them in physical form. Man is a combination of earth and spirit of life; material and spiritual. Man is a special creation. God is Spirit and He created spiritual beings: angels, cherubs, seraphs, and all kinds of beings in heaven that we do not know about. They are spirits, as Psalms 104:4 tells us, "Who maketh his angels spirits; his ministers a flaming fire?" (KJV). The angels are not made of earth. The physical world, the earth, the stars, the animals, the trees and everything else, are created out of a physical substance. Man is the only creation made of earth and spirit. God created man as a mixture of physical and spiritual and set him to rule over the physical world. Adam, who is both physical and spiritual, represents God, who is Spirit in this physical creation. Man was a bridge between spirit and material in this physical world. When we sinned we gave the rule of this world to Satan because we submitted to Satan, the ruler of this world, and we crowned him King. Therefore, "… the anxious longing of the creation waits eagerly for the revealing of the sons of God" (Rom. 8:19).

All of creation waits eagerly for us to be revealed. Man was created as a connection between the spiritual world and the physical world. Jesus came from the spiritual world and the special thing He did was to wear flesh and blood, and become physical too. He became a man. He became both spirit and flesh; the second Adam. He, who was all God, became all man. Before sin we were not gods, but we were completely spirit and completely flesh. When we sinned, the first result was that we died in the spiritual realm. Death and blindness were first of all to the spiritual world and therefore, despite the draw we have to the spiritual world, it is hard for us to see and understand it.

Due to the fact that He was clean of sin, Jesus preserved the connection we did not keep, between the spiritual world and the physical world. That is why He is called the Last Adam.[6] He was the Adam the first Adam had failed to be, he kept the bridge between flesh and spirit. Even in His death he kept up this connection. We have to understand that when God shared Himself with flesh and blood He partnered with creation, with the material. He partnered with man! He partnered with us, the same special creation that is both spirit and flesh. God came down to live among us, a combination of spirit and physical together, died and rose again, and now sits on the right hand of the Father in Heaven; the right hand of the throne in the temple. Today, in heaven, sits a man. We have partnership with God in a special way, a partnership no other created being has. It is not that you and I partnered with God, but that God shared of Himself and partnered with us. When we see Him we will recognize Him. He will still have holes in His hands and feet and marks on His head from the crown of thorns. We will recognize Him.

We need to understand that our sin not only cut us off from God, as is written in Isaiah 59:1-2, "Behold, the Lord's hand is not so short that it cannot save; Nor is His ear so dull That it cannot hear. But your iniquities have made a separation between you and your God,

And your sins have hidden His face from you so that He does not hear." Our sin not only separated us from God, not only killed us physically and spiritually, it also made us blind. We are not able to see or understand the spiritual world in which we live. We have a spiritual hunger, we feel that something is missing, and that there is something beyond the physical world we see around us. The world seeks spiritual things. We see the New Age movement, witchcraft, people delving into the esoteric and crystals, and so on. People are seeking the spiritual world because their hunger is real. Every man has this hunger to understand, to see, and to experience the fact that we are more than just physical beings. But every touch of the spiritual world not done in God's ways brings us more death to our life and puts us more under the curse. That is why Jesus came to restore us to that same meeting place between flesh and spirit, and perhaps the same Tabernacle in heaven that God made was created from the beginning so that His creation of flesh and spirit would also be in the presence of the God of Spirit. The role of the Tabernacle was to be a meeting place between created man and the eternal, holy God. That is why God instructed man to build a Tabernacle on earth according to the pattern of the heavenly temple. It was to remind us that we were created in order to meet with Him, and to be in His presence. Sin causes us to forget important things. That is why God commanded us to observe the Sabbaths and the Feasts: so that we would remember who He is and what He has done.

We are not told exactly why God pitched the Tabernacle in heaven, but perhaps He did so as a meeting place in heaven, as is written in Job 1:6, "Now there was a day when the sons of God came to present themselves before the Lord, and Satan also came among them." Perhaps it was created as a meeting place for that purpose before sin. After sin came, when there was a need for atonement, He created the earthly Tabernacle for us as an exact copy, detail for detail, to reflect the heavenly Tabernacle, and so that we would remember what we need to aim for. And perhaps so that we would remember where we need to get to in order to meet with God. Jesus, who came to the world, reminds us again of the meeting between man and God, and opens the way back so that we can once again worship God in Spirit and in truth. Jesus came and dwelt among us as an earthly Tabernacle. In Him heaven and earth met, spirit and flesh, and in Him we meet God and live in His presence. He cannot be destroyed like the earthly Tabernacle, He serves forever in the true temple that is in heaven. That is where God wants to restore us to Him, to the same heavenly temple where we stand before Him together with all creation; the place where His throne is; the place where we worship Him in Spirit and in truth.

Jesus came and died and rose again. His death was a real death, a real cutting off from heaven. That is why He cried out, "*Eli Eli lama sabachthani*?" (My God, My God, why have You forsaken me?). When He took our sins upon Himself He was cut off from heaven. By His great love, God saw that we as men had fallen, failed, sinned, and destroyed that bridge, that special creation which is both spirit and flesh. That is why Jesus came as both spirit and flesh. He came to restore us to the place we had fallen from, to resurrect our spiritual life, so that we would see and understand the world around us – not only physically but spiritually also. He came so that we could live our lives in this physical world as representatives of the spiritual; so that we could be the Tabernacle in which God dwells in the world. Our fellowship with God is not just a fellowship of outward laws that pertain to the physical, but rather is in Spirit. It is a worship that is in Spirit and in truth. What wonderful grace God has that He did not wipe us out or throw us out because of our sins. Nor did he say, "I am done with them, and will start all over." He took us in His love. He partnered in our sufferings, sin, and death, in order to restore us to Him; to the place we had fallen from. He did this knowing we would never deserve it. What wonderful grace!

"And the Word became flesh, and dwelt among us, and we saw His glory, glory as of the only begotten from the Father, full of grace and truth" (John 1:14).

---

[1] Philo of Alexandria "The Special Laws" 67 and other places

[2] A commentary on the book of Exodus /by U. Cassuto; translated from the Hebrew by Israel Abrahams. 1997

[3] Buber, Martin, Darko shel Mikra. Yerushalayim, Mosad Byalik [1964] Pages 54-58

[4] An interesting article by Dr. Shulamit Lederman, Bar Ilan University in Hebrew http://www.biu.ac.il/jh/parasha/teruma/led.html#_ftn3

[5] I Kings 10:1-5; II Chr. 9:1-4

[6] Rom 5:12-21

CHAPTER 9

The Ideological Pattern
of the Tabernacle

Now even the first covenant had regulations of divine worship and the earthly sanctuary. For there was a Tabernacle prepared, the outer one, in which were the lampstand and the table and the sacred bread; this is called the Holy Place. Behind the second veil there was a Tabernacle which is called the Holy of Holies, having a golden altar of incense and the Ark of the Covenant covered on all sides with gold, in which was a golden jar holding the manna, and Aaron's rod which budded, and the tables of the covenant; and above it were the cherubim of glory overshadowing the mercy seat; but of these things we cannot now speak in detail. Now when these things have been so prepared, the priests are continually entering the outer Tabernacle performing the divine worship, but into the second, only the High Priest enters once a year, not without taking blood, which he offers for himself and for the sins of the people committed in ignorance. The Holy Spirit is signifying this, that the way into the Holy Place has not yet been disclosed while the outer Tabernacle is still standing, which is a symbol for the present time. Accordingly both gifts and sacrifices are offered which cannot make the worshiper perfect in conscience, since they relate only to food and drink and various washings, regulations for the body imposed until a time of reformation (Heb. 9:1-10).

The Scriptures have four names for the Tabernacle:

1. The Sanctuary, or *heychal*, which comes from the verb *lehachil*, meaning "to contain."
2. Temple, or *mikdash*, which is a Holy Place, consecrated for a certain purpose.
3. Tabernacle, or *mishkan*, a dwelling place, or a habitation.
4. Tent of Meeting, or *Ohel Mo'ed.*

So what is the Tabernacle? The word *mishkan* means a dwelling place or habitation; to be present in a place. It is the word that the word neighbor (*shachen*) comes from in Hebrew. The idea in Hebrew is that this is the habitation of God, the place where the God is dwelling. It is important to remember the meanings of the words when we talk about the ideological significance of the Tabernacle.

I Dwelt Among Them
    In the previous chapter we talked about the physical pattern of the heavenly Tabernacle. In this chapter we will talk about the ideological pattern. We will examine what ideas the Tabernacle teaches us. In Exodus 25:8 God says, "Let them construct a sanctuary for Me, that I may dwell among them." The first thing written here is

that the people of Israel have to make a Tabernacle; a sanctuary. Then God says that he will come and dwell among them.

The Tabernacle was erected in the center of the camp of Israel. It was central to the identity and existence of the people of Israel. The Tabernacle was erected according to a pattern of something much deeper, and much more exalted. We know that the centrality and significance of its position symbolize something very important for all believers in Jesus, not only the nation of Israel. We know that Jesus came and dwelt among us.[1] To dwell means to live, to be within, to be next to, or to be a part of. The idea in this verse is that we have to prepare a place. Just as the people of Israel prepared a place for God to come and dwell among them, we too have to prepare a place in the center of our lives as the place for Jesus to live in.

"I will consecrate the tent of meeting and the altar; I will also consecrate Aaron and his sons to minister as priests to Me. I will dwell among the sons of Israel and will be their God. They shall know that I am the LORD their God who brought them out of the land of Egypt, that I might dwell among them; I am the LORD their God" (Ex. 29:44-46). God consecrated the place, and made it entirely His own. He prepares the people to serve Him in the place He chose, and He prepares the place for service. God says "I will dwell among the sons of Israel." The Hebrew word *betoch*, which is translated as "among," actually means "within." It can also mean "within a group," or "within an individual." In verse 46 God says His intention is to dwell within the people, so that they will know that He is the Lord their God who brought them out of Egypt. He dwells within the people of Israel and within us so that we will know Him, and what He has done – and will do – for us.

The word "to know" is complex because it does not mean an intellectual knowledge. It refers to the more intimate knowledge we find in Genesis 4:1, which states, "Now the man had relations with [*knew*] his wife Eve, and she conceived and gave birth to Cain." This kind of knowledge means an intimate relationship. That is why God dwells within us; within the people of Israel. His purpose is that we get to know Him intimately.

"He shall make atonement for the Holy Place, because of the impurities of the sons of Israel and because of their transgressions in regard to all their sins; and thus he shall do for the tent of meeting which abides with them in the midst of their impurities" (Lev. 16:16). This verse is especially interesting because usually when we think of the presence of God (the *shechina*), we think He dwells only in Holy Places. But here we read that the Tabernacle dwells among them in their impurities! Among other things, God is trying to show us through the Tabernacle that He comes and dwells within the filth. God uses the word "within" (*betoch*) again. God dwells within the people of Israel, within all the impurities, because the people of Israel are impure. How can the holy God dwell among the impurity? By means of His atonement, as we read here in verse 16, "He shall make atonement for the Holy Place."

God atones for their impurities, and thus can come and dwell within their filth. There are many layers of meaning here. First of all, the verses speak of the grace of God. God does not demand, "First be holy, and then I will come and dwell within the people of Israel." He says, "The people of Israel are sinners. I know they are sinners, but I atone for their sins. I atone, not they. I come and dwell within them. They are full of sin and filth, but I atone and come to dwell within them."

Many believers think that we have been made holy

or consecrated, and now we need to live completely separate from the world. God does not say, "I am holy, and therefore I live apart from the world." He comes within the filth, into the dirt, into the sinfulness. He did not allow sin to separate Him from the world. If He had, then Satan would have won, and achieved his intent of completely separating man from God. Holiness came to dwell within the sin, and to conquer it; thus making the sinner holy. Jesus also said to His disciples that He did want them to be out from the world, but to be in it, be different, and win it over.

Our task, as the disciples of Jesus, is to be in this world, within this world, and to influence it – not to let the sin of the world separate us or cut us off from society around us. We have to be "holy within the sin" in the world around us, not "saints separated from the sin." We must not let Satan win by taking us away from the people God has placed us among.

The book of Exodus tells us, "Then the cloud covered the tent of meeting, and the glory of the LORD filled the Tabernacle. Moses was not able to enter the tent of meeting because the cloud had settled on it, and the glory of the LORD filled the Tabernacle" (Ex. 40:34-35). The word *shechina* is not in the Scriptures. It was coined to describe what is said here – that the glory of the Lord filled the Tabernacle so that even Moses could not enter in.

Let's summarize what we have seen so far: The people of Israel built a Tabernacle just as God had told them to so that God could dwell there. This was done in order that the people of Israel would know that He is God, that they would be intimate with Him, and that they would know all the good things He does. God knows that the Tabernacle is impure, and that He is within the impurity, because humans built it. God Himself consecrates it. He is the one who atones for it, and comes to dwell within the sin and the filth. He not only lives within the filthiness by means of the atonement and consecration of the place, He also fills the place so much that there is no more room there for the filth. He does the job from the inside. He does not say, "You have to be sanctified, prepare and do things, and then I will come and fill you." No, He tells them, "Prepare the place just as I say, and then I will sanctify it and I will fill it and I will dwell there. And because I dwell within you, you will know me and I will fill the place so much that my holiness will push out all the filth." That is a wonderful picture of holiness conquering sinfulness. Holiness gets into the filth not by the filth becoming holy, but by the grace of God.

That reminds us of our own lives. If we prepare a Tabernacle according to our own conditions, God will not fill it. He will not dwell there. We have to prepare the sanctuary, the *mishkan*, or our hearts, according to God's conditions. Then God will come and dwell within us. But that is not because we are now holy; it is because of His grace. His purpose in coming to dwell within us is for us to get to know Him better, that we may have intimacy with Him, and that the world around us will see Him through us. He fills us with the glory of God, and He does that by His grace and the atonement He made for us. If we allow Him to fill us and prepare ourselves to worship Him in the way He has called us to, He fills us with His glory. The glory of God is revealed through us to others around us.

The central idea of the Tabernacle was that God comes and dwells within us sinners (those who have prepared their hearts by His plan), and His holiness fills the place of meeting until sin has no more place there. That is the clear and wonderful pattern of God's grace, "'Not by might nor by power, but by My Spirit,' says the

Lord of hosts" (Zech. 4:6).

Again, it is very important to prepare the place in God's way, not in our own way. Only then will He in His grace come and live in the filth of our lives. We must remember that we have to clean up the dirt, get it out from the darkness into the light, and confess it before Him. We have to erect the Tabernacle of our hearts according to His plan and His will. Not every house is a Tabernacle to God. Only the one that is built according to the plan God has given is suitable for His presence. There is only one way to come to God, and that is His way. Any other way is sin. We cannot keep living in sin. Let us remember what happened when Nadav and Abihu, the sons of Aaron, entered the Tabernacle in a way God had not commanded, because they were drunk. The fire came out and consumed them.[2] Remember what happened to Korah and his followers. They rebelled against Moses and were consumed by the earth.[3] We have to leave those things that prevent us from drawing near to God, and prepare our hearts the way He wants us to prepare them. And then He comes, by His grace, and dwells in us in the filth. He atones for the filth in our lives, He fills us with holiness until His glory fills the sanctuary as it is written, "the whole earth will be filled with His glory . . . and His train filled the temple."[4] And when He fills the Tabernacle then the sin cannot get in – there is no room for it.

The Tabernacle's Prophetic Significance

The Tabernacle has prophetic significance. "For thus says the LORD God, 'Behold, I Myself will search for My sheep and seek them out. As a shepherd cares for his herd in the day when he is among his scattered sheep, so I will care for My sheep and will deliver them from all the places to which they were scattered on a cloudy and gloomy day'" (Eze. 34:11-12). Again, the Hebrew uses the term *betoch* – "within", translated here as "among." God gave us the Tabernacle and also promised that He would come and dwell within the people of Israel. He says here that not only will He be present in the Tabernacle, within the people, in the sin, but also that He Himself will seek His sheep as a shepherd who lives within the flock. The Tabernacle did not drive out the filth enough. Ezekiel lived in the days of the destruction of the first temple. After the temple had stood for hundreds of years, it was destroyed because of sin. The sins of the people became so many that the place God had sanctified for Himself among the people of Israel was desecrated. The filth overcame the holiness. These verses tell us that now God is going to do something else, something better. He says that just as a shepherd seeks his flock and lives among them, I will come (note that it is God talking of Himself here) to be within my flock.

The Tabernacle will no longer be a building among the people. God says, "I myself will come and dwell within them." Just as a shepherd comes to be with his sheep, and as the sheep know their shepherd, we the sons of Israel, the flock of God, will know God. When Jesus came he said, "I am the good shepherd, and I know My own and My own know Me . . . I have other sheep, which are not of this fold; I must bring them also, and they will hear My voice; and they will become one flock with one shepherd" (John 10:14, 16).

Zechariah 2:10-11 develops this idea further, "'Sing for joy and be glad, O daughter of Zion; for behold I am coming and I will dwell in your midst (Heb. "inside you"),' declares the LORD. 'Many nations will join themselves to the LORD in that day and will become My people. Then I will dwell in your midst [Heb. "inside you"], and you will know that the LORD of hosts has sent Me to you.'" God is speaking to the daughter of Zion, to the sons of Israel, and says, "Sing for joy and be glad!" That is, be glad, sing, rejoice, dance, and praise. Why? Because "I am coming." This is exactly what we say of God at Passover, "Not an angel, not a seraph, not cherubim, not a messenger – it is I, myself, who came and delivered you." That is a reason to party! Not only will God come and live within the people of Israel but also many nations will join themselves to Him and become a nation to Him (Zec. 2:11). This is found in the Old Testament, the *Tanach*, not the New Testament. He adds here that when this happens, then you will know that God sent me. That is also part of the prophetical plan for the Tabernacle.

Ezekiel 43:7 has another prophecy, "He said to me, 'Son of man, this is the place of My throne and the place of the soles of My feet, where I will dwell among [Heb. "inside"] the sons of Israel forever. And the house of Israel will not again defile My holy name, neither they nor their kings, by their harlotry and by the corpses of their kings when they die.'" God is speaking about the place where His throne is which we saw in the previous chapter was in the sanctuary in heaven, in the Holy of Holies. He says that where His throne dwells, the soles of His feet will be there too. In this verse He says, "where I will dwell among the sons of Israel forever." God set the His throne within us for eternity, not because we are good enough, but because He wanted to do so.

Let's go even deeper. We are trying to understand things that are difficult to take in. We are not capable of describing God and spiritual things by human words and thought. So, things may, on the surface, seem to be contradictions and impossibilities. But we have to simply take them on faith because they are written in the Bible.

The presence of God is present in the sanctuary. In

Isaiah chapter six we saw that God inhabits the sanctuary. Here we have read that God dwells in His sanctuary. In Colossians 1:13-20 we read:

> For He rescued us from the domain of darkness, and transferred us to the kingdom of His beloved Son, in whom we have redemption, the forgiveness of sins. He is the image of the invisible God, the firstborn of all creation. For by Him all things were created, both in the heavens and on earth, visible and invisible, whether thrones or dominions or rulers or authorities—all things have been created through Him and for Him. He is before all things, and in Him all things hold together. He is also head of thebody, the church; and He is the beginning, the firstborn from the dead, so that He Himself will come to have first place in everything. For it was the Father's good pleasure for all the fullness to dwell in Him, and through Him to reconcile all things to Himself, having made peace through the blood of His cross; through Him, I say, whether things on earth or things in heaven.

Try to understand what we are told here. God has transferred us to the Kingdom of His Son, who is the image of God. God shows Himself to us in His Son. The word "image" is like a photograph, which is a two-dimensional image of a three dimensional object. Here too, in a certain way, Jesus the Son of God, who came in the flesh, is a revelation of the invisible God in earthly form. He came in the flesh in order that we would see who God is. Even though all the fullness of the Godhead dwelt in Him, we could not see all of that in full because we are not able to comprehend God. Jesus said, "He who has seen Me has seen the Father."[5]

"He is the image of the invisible God, the firstborn of all creation." Firstborn does not necessarily mean "born first," but rather, "a place of authority, the first, or the head." He is the Word of God (*mimra de-ya)* through whom and by whom everything was created. This is Jesus. He created all things. In Him were all things created: all that we see (that is the physical world), and all that we don't see (that is the spiritual world). "All things were created by Him and for Him." This passage of Scripture has a lot of prepositional phrases: in Him, by Him, for Him. These are human words that help us to better understand the full picture.

It is written that it was God's will to have all the fullness dwell in Him. The word "dwell" reminds us of the Tabernacle – the dwelling place of God. The will of God was that everything would dwell in Him, in the Messiah. When God's will was for all the people of Israel to be holy, He came and dwelt among them. His holiness within the filth filled the Tabernacle. The intention was that it would take over the people of Israel. It is also God's will that all things dwell in Him. And how will that be? Just as in the Tabernacle it was through atonement, here too it is through atonement, as we read "through Him (or "in Him") to reconcile all things to Himself."

Let's go back to Colossians 2:9-10, "For the entire fullness of God's nature dwells bodily in Christ, and you have been filled by Him, who is the head over every ruler and authority" (HSCB). Just as we read in the previous verses, the purpose was that all things would dwell in Him. In Him all things were created, and all things will return to dwell in Him. I don't know for sure what exactly "all" includes. I do not think we can understand what "all things" includes. Perhaps all of the universe, or all of creation. But there is even more – the Godhead dwells in Him physically. Here we read, "For the entire fullness of God's nature dwells bodily in Christ." Anyone who claims that Jesus is not God, or that He is less than God, has a serious problem with the Bible. Here we read, "In Him all the fullness of God dwells," and later on we are told something else that seems a bit confusing: "You are filled by Him." It is easier for us to understand that all things dwell in Him, including the Deity, but here He is speaking about believers when he says, "You are filled by Him." He is speaking of the congregation of believers, those who belong to him – including us personally. He tells us, "You are filled by Him." So does he fill us, or is He filled by us? Do we fill Him, or does He fill us? Both. Because He fills everything, we fill Him and He fills us.

The word for baptism in Greek, *baptizo*, is taken from the cloth-dying profession. In the process of dying, the cloth is fully dipped in the color. While it is being soaked in the color it is stirred around so that the color will get into all the threads of the fabric. The fabric is in the dye, and the dye is in the fabric. Baptism in water symbolizes the baptism into Messiah[6]. When we totally belong to the Messiah, we are in Him and He fills us. On one hand this happened when we gave ourselves to the Messiah, and He came and dwelt within us. On the other hand, this is a process that goes on for the rest of our lives. It is a process where the Messiah is soaked into every thread, and every part of our lives. It penetrates the inner workings of our souls, and fills us completely. We are in Him and He is in us.

In Ephesians 1 the apostle writes that our inheritance is in Him when he states, "[W]e have obtained an inheritance."[7] But it is also written that we are His inheritance, "[T]he riches of the glory of His inheritance in the saints…"[8] That seems like a contradiction. We are

His inheritance, and He is our inheritance. Again we are using human words to describe spiritual things. We are trying to understand concepts that are difficult for the human mind to take in. In daily life we see something similar in the life of a married couple. The man is in the wife and the wife in the husband. They have become one flesh.

In Ephesians 1:23 we are told again that the believers are "His body, the fullness of Him who fills all in all." He is full, and we are the fullness of Him; He fills, and we fill. Full. That is, there is no room for anything else. Again, these are ideas and concepts that our logic cannot grasp because we think in terms of A, then B, then C, then D. But here we have A, B, C, D, and E together as one. This is about God and what He has done. That is why we have one of two choices: to accept what is written and live by it –even if we don't under-stand it all – or to reject these things because we cannot accept them without understanding them. If we choose to believe only when we understand God, then we are limiting God to the limits of our understanding. But God is always above and beyond our understanding.

We see this in the people who came to Jesus for healing. When they asked Him to heal them, He placed His hands on them and healed them. But when they asked Him to place his hands on them, He did some-thing different. Either He spat and made mud to spread on the eyes, or He put His fingers in their ears and said, "Open." God always does things His way, not our way. So either we accept his way, even without understanding it completely, or we do not accept it. The choice is up to us. I have been married almost twenty-eight years but there are still things I do not understand about my wife. In order to love and build a relationship, perfect understanding is not necessary. There has to be a little bit of understanding and a lot of acceptance, love, and fellowship. Then the situation is that I am in her and she is in me, even if I don't fully understand her.

Our fellowship is with the One in whom we live, by His grace. We allow Him to fill us with His holiness even when we are still impure, and allow Him to purify us. What wonderful grace! He fills all things! As we read in Isaiah 6, His train fills the temple. God is eternal, but again, "eternal" is a concept we cannot comprehend because we are limited. We have an end. So on one hand we are told that His train fills the temple, and on the other hand it is written that the entire earth is filled with His glory and we fill Him. We are a temple sanctuary that holds the holiness of God. The role of this holiness is to dwell within us – in the sin – and purify it.

Some believers say that we have to be like the mannequins in the shop windows, out there for the world to see. They say that people will look at us and be amazed at our specialness, and our holiness – and that will draw them to Jesus. Jesus never told us to be mannequins. Mannequins are made of plastic. They are not real. God told us to live in the world and to be real. We have to touch pain, sin, and curses; and live in all these to change the world. God did not call us to withdraw from the world and cut ourselves off from it. We are called to live in the world, but to be different. It is a mistake for a believer to say, "Those people are sinners, so I will cut them out of my life. I will stay in my holy bubble and prevent them from getting close, so that they will see only my exhibition of holiness and not my weaknesses!" If we act like that we are not fulfilling the role God has called us to – to tabernacle within the people in their impurity. God wants the holiness within us to draw near to the world around us, to connect with it, and love it. We need to touch the people around us with the reality of our lives while keeping pure in our own lives - not to be mannequins for show. We have to change the world by touching it, just as Jesus did. The holiness is within the filth, touches it, and changes it. People in the world are hungry for real people, not for a show. And who is better for that than believers who are filled with God, who live in the filth and drive it out? That is what we are called to do. That is what the pattern of the Tabernacle teaches us.

The Heavenly Jerusalem

Another aspect is mentioned in Revelation 21:22, "I saw no temple in it, for the Lord God the Almighty and the Lamb are its temple." As we said above, we are the sanctuary filled by God. But here we see the holy city that comes from above, the heavenly Jerusalem. We are told that God is its temple. We have seen that we fill Him, and that He fills us. We have seen holiness coming to live among the filth to change it from the inside. We have seen grace shown to each one of us so that the same grace can be shown to others through us. We have seen that God dwells in us not because we deserve it. We have seen our need to prepare our hearts in the way He has commanded, but the rest is His work. He is the alpha and the omega, the beginning and the end.

He is the tree of life because life is in Him.[9] When man sins he is cut off from the tree of life. In Genesis 3:24 we read, "So He drove the man out; and at the east of the garden of Eden He stationed the cherubim and the flaming sword which turned every direction to guard the way to the tree of life." When God drove man from the Garden of Eden He placed cherubim at the east of the garden to protect the tree of life. In the Hebrew text the word for "stationed" is the same as "tabernacle."

This is the first time this word appears in the Bible, and it is used to describe the action God took in order to separate between us, to separate us from life. Later, God uses the Tabernacle to change the meaning of this word into a source of life. God did something similar with the woman. Sin entered the world through the woman, but God, by His grace, also entered the world through a woman when He brought salvation from sin

In Revelation 22:13-14 we are told, "I am the Alpha and the Omega, the first and the last, the beginning and the end. Blessed are those who wash their robes, so that they may have the right to the tree of life, and may enter by the gates into the city." At first, the cherubim were placed to separate us from God. Then, in the Tabernacle, their place was the place that was inhabited by God, who "dwells between the cherubim" (HCSB).[10] God came and dwelt within us, and the place that separated us became the meeting place. He broke down the barrier that separated between us. As it is written, "I am the Alpha and the Omega, the first and the last, the beginning and the end." He continues to say, "Blessed are they who wash their robes, that they may be entitled to the tree of life," that same tree of life that we were cut off from. They receive the right to the tree of life when they wash their robes in the blood of the sacrificial lamb. We see the separation, the barrier that came as a result of sin. We see the breaking down of the separation, and the placing of the entry to the Tabernacle through a gate. The gate is Jesus (John 10).

Again we see that there are layers upon layers of symbols, as well as layers upon layers of patterns. The believers in ancient days understood the connection. There is a mosaic[11] in one of Rome's ancient churches. The first thing that strikes the eye is the cross in the center of the mosaic. But underneath the cross there is the tree of life. This is the tree of life that God planted in the Garden of Eden, the same tree we were separated from. This is the tree that became the cross of Jesus. The cross of Jesus is the tree of life, through which we have life. God came and broke down the barrier that separated us from Him, and instead of us going to taste of the fruit of the tree of life, He came down to us and tasted of the fruit of death so that we would have life. If we want to eat from the tree of life, there is only one way to do so: to pass through His death. Death to ourselves is the only way to a new life in Him. That is the only way we can taste of the tree of life. We have already tasted the fruit of the tree of the knowledge of good and evil, and God hid or disguised the tree of life as what seemed to be a tree of death: the cross. Again, one thing inside another: death in life, life in death.

The Tabernacle Jesus passed through is greater and more perfect. He passed through it in order to give us life. When we observe the Lord's Supper we remember the tree of life that appeared as a tree of death. We celebrate the fact that God broke through the blaze of the fiery sword, the cherubim who stand guard, the wall that separates us, and came to dwell within us - holiness within the filth – to change us so that our lives would be changed and we would receive the life that is in Him.

Matthew 8 tells of a leper who asked Jesus to heal him. Jesus did something against the Torah, against common sense, and everything the society around Him thought. He touched the leper and healed him. Instead of the leprosy infecting Jesus, the holiness of Jesus drove away the leprosy. Jesus did not close the world outside of Himself. He did not distance Himself from the world. Jesus dwelt in the sinful world and purified the sin in the people who allowed Him to touch them. He calls us to live as He did.

Every one of us should ask himself, "Am I building a Tabernacle? Am I building it God's way so that God will come and live in it? Or am I telling God to come to me on my terms? Am I serving Him in the Tabernacle His way? Am I letting His glory fill this Tabernacle so that He can consume and cleanse all impurity, and consecrate and hallow everything around? Am I prepared to live in this world, to touch the filth, and let God wash my feet every day, as He did to the disciples at the last supper? Am I ready to tabernacle in this world, to live in the world, to touch people, and not to hide away in a kind of ghetto? Am I prepared to be real in an unreal world?"

This is what God did, and He calls us to do the same. I can either accept it or reject it. If we wait until we understand everything, it will never happen. We do not even understand ourselves at times. But He loves us and accepts us. He sanctified us by His blood, and He dwells within us forever. We do not have to work for it since Jesus has already done all the work. That is part of what the Tabernacle means for us. May we also learn and become those who reflect the Messiah in this dark world.

---

[1] John 1:14

[2] Lev. 10:1-2

[3] Num 16:1-34

[4] Isa 6:1

[5] John 12:45

[6] Gal. 3:27 "For all of you who were baptized into Christ have clothed yourselves with Christ"

[7] Eph. 1:11,13. It is highly recommended to read the entire chapter.

[8] Eph. 1:18

[9] John 1:4

[10] 1 Chron. 13:6

[11] The Apse Mosaic at San Clemente in Rome dates from circa 1120. It was based on examples of drawings found in the catacombs.

CHAPTER **10**

The Physical Pattern of the Tabernacle

W e have seen that the ideological pattern of the presence of God "within" the people. That is, He not only dwells among us, He dwells within us. In Lev. 16:16 we are told that God lives within the filthiness of the sons of Israel. That is to say, the Tabernacle as a pattern shows us that the holy God comes to dwell within our filth.

We also examined the prophetical significance that speaks of things to come, some of which have already been fulfilled. In Ezekiel 34 it is written that God will come to be among us, among his flock. In Zechariah chapter 2:10-11 we read that God, the Holy One of Israel says, "I will dwell in your midst." He will dwell among the people just as He did in the Tabernacle and the Temple. This is talking of Jesus, who is God, and who took on flesh and lived among us. This is not by accident. God spoke and prepared us for His coming. In Ezekiel 43:9 we are told that He will dwell within us forever.

We have also seen that the physical pattern represents the heavenly Tabernacle, mentioned in Isaiah 6. In Revelation 8 and 11, and in Hebrews 8:1-2, we saw that this is the Tabernacle built by God, not by man. It does not belong to this creation. It is "heavenly." This is the heart around which everything in heaven is centered (Heb. 9:11, 24).

In this chapter we will discuss the physical pattern. The physical pattern focuses on three things: the structure itself, and the materials it is made of; the priests, especially the High Priest and his garments; the sacrificial system, and the role the priest fulfilled in the holy service. All these things are described in great detail in the word of God.

Many books have been written on these subjects, and I recommend reading them on your own, so I won't go into very great detail here. We have already seen that when God gives the pattern, there are many layers with deep significance. Here we will taste only a bit of this in order to encourage us to study more deeply on our own.

God gave very exact instructions regarding the materials to build the Tabernacle, and what to do with them. We know that God does not do anything without a reason. In fact He tells us that the reasons is that the Tabernacle reflects something greater and more real. Every material used to build the Tabernacle symbolizes something.

In John 2:18-22 we read:

The Jews then said to Him, "What sign do You show us as your authority for doing these things?" Jesus answered them, "Destroy this temple, and in three days I will raise it up." The Jews then said, "It took forty-six years to build this temple, and will You raise it up in three days?" But He was speaking of the temple of His body. So when He was raised from the dead, His disciples remembered that He said this; and they believed the Scripture and the word which Jesus had spoken.

Jesus was referring here to Himself as the temple. He used the same terminology used by those around Him when they spoke of the temple, and this is why they were confused. They thought He was speaking of the temple, when at the time He was speaking of the temple of His body. If Jesus Himself compared His body to the temple, then we also have to understand the temple to be a symbol of Jesus.

The more deeply we examine this, the more we see the many ways in which the sanctuary symbolizes Jesus. In effect, everything points to Jesus and on those who are found in Him. If we start from what Jesus said, we will begin to see and understand things we haven't noticed before.

The Parts and Utensils of the Tabernacle

Let's briefly go over the structure of the Tabernacle and the materials used to build it. Most of it was made of acacia wood, which is the most common tree in the Sinai desert. The acacia tree, which grows in the desert, is hardy and fireproof. Some of the wood used to build the Tabernacle was covered, and some was not. In Isaiah 53 we read of the Messiah as "like a root out of parched ground."[1] That is to say, like a tree that grows in a dry land. The wood of the Tabernacle usually symbolizes humanity: the humanity of the Messiah, or the humanity of those who believe in Him.

The fence was made of stakes of acacia wood that were placed on bases, and covered with white fabric facing outward. This represents the believers who reflect the purity and holiness of God.

The Tabernacle had only one opening – a symbol of Jesus, who said, "I am the door of the sheep."[2] This gate had four pillars, which evidently symbolized the four writers of the Gospels: Mathew, Mark, Luke and John. The gate and the Tabernacle itself had four colors: white, blue, purple and scarlet red. The white indicates purity and holiness. The blue indicates that Jesus is the son of God who came from heaven, as blue is the color of the sky (in Hebrew both sky and heaven are the same word). The purple points to Him as King, and the red represents the blood of Jesus as the sacrifice.

The entrance to the courtyard of the Tabernacle was through the gate. In the courtyard there was bronze-plated altar of acacia wood, on which the sacrifices were offered. The bronze represents judgment, because God had judged Korah and his followers for their rebellion against Moses. The two hundred and fifty men who held bronze censers with burning incense were consumed by fire. The bronze remained, and this was what was used to plate the altar.[3] It also symbolizes the grace of God – as for instance, the bronze serpent, which men looked to for healing from venomous snakebites. Fires burned continually on the brazen alter, as a symbol of God's judgment and grace. Even on the Sabbath the priests prepared the fire and sacrificed on the altar, in effect breaking the Sabbath laws. The altar symbolizes God's place of judgment, and at the same time His grace, because sacrifices were offered up on it to show us that someone else will bear the judgment for our sins. Behind the altar Moses placed a laver, or sink, made of copper and filled with water. The laver was made of copper and was fashioned out of the mirrors of the serving women.[4] The laver and the water symbolizes the word of God. The word of God washes us and makes us clean[5]. It is also written that the word of God is like a mirror because in it we are able to see what we look like and what our spiritual and moral state is.[6] In order to enter the Tabernacle the priests had to pass by the altar, offer a sacrifice, and wash themselves with water in the copper laver.

The Tabernacle itself was comprised of two sections, the Holy Place and the Holy of Holies. It was built of wooden beams overlaid with gold and attached to each other. It was covered with various fabrics and skins, some of them visible and some not. The inner layers were more beautiful, but the outer layer was made of porpoise skins, which are not particularly aesthetic. They symbolize the Messiah, "He has no *stately* form or majesty that we should look upon Him, nor appearance that we should be attracted to Him."[7] It did not look appealing from the outside, but on the inside it was beautiful. The priests entered into the Holy Place to serve there every morning and every evening. The fabric at the entrance was woven with the four colors we saw at the entrance gate: white, blue, purple and red.

Inside the Tabernacle was the menorah, fashioned out of pure gold, with seven candlesticks filled with the oil that feeds the fire, which in turn lights the Holy Place. The oil symbolizes the Holy Spirit, who enlightens through the word of God, as is written, "In Your light we see light."[8] On the other side was placed the table of showbread. The Rambam (Maimonides) confessed that the purpose of the showbread was the one thing he could not understand. The table was also made of acacia wood overlaid with gold, and held twelve loaves of bread sprinkled with frankincense. The twelve loaves were replaced every week and placed in a pile on the table. The priests entered the Holy Place by shifts, and ate the showbread there. The bread stood there for a week, but remained fresh. The bread is a symbol of the word of God that the priests, the believers who serve God (who are called a nation of priests), eat of. It is always fresh. Jesus said. "My food is to do the will of my Father in heaven" (John 4:34).

An altar of incense was placed opposite the entrance, just before the veil. It was made of gold and symbolized the prayers of the saints[9]. The incense was offered on the altar, both in the morning and in the evening. The mixture of spices for the incense was prepared only for the use of the offering on this altar. It was not something used in everyday life. The things we say to God in prayer must also not be the ordinary shallow things we say on the street. They have to be real and pure. They have to be a sweet fragrance rising from our hearts to heaven, by means of our mouth.

A veil made of thick fabric separated the Holy Place and the Holy of Holies. It was embroidered with the forms of cherubs in the four colors we have already seen. The veil separated the two places completely. This is the veil that was torn in the temple on the day Jesus was crucified (Luke 23:45). The veil was not just a thin curtain that was easy to tear. When Jesus was crucified, the doors of the temple opened,[10] the veil tore,[11] and the inner sanctuary became one room. The Holy Place and the Holy of Holies became one. All the priests now had a way into the Holy of Holies – not just the High Priest.

The High Priest entered the Holy of Holies just once a year, on the Day of Atonement, after offering an atoning sacrifice for himself and for the people. There was no outside light in the Holy of Holies, only the light of the *shechina*, God's presence. God Himself was the light here. The Ark of the Covenant was placed in the Holy of Holies. In it were a golden jar of manna, Aaron's rod and the tablets of the Law. This was a meeting place between the holy God and sinful man. As in every covenant between two parties, the meeting place held tokens of the covenant. The tablets of Law testified to the conditions of the covenant between God and man. The rod of Aaron reminded them that it is God who appointed the leader-priest, it was not by man's choice, and the manna reminded them that God had supplied all their needs as they wandered for forty years in the desert.

The Ark of the Covenant was made of wood and overlaid with gold. Gold symbolizes God, and the wood symbolizes humanity, so that the Ark is a symbol of Jesus, God-man, and the point of meeting between God and man. Two golden cherubim were above the Ark. Their wings stretched from one wall to the other, and they in effect covered the Ark. Two is not a number we come across often in the Scriptures in relation to God. Usually the numbers three or seven are used. The reason there are two cherubim in the Holy of Holies could be that there were three cherubim before the creation of the world. The third cherub, the anointed one mentioned in Ezekiel and Isaiah,[12] was the cherub that rebelled against God and was cast out of heaven. He is known as Satan. This could be the reason why there are only two cherubs here.

The High Priest

The High Priest and his garments also pointed to Jesus. Bells and pomegranates were sewn on to the hem of his robe, and these rang when he entered the Holy of Holies, which the High Priest entered only once a year. There is no light there. The Jewish sources also say that a thread was tied on to his foot so that he could be pulled out if God killed him there for sin.[13] He wore a bonnet on his head, with a golden plate on it with the words "Holy to the Lord." That is, he belonged entirely to God. The thoughts of the priest were not focused on leaving the world, or on belonging to the world. His thoughts focused on the fact that he belonged to God.

On his breast he carried a plate of twelve precious stones. The name of a tribe was engraved on each stone. That is how he bore the people of Israel, the believers, on his heart. An onyx stone was placed on each shoulder, with the names of six tribes on each. He bore the sons of Israel on his shoulders when he entered the Holy of Holies. We are called to be priests. As priests we are called to bear the believers close to our hearts, in a personal way. The priest had a precious stone for each tribe on his heart. I hear many people saying, "I love the people of Israel a lot, but I have a problem with Jacob, Moses and Yossi. I have a problem with the Israelis, I cannot stand them. But I love the people of Israel a lot." It is easy to love in general, but God wanted us to love each one personally. God created each one of us as a special, precious stone in different shapes and shades. That is how the High Priest bore us on his heart, loving us together and separate. We have to remember the uniqueness God has given to each one of us. It isn't always easy to love others. That is why we read of "the burden of the word of the Lord."[14] A burden is something that is not easy to carry. We are called to bear each other's burdens.[15] We are told to bear with each other in love.[16] God calls us to carry each other, to help each other, and to bear the burden even when this is difficult.

The process of building the Tabernacle in the desert began by building the Ark of the Covenant and the Holy of Holies. The rest of the Tabernacle was built around this. That is, the process began from the inside to the outside. We also go through a similar process of building the life of Messiah in our lives. This begins with a new birth when God's spirit comes to dwell in our hearts and awakens our spirit. Then the life of Messiah grows in us in ever widening circles from the inside out, influencing our thoughts, and then our actions. It is not the outward acts that change our inner man; it is the new inner man that changes our thoughts, and then our actions. So the building of the Tabernacle of God in our lives is also done from the inside out.

The process of transition from the world to intimacy with God is parallel to the process of entering the Tabernacle. We come in through the gate, which is Messiah. The altar of sacrifice symbolizes the sacrifice Jesus made for our sins. The bronze laver symbolizes the word of God, and from there we go to the Holy Place (where fewer people come in), which contains the menorah, the table of showbread, and the altar of incense. These symbolize the light of God, the Holy Spirit, the word of God, and prayer.

Only the High Priest goes beyond the veil to the Holy of Holies – the closest place on earth to God, where the Ark of the Covenant and the presence of God are. This is a process of leaving behind the world, and growing closer to God in a more personal and deep way. Again, it is from the outside in. The process begins in the world and ends before God in a place so close that only you and He are there. The new covenant He made with us is the basis for this intimate relationship.

Where Is the Altar of Incense?

In Heb. 9:3-4 we read, "Behind the second veil there was a Tabernacle which is called the Holy of Holies, having a golden altar of incense and the Ark of the Covenant covered on all sides with gold, in which was a golden jar holding the manna, and Aaron's rod which budded, and the tables of the covenant." At first glance there seems to be a mistake here. We read that the altar of incense was within the Holy of Holies. That is very interesting because in the description of the Tabernacle and the priestly duties,[17] we are specifically told that the altar of incense is in the Holy Place, not the Holy of Holies. The priest burns incense on it every time he goes in, both morning and evening. In fact, all the other places in the Bible tell us the altar of incense was in the Holy Place, but Hebrews 9 describes the altar of incense as being in the Holy of Holies.

Christian commentaries have also seen the problem with this. One of the ways they tried to resolve the difficulty is by saying that the Greek does not say "golden altar of incense," but rather "a thing," or "a place" where the incense was burned. They claimed that this shows the meaning here was not to the golden altar, but the censer on which the High Priest burned incense, and entered with into the Holy of Holies on the Day of Atonement. When he comes into the Holy of Holies with the blood, he places some of the incense from the altar onto the censer, which is like a tray. These commentators think their explanation solves the problem, because the censer is taken into the Holy of Holies. But I have a serious problem with this interpretation. I wonder, why would the author of Hebrews write about a censer instead of an altar of incense? The source of incense is not the censer, it's the altar. The censer is not the main object; it is only an instrument to bring the incense into the Holiest of Holies. It is just a tool of service to the altar. There are other instruments that serve the table of showbread, the altar and the menorah.[18] Every item in the Tabernacle has utensils that serve it.

In the descriptions of the Tabernacle God always refers to the altar of incense itself, and not the censer.

So we have to wonder why the censer would be mentioned here, but not the altar of incense. I do not think this interpretation is correct. We need to keep in mind that we are allowed not to understand all things.

Another attempt to understand these verses explains that, from the verse, "in which was the altar of incense," the Greek word "in" can be understood to mean "relating to," or "belonging to." That is, a preposition indicating belonging. Since the incense altar was on the Holy side of the veil, and incense was brought into the Holy of Holies by the High Priest. Therefore it related to the Holy of Holies. I believe that this explanation is faulty, because the author is describing where things were placed in the Tabernacle, and not what they related to. For instance, when he says, "beyond the second veil," he is referring to a place, not a belonging.

In the Mishna[19] there is a discussion about the veil that was between the Holy Place and the Holy of Holies. That discussion speaks of the veil as either being too big and folded over on the top – creating a kind of corridor – or that there were two veils, and the space between them created a kind of passageway through which the High Priest entered from the southern side, turned north, and entered the Holy of Holies from the north side. After coming in to the Holy of Holies, he turned left and walked south with the veil to his left, until he reached the Ark. The width of this passageway was one *ama*, which is about 1.5 feet. The width of the altar of incense was also one *ama*. Is it possible that the altar of incense stood in the entry to that corridor, which would make it stand both in the Holy Place and in the Holy of Holies? I do not know, nor do I want to give an answer simply to pacify an unresolved dilemma. We need to realize that we have to live our lives in the understanding that there are things about God we do not understand. Just as was said above, we will never understand God entirely. He is far higher than our human understanding. It is hard for us when we do not find answers, but we have to beware of adopting unsatisfactory answers. We have to hold on to what we don't understand. We study and try to understand with the hope that maybe one day we will. If not, then that will be one of the things we ask God about when we see Him. Can you live with a question mark?

What is written here is absolutely true even if I don't understand it. We have to make the decision to accept the word of God as perfect and complete. We cannot say the Scriptures made a mistake here, because if they are wrong here, then maybe they are wrong about other things too. Either the word of God is true, or it isn't. It cannot be right about one thing and wrong about another, yet still be considered as God's word. The choice is ours. Do I receive it as one hundred per-cent true, even when I don't understand? If the word of God is perfect, then the problem lies in my lack of understanding – not in God's word. When I decided to receive the word of God as perfect, even when I did not understand it, my life began to come together. My relationship with God came right because I began to eat of the showbread, and I began to see through His light.

How Do We Approach the Scriptures?

How do we deal with things we do not understand in the Scriptures? It is extremely important to study, to look closer into them, and to think; not to compromise with unsatisfactory answers, even if they come from someone who seems to understand the Scriptures. If one of you discovers the answer, and this answer covers all the aspects and is satisfactory, then I will be glad to hear of it because I myself do not have all the answers. Each and every one of us is called to study the word of God for himself, not only through others who teach us, but personally and ourselves. There was a very long time when I read the Scriptures, and my understanding was affected by what I had heard taught about those verses. I read the Scriptures but I wasn't really reading what was written. I was remembering what I had been taught about the verses I was reading. One day someone challenged me, as I am doing here, and told me that was not the right way to go about it. So I prayed and said, "God, I am putting all those teachers to the side. Teach me Yourself. Give me the ability to read the Scriptures without hearing what I learned in the past from others. Speak to me in a new way through Your Word, You and no other teachers." Wonder of wonders, it began to happen. Things I had not understood before became clear to me. The moment I silenced the voices of the teachers who had spoken to me, I was able to hear the voice of the Scriptures.

Although it is good to learn from others – particularly from God-fearing teachers who have received wisdom from Him, know how to teach, and "divide faithfully" the word of God – this must not come in place of personal study. The voices of the teachers must not silence or replace the word of the Scriptures themselves. God wants to speak with each and every one of us in a new way through the Scriptures. He wants to give us fresh bread from the table of showbread. He wants to feed and water us with fresh food and water. Not like the eagle that chews the food into little pieces, so that the eaglet can swallow it. He wants us to catch our prey. It is all right to eat already-been-chewed food, or small cut-up pieces, when we are tiny chicks, but we must not stay small for a long time. God does not want someone else to chew the cud for us.

When I was living in Africa we visited the enormous Krueger Park (which is about the same size as the state of Israel), a place where wild animals roam about free. We saw a lot of animal droppings. In one place I saw tiny droppings that seemed to be goat droppings. Our guide told me, to my surprise, that those were giraffe droppings. He explained that the giraffe has a few stomachs; it chews the cud and thus makes optimal use of all the food it swallows. The difference between the giraffe's tiny droppings and the enormous droppings left by elephants was amazing. It is all because of the use the giraffe makes of its food, and as a result of chewing the cud. What does the use of food and chewing the cud have to do with the word of God? The answer is meditation.

Mediation on the word of God is very different from the meditation common to eastern religions. In eastern religions, meditation is intended to empty the mind of any thoughts but the mantra. Meditation on the word of God, however, is exactly the opposite. It is filling the thoughts with the word of God, trying to understand, then remembering it few times during the day and thinking about it again and again, trying to understand. God wants us to feed on His word by ourselves, and like what the cow is doing, we are to let it come up again and again into our thoughts during the day. It is important to first fill your mind with the word of God. "Chewing the cud" can be done throughout the day in any place. Sometimes my best sermons have come together in the most unlikely places. I sit somewhere, and my thoughts are occupied with the word of God. I chew the word of God, and I get an idea and my understanding is increased. That happens a lot during the week, but only towards the end of the week do I begin to write down my thoughts and organize them for teaching.

I hope and pray that each and every one of us will become an expert in the word of God. Let us not read the Scriptures wondering what this or that teacher would have thought about it. Instead, let us ask, "God, what are you telling me in this verse?" It is vitally important that each one of us study and learn the word of God for himself. Get yourself a computer program that helps you search the Scriptures, buy a concordance, buy books, study, and check out for yourself. Do not rely only on lessons taught by others. Examine the Scriptures for yourselves. Our basic premise is that the word of God is truth and God is always right. God wants to reveal Himself to us. He wants us to get to know Him. From this starting point we can try to understand and resolve things. True, not everyone is called to be a teacher or a preacher, but each one of us is called to be a priest. Each one of us is called to enter the Holy Place and minister in the Holy Place. That is, to eat the showbread himself: to eat from the word of God. We must not say, "Another priest ate, that's good enough." Each one of us is called to serve in the light of Messiah, not to make do with someone else's service in our place. Each one of us is called to be filled with the anointing oil, to receive light from God, and be a light in the world. Each one of us is called to pray and offer up the incense of prayer. And since the veil has been torn and is open, we can all enter in and be a part of what happens in the Holy of Holies.

If there are questions or problems, check it out for yourselves. Examine the Scriptures for yourself ("examine" in the Bible means to research, search, investigate, and check). Do not make do with what others have told you. You can certainly use what others teach in books and commentaries, but in the end, each one of us will stand alone before God. Know that what you believe is true. Not because a teacher you admire told you it's true, but because you came to that understanding through thought, study and checking what the word of God says. If there are things you do not understand yet, put them on the long list of things in the Scriptures you don't understand, and ask God about them when you see Him face to face. I want to encourage you to work towards shortening that list. Make sure you are always increasing in understanding by studying things on your own. Serve in the Holy Place by yourselves; receive the revelation of the Spirit by yourselves.

God called us to be priests and to enter into the Holy of Holies. He paid the price for us through the sacrifice of Messiah Jesus. He offered the sacrifice on the altar to atone for our sins so that we would be able to enter into the Holy Place; not so that we would just stand outside in the courtyard, encouraging other priests like our teachers and pastors. He sent the Messiah as atonement so that we ourselves would enter into the Holy Place, and serve in the Holy of Holies. Just as we say at the Passover Seder "each one of us must consider himself as having come out of Egypt personally, because not only our fathers came out of Egypt, God brought each one of us out." That is what is important. That is why I have expanded on the problem of understanding exactly where the altar of incense was placed. I wanted to challenge you: study the Scriptures! That is a part of the ministry you have been called to. God saved you in order that you might minister in the Holy Place.

The priests entered the Tabernacle twice a day to fill the menorah with oil, and to offer up incense. How many times a day do we come to be filled with the Holy Spirit and the word of God by coming into God's presence in prayer? The priests ate the showbread, which was always fresh. Do we eat the fresh word of God regularly, or do we only eat what others have chewed and digested for us? The word of God is food for our souls. If we do not read and study the word of God, we will die of starvation. If we only read a little and study a little, we will be weak and sick. We have to eat in order to grow and get stronger. We have to learn to feed ourselves. It does not matter if you are in the army, at work, or at school – give time to reading the Scriptures. If you don't have a lot of time, begin with ten minutes a day. Read a chapter, or one page a day. It doesn't matter what time of day, whether just before bed or first thing in the morning with a cup of coffee. You can always find the time. God's desire is that all of us will be wise and that we will all know the Scriptures. That is his desire, and a part of what God wants us to do.

Our prayer to God as we read His word should be "open my eyes that I may see your law."[20] Open my eyes, and I will learn wonderful things from Your law, from Your word. "In Your light we see light."[21] I will see light by the Holy Spirit as I pray, "God, give me Your Spirit as I read the Scriptures, open my eyes, unveil my eyes as I read Your word."

God has called us to be a kingdom of priests and a holy nation. Are we, then, serving in the Holy Place?

---

[1] Isaiah 53:2
[2] John 10:7
[3] Num. 16
[4] Ex. 38:8
[5] Eph. 5:26
[6] James 1:23-25
[7] Isa. 53:2
[8] Psa. 36:9

[9] Rev. 8:3-4

[10] Tractate Yoma 39b tells that forty years before the destruction of the temple strange things began to happen in the temple. The Doors opened of their own accord, until Yochanan ben Zachai rebuked the sanctuary and understood that destruction was soon to come.

[11] Matt. 27:51

[12] Eze. 28:12-19, Isa. 14;12-15

[13]Zohar, parashat Amor 102:a

[14] Zech. 9:1, 12:1, and other prophets who used the word "burden" for the message from God

[15] Gal. 6:2

[16] Eph. 4:2

[17] Ex. 40:2-8, 30:1-10

[18] For example: Ex. 25:38 mentions snuffers and trays; Ex. 27:3 mentions shovels, basins, forks and firepans.

[19] In Tractate Yoma 5a we are told that there are two veils with a gap in between them, or one large one that creates a corridor through which the High Priest passes.

[20] Psa. 119:18

[21] Psa. 36:9

CHAPTER **11**

The Worship Pattern in the Tabernacle

Now that we have seen that there is a sanctuary (Tabernacle) in heaven, and we have looked at the ideological, the prophetical, and physical patterns, we will now look at the pattern of worship in the Tabernacle.

Worship in Heaven and Worship on Earth
Let's look at Hebrews 9:1-14:

Now even the first covenant had regulations of divine worship and the earthly sanctuary. For there was a Tabernacle prepared, the outer one, in which were the lampstand and the table and the sacred bread; this is called the Holy Place. Behind the second veil there was a Tabernacle which is called the Holy of Holies, having a golden altar of incense and the Ark of the Covenant covered on all sides with gold, in which was a golden jar holding the manna, and Aaron's rod which budded, and the tables of the covenant; and above it were the cherubim of glory overshadowing the mercy seat; but of

177

these things we cannot now speak in detail.

Now when these things have been so pre-pared, the priests are continually entering the outer Tabernacle performing the divine worship, but into the second, only the High Priest enters once a year, not without taking blood, which he offers for himself and for the sins of the people committed in ignorance. The Holy Spirit is signi-fying this, that the way into the Holy Place has not yet been disclosed while the outer Tabernacle is still standing, which is a symbol for the present time. Accordingly both gifts and sacrifices are offered which cannot make the worshiper per-fect in conscience, since they relate only to food and drink and various washings, regulations for the body imposed until a time of reformation.

But when Christ appeared as a High Priest of the good things to come, He entered through the greater and more perfect Tabernacle, not made with hands, that is to say, not of this creation; and not through the blood of goats and calves, but through His own blood, He entered the Holy Place once for all, having obtained eternal redemption. For if the blood of goats and bulls and the ashes of a heifer sprinkling those who have been defiled sanctify for the cleansing of the flesh, how much more will the blood of Christ, who through the eternal Spirit offered Himself without blemish to God, cleanse your conscience from dead works to serve the living God?

As we have seen in previous chapters, the earthly Tabernacle is built according to the pattern of the Tabernacle in heaven. But it is not patterned after only the physical nature of the Tabernacle and its function.

We also find parallels to the way the worship of God is conducted in the heavenly Tabernacle. There are laws of worship in the heavenly Tabernacle too. Even in heaven, the worship of God is conducted in a certain way. That is why the service of the priests in the earthly Tabernacle reflects the true worship of God in the heavenly Tabernacle.

The priests entered the Holy Place every day; we too must enter the Holy Place every day. There the priests filled the oil of the menorah, cleaned the wicks, ate of the showbread and offered incense on the altar. We already know that the oil is a symbol of the Holy Spirit. We also must be sure to be filled with the Holy Spirit every day so that we can shine with His light. The light is the word of God and the Spirit of God, as it is written, "Your word is a lamp to my feet and a light to my path."[1] We need to read the word of God every day, study it, and fill our mind with it. In the Holy Place the priests cleaned the wicks of the menorah so that its light would shine brightly. They renewed, cleaned, and fixed. The word of God enables us to fix, to purify, and to clean the source of light in our lives, our hearts and our thoughts. He shows us what is wrong with us. We are called to be a light to this world. When we sin, our light is dimmed and begins to smoke. Whoever has seen the untrimmed wick of a candle or a gas lamp knows how smoky it can be. Just as we must cut and clean a wick to make sure that the light burning will not give out black and dirty smoke, so the things God has burned must be cleansed and cut out of our lives.

The High Priest entered the Holy of Holies once a year on the Day of Atonement. Before entering it, he offered up a sacrifice for himself and for the people. Then he took blood from the sacrifice and incense from the altar of incense, and entered into the Holy of Holies.

There he sprinkled the blood on the covering of the Ark, while the incense burned, and filled the place with smoke. That is how he made atonement for the people every year. Jesus the Messiah entered once and for all into the Holy of Holies, poured out His own blood, and offered up prayers and intercessions.[2] When He did that, the veil was torn, and the barrier between the Holy Place and the Holy of Holies was broken down. Every priest who entered into the Holy Place was able to look into the Holy of Holies. When Jesus poured out His blood, the door was opened[3] and the veil was torn, so that we too, as priests, are able to reach the Holy of Holies when we enter into the Holy Place day by day.

The priest entered the Holy Place every day to offer up incense (which symbolizes the prayers of believers in Jesus). We have seen that the incense was a special mixture concocted exclusively for this purpose. We too have to enter every day into the Holy Place, to study the Scriptures, to be filled with the anointing oil, to clean the wicks of our lives, and to offer up prayers to God. Sometimes we pray in order to impress those who hear us. Our prayer is not just for God's ears. Sometimes the incense we offer is impure because it is for those who hear us. But our incense has to be pure. The pure incense accompanies us not only into the Holy Place, but also into the Holy of Holies. As believers, we have to seek to enter further in, to draw as close as possible to the *shechina*, to the Ark of the Covenant that was sprinkled with the blood. There the covenant of God strengthens us. There God provides all our needs as we pass through deserts in our lives. And there we obtain assurance that God will always provide for our needs. It is where we remember that it is God who has chosen us by His grace, having nothing to do with our works. God Himself chose to pay the price for me. Believers in Jesus can, and should come every day into the Holy Place and into the Holy of Holies because the veil has been torn down.

The offerings and sacrifices of the Tabernacle didn't really cleanse the conscience. But today in the heavenly Tabernacle, the sacrifice of Messiah has cleansed our consciences. If your conscience is not clear, that is a sign that you have not yet allowed the Messiah to cleanse that area of your life. You have not yet received the sacrifice of Messiah in that area of your life. You have not yet found rest in Messiah in that area of your life.

There are different kinds of offerings and sacrifices in the Tabernacle. There are sin offerings, burnt offerings and sacrifices of thanksgiving. These were simply a shadow of the sacrifice of the Messiah. In the heavenly Tabernacle Jesus was the true sacrifice that replaced all the offerings for sin. We are the ones that are called to offer up the sacrifices of thanksgiving and praise. As is written:

> Therefore I urge you, brethren, by the mercies of God, to present your bodies a livingand holy sacrifice, acceptable to God, which is your spiritual service of worship. And do not be conformed to this world, but be transformed by the renewing of your mind, so that you may prove what the will of God is, that which is good and acceptable and perfect (Rom. 12:1-2).

And again, "Through Him then, let us continually offer up a sacrifice of praise to God, that is, the fruit of lips that give thanks to His name" (Heb. 13:15).

That is how you will worship in the sanctuary in heaven: by giving yourselves as a living sacrifice, holy and acceptable to God. Our songs to God of thanksgiving and praise are the offerings we bring with us into the Holy of Holies. These sacrifices, brought to God in prayer, also cleanse our conscience. When I sin, I feel guilty. When I give myself anew to God and praise Him, look upon Him, and receive His forgiveness, then He cleanses me. This is not a result of works. The commands, the Torah given here, is not a law of works, or food, or drink. We do not live under the external Torah of "thou shalt" or "thou shalt not". Ours is the spiritual, internal Torah of worshipping God from the heart. This is true worship, which is the giving ourselves as a holy, living sacrifice. I do not think God really cares whether I pray with head covering or without; whether I pray facing east or west; or whether I stand on my head, lie down or sit. What is important is that I give myself as a pure and living sacrifice, acceptable to God. When I come before Him in prayer; or through reading the Word and living according to what is written there, thus allowing the Holy Spirit to fill me and change me; or when I trim the wick and allow His light to shine clearly through me - then I am serving in the Tabernacle in heaven that is not of this creation. I am serving in the Tabernacle that is not made by hands, but is far greater and more perfect.

The Tabernacle has three sections: the courtyard, the Holy Place, and the Holy of Holies. As said above, Jesus is the Tabernacle. He said of Himself, "I am the way, the truth and the life."[4] This is reflected in the Tabernacle. The courtyard is the way, the Holy Place is the truth, and the Holy of Holies is the life. All is in Jesus, and Jesus is all in all.

The Way

There is only one way to enter the Tabernacle, and that is through the gate. There is no other gate. The gate is Jesus, who said, "I am the door; if anyone enters through Me, he will be saved, and will go in and out and find pasture. The thief comes only to steal and kill and destroy; I came that they may have life, and have it abundantly."[5] Jesus is the way into God's sanctuary.

The first thing we see in the courtyard is the sacrificial altar. In order to continue further in, we have to receive the atoning sacrifice of the Messiah. Whoever tries to climb in or slip in without going through the gate and the altar cannot come in. He is a robber and a thief. Whoever does not receive the sacrifice of Messiah does not enter the Tabernacle. Whoever tries to offer up his own kind of sacrifice – whether these are works or other things – cannot come in. The first step on the way into the Holy of Holies is the blood of Messiah poured on the altar as a sacrifice. Jesus is the way to receive atonement from God so that we can come in closer and understand the word of God.

Right after the altar, but not yet in the sanctuary, we find the bronze laver. We have seen that it was fashioned out of the mirrors of the serving women and symbolizes the word of God, which shows us who we really are. The laver (the sea) was filled with water. The priests washed their bodies here to prepare themselves for the divine service. We have to cleanse ourselves before we enter the sanctuary. The water also symbolizes the word of God, which cleanses us and prepares our heart for the true worship of God. Without the word of God we cannot enter the sanctuary. The way into the Tabernacle is through the gate, which is Jesus. The altar is the sacrifice of Jesus, and the word of God is like water that drips on a rock, eventually splitting it, so the word of God softens and breaks our hard hearts. The word of God prepares us to enter through the door into the Holy Place. That is the way.

The Truth

When we enter in to the Holy Place we recognize Jesus as the truth. The golden menorah in the Holy Place symbolizes the Spirit and word of God as the only light there. The showbread is the word of God, and fellowship with the believers in Jesus. The altar of incense is prayer. The moment we enter in, we are living in God's truth. This truth includes being filled with the Holy Spirit, and with the word of God. Our lives have to reflect His light. The word of God lit by the Spirit of God makes us shining lights that reflect Jesus more and more.

The fellowship with other believers is a part of our life in truth. We are told that just as iron sharpens iron, so a man sharpens his friend.[6] We need each other. We need the difficulties and problems that come up between us in order to rub off our rough edges. The believers around us help us see ourselves as we really are. The believers God has placed us among help us to grow. If we had the choice, most of us would wish that certain people, especially the most difficult of them, would just leave our lives. But we have to thank God for these people too; and perhaps especially for them because they are the ones who help us to change into the image of Messiah.

I remember an elderly man who did not wash himself or his clothes much. He lived alone, and often smelled rather unpleasant. He used to visit us at our home, and tended to turn up at the most inconvenient times. It was not unheard of for him to knock on our door at ten o'clock at night when my wife and I were already in bed, and sometimes he would even bring other guests with him. Our immediate reaction was to ask him to come back tomorrow at a normal hour, but we chose to thank God for bringing him, and asked Him to give us the strength to serve. It wasn't easy, but God used him to teach us to love, and to soften our hearts. It doesn't matter if he was a strong believer or not, God used him to teach us things we found difficult to learn.

Life in truth includes real prayers from the heart. These are not wishes someone else wrote down for us, which I parrot to show how beautifully I pray. They are not prayers for world peace, or for all the believers. They are true prayers that come from the heart. One of the gifts of the Spirit that helps us to pray in truth is the gift of tongues. This helps us to pray in truth, to pray from deep within us without going through the filter of our thoughts. These prayers express very deep things that our words cannot express.[7]

The Life

The Holy Place symbolizes life in truth, but truth is not the end goal. We mustn't stop here. The truth guides us on to life, and life is found beyond the veil in the Holy of Holies. The word of God prepares us to move from the courtyard into the Holy Place, and it is prayer that brings us into the Holy of Holies. When he entered into the Holy of Holies, the High Priest took with him blood from the sacrificial altar, and burning incense from the altar of incense. Our prayers move us on from truth into life, not because of our skill at praying, but because of Jesus' sacrifice.

The life, as the Holy of Holies, has only the light of Messiah. There is no other light and no other life.[8] This is where the Ark of Covenant – God's testimony of His covenant – is. Just like the pillar of stones Jacob and Laban set up,[9] it is the place of meeting between the two parties of the covenant. Here, heaven and earth meet. Here, fellowship with God is intimate. We draw the intimacy from the covenant God has made with us, from the fact that God has chosen us, and from the fact that God supplies all things. Here we live in deep intimacy with God. This is the place where the only light is His light. The light of the world outside does not touch us. Nothing else shines here. The only light is given by the presence of God. In this place the believers live in the Spirit and in intimacy with God. That is what we have been saved for.

In the courtyard, the atonement allows us to enter the Holy Place where sanctification, the filling of the Spirit, fellowship, and prayer open the way to intimacy with God. In this place we know Him who is from the beginning, as we are told in 1 John 2:12-14:

> I am writing to you, little children, because your sins have been forgiven you for His name's sake. I am writing to you, fathers, because you know Him who has been from the beginning. I am writing to you, young men, because you have overcome the evil one. I have written to you, children, because you know the Father. I have written to you, fathers, because you know Him who has been from the beginning. I have written to you, young men, because you are strong, and the word of God abides in you, and you have overcome the evil one.

John divides the body of Messiah into three: children, young men and fathers. This is a division not by age, but by maturity in relations with God. Children are those who know that their sins have been forgiven and know God. They have come in through the door of the sheep that Jesus talks of in John 10, when He says He is "the door of the sheep." This is what the gate of the Tabernacle symbolizes. These children are in the courtyard. The young men have overcome evil, and entered into the Holy Place. They are strong, and the word of God lives in them. They know the Scriptures; they fight against sin and evil, and are victorious. They have experienced victories in the battle against sin, and have overcome things that before had subdued them. The fathers – and sadly I must say that there are all too few fathers in the body of Messiah – are those who have "known Him who was from the beginning." They live their lives in the Holy of Holies, intimate with God. In all that happens to them, they recognize the rule and hand of the One who planned their lives from the beginning; the One who rules over all, and is the Alpha and the Omega of all things. They know the One who has created all things, from whom all things come, and to whom all things will return.

Some of us are still children, but a child always wants to grow up. I remember when I was six years old and saw the thirteen year olds. I thought to myself, "Wow, they are so big; I want to be like them!" When I got to be thirteen years old I wanted to be sixteen, and so on until I grew up. There is always the desire to grow, and that is very good. That should be the desire of each one of us, to progress beyond the point we are in at the moment. Not to stay a child, and not to stay a young man. It is not enough to be strong to overcome evil, or to know the Scriptures and let the word of God dwell within me. We have to strive to enter the Holy of Holies. We have to go in deeper to the place where we always know the One who has been from the beginning. This is the place where I am a father to others, not just a big brother. In my younger days I always sought someone to learn from. Unfortunately, most of what I learned from others was learned from bad examples. We have to pray that we will be a good example. We need to be good fathers to those who seek fathers, so that people will learn from us and say, "That's what I want to be like." In the family, our duty as fathers is to give our children the tools they need to contend successfully with the difficulties of life. The most important thing for a mother or father is to see their children acquire the tools that will help them to live life in the best way possible. Good parents want to see their children grow up and succeed even more than they.

A child needs to want to learn, develop, and grow. One of the dangers young men face when the word of God dwells within them and they overcome evil is to think: "I have made it! I have gotten there, I know things now." We mustn't remain forever in the Holy Place. The veil has been torn, and the way is open. We need to press on into the Holy of Holies. Outside the gate is judgment and death. Only in the presence of God is life, and the more we rely on Jesus, the more life we have.

Very often when we think of death and life, we think that death begins where life ends. The picture painted in the Scriptures is a bit different. The understanding of life and death in the Scriptures, whether physical or spiritual, is that of a scale that at one end is total life, and at the other end is total death. In between these are all kinds of stages. The more distant a man is from total life, the more death is in him. The more distant he becomes (whether from illness, weakness, etc.), the more death he has until death wins. The opposite is true too. The sicker we are, the closer we are to death, and the healthier we are, the closer we are to life, with all kinds of stages in the middle. I think some doctors see it that way too. A man who is in a vegetative state isn't dead, but he isn't really alive. A sick person has less life than a healthy person. A healthy person who is full of energy and joy is said to be "full of life." Most people live somewhere in between. During life, and as they continue to grow older, they become more full with death until they die completely. It is the same in spiritual life. If we allow sin in our lives, we are allowing death to harm the life of Messiah, and to decrease the amount of life we have. In Genesis 25:32, Esau describes his weariness and weakness as, "I am going to die" (Darby), meaning, "I am in the process of dying." The progression from life to death isn't sharp. It is like a candle that dies down slowly. Perhaps that is why the word "life" in Hebrew, *hayim*, is in the plural.

Judgment and death are outside the gate, but the fullness of life is in the Holy of Holies. As is written in John 1:4, "In Him was life and the life was the light of men." The sanctuary is Jesus, and it is written that the life is in Him. The life is the source of light for man. The more I am in Him, the more light and life I have. Outside, the sun lights up the world. In the Holy Place there is only the light of the menorah. In the Holy of Holies there is no light at all except for the light of the *shechina,* the presence of God. In terms of the light of this world, we will be in a darker place, but we have more life and more of God's light.

Our goal has to be to distance ourselves from the world's light, and to be as far inside as we can, to be as close as possible to Him. Psalms 36:10 says, "For with You is the fountain of life; In Your light we see light." So our purpose must not be to seek the light, the understanding, and strength in the world, but to be as much as possible in God's light. In Him is the source of life, like a wellspring of life for all. Ezekiel 47:9 describe the river of life that flows from the Tabernacle, "It will come about that every living creature which swarms in every place where the river goes, will live. And there will be very many fish, for these waters go there and the others become fresh;

so everything will live where the river goes."

We must seek to be like a child who desires to grow and mature. It is not healthy to stay in the courtyard, receiving forgiveness and atonement again and again. It is good to know I do have forgiveness, but I need to continue on into the Holy Place. I need to grow from a child into a young adult. We need to move into a place where we have more of His life and strength, where God's word is in our hearts and we overcome evil. But we should not remain long here either. We have to seek to know the One who has been from the beginning, and to become fathers and mothers to others. In the Scriptures the word "to know" indicates an intimate knowledge, not an intellectual understanding. We have to aim to live in the source of life all the time, to live in His light all the time, and thus to be a source of help, life, and light to those around us. Death rules outside the gate. We can make do with a kind of life that is more life than death, but that is not enough. We must aim to get deeper and closer into the Holy of Holies, not to just make do with where we are at the moment.

We have laws of service in the sanctuary that we are called to use in order to draw near to God. We are told how to worship God. We must receive the atonement of Messiah, give a sacrifice of thanks to God, read the word of God, and allow it to soften our hearts and purify us. We need to enter into the Holy Place and fellowship with Him, to be filled with His Spirit and His word, clean the wick, be filled with oil, offer up prayer for others, as the High Priest carried the people of Israel before God. Through our prayer we pass through the torn veil into the Holy of Holies, to the place where the light of God shines, and where God's covenant with us as an anchor to our souls against the storms of this world.[10] This is the place where the blood of Jesus was spilled.

The life of God flows here continually and the covenant with God is the foundation of our lives. Here I understand that God has chosen me and will never leave me. Here the cherubim shelter me under their wings. The source of life is here, and we seek to come here to the place full of God's life, to get to know the One who has been from the beginning. The laws of worship are not legal external rules of what to wear, what to eat, or what to drink. They are internal laws through which my conscience is cleansed.

---

[1] Psa. 119:104

[2] Heb. 5:7

[3] Jewish literature also mention this instance: During the last forty years before the destruction of the Temple the lot ['For the Lord'] did not come up in the right hand; nor did the crimson-colored strap become white; nor did the westernmost light shine; and the doors of the Hekal would open by themselves, until R. Johanan b. Zakkai rebuked them, saying: Hekal, Hekal, why wilt thou be the alarmer thyself? I know about thee that thou wilt be destroyed, for Zechariah ben Ido has already prophesied concerning thee: Open thy doors, O Lebanon, that the fire may devour thy cedars. Tractate Yoma 39b

[4] John 14:6

[5] John 10:9-10

[6] Prov. 27:17 Iron sharpens iron, so one man sharpens another.

[7] Rom. 8:26 "In the same way the Spirit also helps our weakness; for we do not know how to pray as we should, but the Spirit Himself intercedes for *us* with groanings too deep for words."

[8] John 1:4 "In Him was life, and the life was the Light of men."

[9] Gen. 31:43-54

[10] Heb. 6:19 "This hope we have as an anchor of the soul, a *hope* both sure and steadfast and one which enters within the veil."

CHAPTER 12

Jesus Prepared a Better Covenant

J esus is the mediator of a better covenant (Heb. 8:6). In this chapter we will discuss why the covenant mediated by Jesus is better. There are several types of covenants, but they can be divided into two main types. First, there is one made between a strong side and a weaker side, such as one between a conquering king and a conquered king, or between God and man. The second is a covenant between equals, or a covenant of brotherhood.

The Covenant Between a Strong Side and a Weak Side

Such a covenant involves promises from the stronger side regarding what the weaker side will receive. These may be promises of protection, or demands on behalf of the weaker party. In ancient days, if a treaty was struck up between states, peoples, or kings, it was engraved on stone and placed on the border between the two peoples. The treaty was engraved on two stones, or on two sides of the same stone, so that one side faced the strong side – the conquering king – and the other side faced the weak side. In this way, both of them could see the treaty at their point of meeting. Usually they commemorated the treaty at least once a year. We see a good example of this in Genesis 31:43-54:

> Then Laban replied to Jacob, "The daughters are my daughters, and the children are my children, and the flocks are my flocks, and all that you see is mine. But what can I do this day to these my daughters or to their children whom they have borne? So now come, let us make a covenant, you and I, and let it be a witness between you and me." Then Jacob took a stone and set it up as a pillar. Jacob said to his kinsmen, "Gather stones". So they took stones and made a heap, and they ate there by the heap. Now Laban called it Jegar-sahadutha, but Jacob called it Galeed. Laban said, "This heap is a witness between you and me this day". Therefore it was named Galeed, and Mizpah, for he said, "May the Lord watch between you and me when we are absent one from the other. If you mistreat my daughters, or if you take wives besides my daughters, although no man is with us, see, God is witness between you and me". Laban said to Jacob, "Behold this heap and behold the pillar which I have set between you and me. This heap is a witness, and the pillar is a witness, that I will not pass by this heap to you for harm, and you will not pass by this heap and this pillar to me, for harm. The God of Abraham and the God of Nahor, the God of their father, judge between us". So Jacob swore by the fear of his father Isaac. Then Jacob offered a sacrifice on the mountain, and called his kinsmen to

the meal; and they ate the meal and spent the night on the mountain.

When Laban chased after Jacob, he could well have killed him. God revealed Himself to him, stopped him, and commanded him not to do that. Instead, Laban suggested making a covenant with Jacob. They set up a stone as a memorial in their place of meeting, on the border between them. The word *sahadutha* in Aramaic means "witness" or "testimony." Jacob called it *Galeed,* which means the same thing: a stone set up as a perpetual testimony or witness to us. Laban laid down the conditions for Jacob. The covenant between them involved several factors: they took a stone and set it up on the border, they called on God to be their witness, they sacrificed and ate together, and there were conditions each side had to respect. These were the conditions Laban gave to Jacob so that Jacob would not be harmed.

We see similar things in the covenant God made with the people of Israel in the Sinai desert. The covenant was written on two tablets of stone. It was written on both tablets not because there wasn't room to write it on one, but because one stone turned towards the sons of Israel and one turned, symbolically, in God's direction. The stones were placed in the Ark of the Covenant in the Holy of Holies where the presence of God was. Here too the covenant written on stone is placed at the point of meeting between God and the people of Israel. When the people of Israel entered the Promised Land and renewed their covenant, they climbed up Mount Gerizim and Mount Ebal and there wrote the covenant on stones using lime.[1]. In this incident too, the covenant is written on stone.

The Law demanded that the king write the law, or the

covenant, for himself.[2] Over and over God emphasizes that we must remember His covenant. That is why the people of Israel were required to make three annual pilgrimages to Jerusalem. They were to remember the covenant and renew it.

An additional thing that was often done when sealing a covenant between a stronger party and a weaker party was the bodily marking of the weaker party to show that he belonged to the stronger one and was protected by him. This was more than the kind of marking cattle are branded with to show they belonged to someone. This was also to show others that someone strong protected him. If they attack him, they will have to deal with his strong protector.

A good example is that of the people of Jabesh-gilead in 1 Samuel 11:1-2, "Now Nahash the Ammonite came up and besieged Jabesh-gilead; and all the men of Jabesh said to Nahash, 'Make a covenant with us and we will serve you'. But Nahash the Ammonite said to them, "I will make it with you on this condition, that I will gouge out the right eye of every one of you, thus I will make it a reproach on all Israel.'" While Saul was being crowned king, Nahash the Ammonite attacked the people of Jabesh-gilead. When they expressed their readiness to submit to him and make a covenant with him, he demanded a physical sign from them that everyone would see. In this case he wanted to humiliate them by disfiguring them. Nevertheless, after making the covenant they would be protected by Nahash the Ammonite and belong to him. We see in this story that part of making a covenant meant to mark people with a sign.

The same thing happened in the covenant between God and the people of Israel, the circumcision, but unlike Nahash, God made the mark in a hidden place.

God put His mark on the people of Israel when He commanded them to be circumcised, in order to remind us, and others, of the covenant he made with us. The sign of the covenant God made with Abraham our Father was commanded to all the generations of Abraham's descendants. This was a sign to memorialize the covenant by which God gave us the land of Israel.

Sealing a covenant involved a sacrifice. Sometimes the sacrifice was divided into parts, and the two parties passed between them as we see in the covenant God made with Abraham our father.[3] In passing through the pieces of the sacrifice, the parties would proclaim, "may this be done to whoever breaks this covenant." Afterwards they drank together and feasted on the sacrifice. Often they ate bread and salt, and drank wine. Even today we use the concept of a "salt covenant" because salt was part of sealing the covenant as we saw in Lev. 2:13, "Every grain offering … you shall season with salt, so that the salt of the covenant of your God shall not be lacking from your grain offering."

A Covenant Between Equals

This kind of covenant is also called a blood-covenant, or a covenant of brothers. We find a good example of this in 1 Samuel 18:3-4, "Then Jonathan made a covenant with David because he loved him as himself. Jonathan stripped himself of the robe that was on him and gave it to David, with his armor, including his sword and his bow and his belt." Jonathan's soul bonded with David, and they made a covenant together. The Scriptures don't describe what they did in order to seal the covenant, but we see here that Jonathan gives David his armor and weapons. Exchanging clothes was a symbolic step to indicate that they exchange roles. From that moment Jonathan considered David to be the next king, and told David that he would be David's second-in-command.[4] Through the covenant Jonathan gave the kingly rights to David. Usually a brotherly covenant, or a covenant of blood, involved mixing the blood of the two parties as a sign of becoming one. This symbolic gesture is known to most of us from movies about Native Americans who would cut their hands and hold the wounds together, mixing the blood. In other cultures, each party would cut their hands and drip the blood into a cup of wine, which they both drank, saying "My blood is mixed with your blood, we are one. We are absolute partners in life. We are family, as one man. What is yours is mine, what is mine is yours." This partnership included family. Many years after the covenant with Jonathan, David sought for his descendants and treated them like his own sons. Usually this covenant also involved sharing a meal together.

The Sinai Covenant and the New Covenant

We have looked at the different means of covenant in order to understand why the covenant Jesus brought us, the New Covenant, is better. Let's compare the Sinai Covenant with the New Covenant.

First of all, the Sinai Covenant was sealed between God and the people, not between individuals. "Behold the blood of the covenant, which the Lord has made with you".[5] In Hebrew "you" here is plural. God made a covenant with the people of Israel, and we know that God is faithful to his covenant even if not all the individuals that are Israel are faithful to it. Until today we see the faithfulness of God toward us. God protected the people of Israel, and brought us back to the Promised Land, but not because we, as individuals are faithful. When we personally are not faithful, God disciplines us individually. There are consequences to our unfaithfulness. But as a people, despite the punishments, God is faithful to the covenant He made with us. Individuals within the people have been called to know Him, and walk in His paths. The entire nation is also called to walk in His paths, but the covenant made in Mt. Sinai was made with the people so the behavior of an individual cannot alter its promises. The lack of faithfulness of one of the parties, the nation of Israel, has consequences. There is punishment, such as exile. But the second side of the covenant, God Himself, nevertheless remains faithful.

The Sinai Covenant was engraved on tablets of stone and placed in the Holy of Holies. The conditions of the covenant were too difficult for the people of Israel to observe. The Torah details the conditions of the covenant, and we know that no man can observe all the Law. We can keep part of it, but not all of it.[6] God, who of course knew that, established the sacrificial system of sin and guilt offerings so that individuals could remain a part of the people even if they broke the conditions of the covenant. The sacrifices were given to atone for breaking the covenant. Sinful individuals had to go to the Tabernacle and offer a sacrifice in order to receive atonement, so that they could continue to share in the covenant of the people.

The tablets of stone were placed in the Holy of Holies. Not everyone had access to them, only the High Priest who represented the people. Once a year, on the Day of Atonement, he entered the Holy of Holies, the place of meeting between God and the people, in order to sprinkle the blood on the Ark of the Covenant to remind us that the blood of the sacrifice is what allows us to remain in covenant with God.

A covenant involved a renewal or reaffirmation, once a year. The Day of Atonement was the day the entire people came together symbolically, represented by the

High Priest, into the Holy of Holies, the meeting place, and reaffirmed that the covenant is in effect only by the blood of the sacrifices. The blood was meant to show that we are weak and helpless and in need of the sacrifice to atones for us, that we come before God with the sprinkling of blood to remember and be reminded of that.

The differences between the elements of the Sinai Covenant and the New Covenant Jesus has made with us are seen clearly in the famous prophecy in Jeremiah 31:31-34:

> "Behold, days are coming," declares the LORD, "when I will make a new covenant with the house of Israel and with the house of Judah, not like the covenant which I made with their fathers in the day I took them by the hand to bring them out of the land of Egypt, My covenant which they broke, although I was a husband to them," declares the LORD. "But this is the covenant which I will make with the house of Israel after those days," declares the LORD, "I will put My law within them and on their heart I will write it; and I will be their God, and they shall be My people. They will not teach again, each man his neighbor and each man his brother, saying, 'Know the Lord,' for they will all know Me, from the least of them to the greatest of them," declares the LORD, "for I will forgive their iniquity, and their sin I will remember no more."

The New Covenant is not a Christian invention. It is a prophetic promise given to the people of Israel. We have seen that the covenant made in the Sinai was a covenant with the people. Not everyone knew God intimately and personally. Even though God always had a *sha-ar yashuv,* a remnant[7], – that small part of the people who knew Him and walked in His ways – most of the people did not truly know Him. In the New Covenant we see something else. God promises that He will make a new and different covenant with the people, "not like the covenant which I made with their fathers," and tells us how it will be different. After saying that "they broke My covenant even though I was as a husband to them," He was angry and punished them. Then He says, "But this is the covenant which I will make with the house of Israel . . . I will put My law within them and on their heart I will write it."

God is speaking here to the manner of writing the covenant, and tells the people that He will write it on their hearts, not on tablets of stone. He says, "I will not place my Law in the Holy of Holies in the meeting place only the representative could enter. I will prepare another meeting point in them. The Holy of Holies – the meeting place where the covenant is written, and where the witness stone is placed – is no longer outside of the people; it is no longer in a place only the representative of the people have access to once a year. It is within every single person who accepts the conditions of the New Covenant. God writes the covenant on our hearts. He puts it within us. The Holy of Holies is no longer a place outside of us. The meeting place between God and us is within us. That is why the Scriptures call us, as a body[8] and as individuals[9], "the Temple of God." God says that He will come and dwell within us. When we receive the New Covenant in Jesus, He comes and writes the covenant on our hearts. He comes and dwells within us. The meeting place is within us. That is why we are called to prepare our heart and purify it.[10]

The People of God

When God said through Jeremiah, "I will be their God and they will be My people," He was speaking of a people who had His covenant written on their hearts. That is to say, this covenant is not a covenant the people make with God as a people, where the covenant is outside of the individual person. Here everyone who has the covenant written within him becomes a part of God's people. That is why, whether you are Jew or Gentile, as long as the covenant is written on your heart – you are part of the people of God. We have become a people that have the covenant written within us, the same people that once were not a people, since we are not made of a people, but rather of individuals from many peoples. This is mentioned in the song of Moses,[11] through which God will provoke the people of Israel to jealousy.

In this covenant, not only the remnant know God, but "all will know Me from the smallest to the greatest." It does not matter what people you belong to, your age, the amount of wisdom you have, or how big or famous or beautiful you are. What is important is that God has made this covenant with you, and it is within you. He put His Law in your heart. If you have a part in this covenant, God knows you. You know Him personally, and you have the possibility for intimate relationship with Him. Not only the pastor or the pope, not only special people, but all of us know God; from the smallest to the greatest. The purpose of our lives is to know Him better. It is to be increasingly purified so that more of Him will dwell within us, and be seen through us. And also that we do not hide the holiness, the light, the love, and the life of God that dwells within us.

He is the one who forgives. I don't have to make a pilgrimage to Jerusalem every time I sin, to purchase a sacrifice, and go to the priest so that he can offer it up for me in the Temple, the meeting place of God and man. Jesus is the sacrifice, the covenant is written on my heart, the meeting place is within me, and the possibility to receive forgiveness is always there, in an instant. Every time I sin I wish to recognize the sin as quickly as possible and immediately repent of it. There is no need to punish myself over several days, to be sad, to flagellate myself, and only then ask for forgiveness. The atonement of Messiah's sacrifice can and should be received immediately to receive forgiveness so that I can continue to be in the Holy of Holies.

A New Heart

> Then I will sprinkle clean water on you, and you will be clean; I will cleanse you from all your filthiness and from all your idols. Moreover, I will give you a new heart and put a new spirit within you; and I will remove the heart of stone from your flesh and give you a heart of flesh. I will put My Spirit within you and cause you to walk in My statutes, and you will be careful to observe My ordinances. You will live in the land that I gave to your forefathers; so you will be My people, and I will be your God. Moreover, I will save you from all your uncleanness; and I will call for the grain and multiply it, and I will not bring a famine on you (Eze. 36:25-29).

In these verses God says that not only will He write his Torah on our hearts, He will also replace our heart of stone with a soft heart. You don't have to be a prophet to know that we have a hard heart. God will give us a heart of flesh instead, and will write His law on this heart.

I remember that, before I became a believer in Jesus, I was tough, and never cried. Tough men don't cry. When I began to believe in Jesus I began to cry. In fact, the first thing I did when I gave my life to Jesus was to cry, because my heart changed from a heart of stone to a heart of flesh, and I began to feel. Sin has turned our hearts into stone, and in order to make sure the New Covenant will not be another covenant written on stone, God promises to change our hearts.

Further, God has promised that He will do much more than give us a new heart, or write His Torah on our hearts. Since He knows that it is hard for us to walk in His ways and keep His commandments, he will give us the Holy Spirit. The Spirit will give us the power to walk in His ways and if we leave His ways He will point out the sin, reprove us,[12] and remind[13] us of the atonement we have in Jesus. The Holy Spirit will help us and give us power, as promised in John 1:12, "But as many as received him, to them gave He power to become the sons of God, even to them that believe on his name" (KJV).

The Mark of the Covenant

As with other covenants, the New Covenant includes marks In the flash, but unlike other covenants, God did not put these marks on those who make a covenant with Him. Instead, the marks are on the body of Jesus who represented both sides in the Covenant – both God and man. The marks of the cross on His body are always before God, where Jesus intercedes for us.[14] Generally the weak side receives the mark of the covenant, but in the New Covenant God marked Himself for us, the weak ones.

The Messiah shared Himself in flesh and blood, and poured His blood out for us. God not only made a covenant with us, the strong with the weak, He also made a covenant of brothers with us, a blood covenant. He exchanged His life with us, giving up His life for ours. He exchanged His garments for ours. He who knew no sin wore sin for us so that we could wear His righteousness. Jesus was the perfect man. As man, He took on the marks of a blood covenant. Today Jesus sits in heaven on the right hand of the Father, God who took on flesh, man with the marks of the cross, those same marks He showed His disciples after He rose from the dead. Thomas, who did not believe, was invited by Jesus to see the marks in His hands, and put his hands in the hole in His side. God marked Himself when Jesus was flesh and blood, completely human, and thus always remembers His covenant with us. God mixed His blood with ours, exchanged clothes with us, exchanged life with us – and that is the Gospel. Martin Luther called that "The Divine Exchange." God gave all of Himself entirely for us so that we would give all of ourselves entirely to Him. But we hold on to things and do not want to give in. We do not want to exchange. We think that what we have is worth more than all that is God's. The moment we replace all that we are with His life, then our lives change from one end to the other. "For if we died with Him, we will also live with Him; If we endure, we will also reign with Him; If we deny Him, He also will deny us" (2 Tim. 2:11-12).

A Better Covenant

The New Covenant is a better covenant because it includes everything. God has done everything for us through it. He only demands that we receive it and exchange our life for His. He made with us a covenant that is both between a strong party and a weak party, and a blood covenant. He has given us everything so that we can walk in His ways. God made a New Covenant with each one who allowed Him to write the covenant within him, and put His Torah in his heart, and who says, "I want to share in the covenant with you, come and dwell within me in Your Holy Spirit, fill me with Your Holy Spirit. Give me Your clothes in place of mine, exchange my sin for Your righteousness." Each one of us who has done that knows God. When we commemorate the Lord's Supper, we remember with joy and thanks the New Covenant God has made with us, which is so much better than the Sinai Covenant. The New Covenant is a full covenant through which God gave us all that is necessary to receive His new life, His righteousness, and the power to be sons of God. All of us who live under the New Covenant know all of that personally, not just as part of a group or people.

We are in a process of purifying the Tabernacle, purifying and renewing our heart. The process whereby God exchanges His life for ours goes on. When we look back on our life, we can see the changes God has made, the purification He has done, and all that He did in our hearts. He has placed the Holy Spirit within us to work in us as He has promised. The New Covenant is a better covenant because it is not just between a strong King and those under him. It is not just a covenant between conqueror and conquered. It is also a blood covenant, a covenant of brothers. "For it was fitting for Him, for whom are all things, and through whom are all things, in bringing many sons to glory, to perfect the author of their salvation through sufferings. For both He who sanctifies and those who are sanctified are all from one Father; for which reason He is not ashamed to call them brethren" (Heb. 2:10-11).

---

[1] Deut. 27:1-26, Josh. 8 30-35

[2] Deut. 17:18

[3] Gen. 15

[4] 1 Sam. 23:17

[5] Ex. 24:8

[6] James 2:10 "For whoever keeps the whole law and yet stumbles in one *point*, he has become guilty of all".

[7] Isa. 10:22

[8] 2 Cor. 6:16 "For we are the temple of the living God; just as God said, "I WILL DWELL IN THEM AND WALK AMONG THEM; AND I WILL BE THEIR GOD, AND THEY SHALL BE MY PEOPLE".

[9] 1 Cor. 6:19 "Or do you not know that your body is a temple of the Holy Spirit who is in you, whom you have from God, and that you are not your own?"

[10] James 4:8, 5:8

[11] Deut. 32:21

[12] John 16:8 "And He, when He comes, will convict the world concerning sin and righteousness and judgment"

[13] John 14:26 "But the Comforter, which is the Holy Ghost, whom the Father will send in my name, he shall teach you all things, and bring all things to your remembrance, whatsoever I have said unto you." (KJV)

[14] Rom. 8:34 "who is the one who condemns? Christ Jesus is He who died, yes, rather who was raised, who is at the right hand of God, who also intercedes for us."

CHAPTER 13

Jesus Gave Better Promises

Hebrews 8:6 tells us that Jesus gave better promises, "But now He has obtained a more excellent ministry, by as much as He is also the mediator of a better covenant, which has been enacted on better promises." Every covenant is based on promises. According to the Merriam-Webster dictionary[1], a promise is, "1) a declaration that one will do or refrain from doing something specified; or 2) a legally binding declaration that gives the person to whom it is made a right to expect or to claim the performance or forbearance of a specified act."

If, for instance, we say, "Take the book." that's not a promise because it is given right away. If I say, "Just wait, I will spank you if you keep acting like that!" I am threatening, not promising. A promise is something good and positive that will be fulfilled in the future. We know the promises of the Sinai Covenant were given through mediators. Hebrews 1:1 tells us that God spoke in the past in many ways through the prophets. In the New Covenant we see the reflection of the dialogue of that time, in that the angels are involved even in giving the Law.[2] The promises are not given directly by God. They are given through mediators: both prophets and angels.

Promises to the Nation of Israel

The promises given at Sinai were given to the entire nation. As mentioned in the previous chapter, the covenant was made with the people, not with individuals, although, the covenant also related to individuals within the nation. The clearest promise is that God will give the people the land of Israel. That is not a promise to an individual; it is given to the entire nation. I think this is true even the Ten Commandments. The first commandment with a reward, "Honor your father and your mother, that your days may be prolonged in the land which the Lord your God gives you"(Ex. 20:12), is a promise to the entire nation. I am not so sure that honoring one's father and mother will lengthen the individual's life, but a nation that honor's their parents is a stronger nation that endures for a longer time on the land God has given it. The first step in the deterioration of a society is the breakup of the family unit. If children despise their parents instead of honoring them, the family unit falls apart. As a result society breaks down, and then the nation breaks down. Its endurance is affected. This commandment is not only for individuals, as God gave the land to the nation of Israel.

The promises to the people of Sinai Covenant include a promise of victory over their enemies. There are many such promises. One example is in Deut. 28:2-9:

All these blessings will come upon you and over-take you if obey the LORD your God: Blessed shall you be in the city, and blessed shall you be in the country. Blessed shall be the offspring of your body and the produce of your ground and the offspring of your beasts, the increase of your herd and the young of your flock. Blessed shall be your basket and your kneading bowl.

Blessed shall you be when you come in, and blessed shall you be when you go out. The LORD shall cause your enemies who rise up against you to be defeated before you; they will come out against you one way and will flee before you seven ways. The LORD will command the blessing upon you in your barns and in all that you put your hand to, and He will bless you in the land which the LORD your God gives you. The LORD will establish you as a holy people to Himself, as He swore to you, if you keep the commandments of the Lord your God and walk in His ways.

Although God speaks here in the singular, He is in fact addressing the nation, because the covenant and the promises were given to the nation as one. "Blessed shall you be in the city and blessed shall you be in the country. Blessed shall you be when you come in, and blessed shall you be when you go out." It may seem as if He is speaking to individuals, but further on we will see that He is speaking to the nation.

Another verse people tend to apply to individuals is Deut. 31:6.which says, "Be strong and courageous, do not be afraid or tremble at them, for the Lord your God is the one who goes with you. He will not fail you or forsake you." The first words of the verse are written in the plural, that is, to the nation rather than to an individual, so applying the verse to individuals in this case is a mistake. The promises and covenant of Sinai were given to the nation. They were intended to influence the individuals within the nation. We see this did not work very well because throughout the history of the people of Israel, even through to today, very few have known God personally.

It is interesting how people who read the Bible, and claim they believe the Bible is the unchanging Word of God, can read these verses and still believe that God has abandoned the people of Israel. They hold on to a belief that Israel is no longer important to God, and has that it has ceased to be His people – their place has been taken by the Christian church. How can they say such a thing when God promises the people of Israel here so clearly, "I will not fail you or forsake you?" After speaking of the New Covenant, the prophet Jeremiah tells us:

> Thus says the LORD, Who gives the sun for light by day and the fixed order of the moon and the stars for light by night, Who stirs up the sea so that its waves roar; the Lord of hosts is His name: "If this fixed order departs from before Me," declares the LORD, "then the offspring of Israel also will cease from being a nation before Me forever." Thus says the LORD, "If the heavens above can be measured And the foundations of the earth searched out below, then I will also cast off all the offspring of Israel for all that they have done," declares the LORD (Jer. 31:35-37).

Sadly, there are many among the nations who believe that Israel has ceased to be the people of God, and that the church has taken their place. They claim that God has become fed up with the sins of the people of Israel. We sinned too much, and He banished us from His presence. But here we read that God will never fail us or leave us. Jeremiah tells us that only if the impossible happens – for example, if the heavens above are measured, and the foundations of the earth are searched out – only then will He tire of the people of Israel because of their sins. I do not understand how such people are able to place their trust in God, because if God promised the people of Israel He would never leave them, but then rejects them because of their sins, how can He be trusted? It sounds as if He is a God who does not keep His promises. Perhaps He will also tire of the promises He gave to us as believers? When I look back on my life, I find many reasons for God to banish me from his presence. If Israel's sin caused God to say, "All right, I promised, but I am not going to keep My promises because I am fed up with you," then what chance do I have? If people believe God has rejected Israel despite His promises, then how can they believe in a faithful God who keeps His word?

A Conditional Promise

There are unconditional promises given to the people of Israel through Abraham, Isaac, and Jacob. The Sinai Covenant also includes unconditional promises, but most of the promises in the Law have conditions attached, and were obtained through great effort. For example, Deuteronomy 28:1-2 states, "Now it shall be, if you diligently obey the LORD your God, being careful to do all His commandments which I command you today, the LORD your God will set you high above all the nations of the earth. All these blessings will come upon you and overtake you if you obey the LORD your God." This passage begins with the words "now it shall be if you diligently obey." The condition placed here is not "if you make an effort to observe the commandments," but "if you diligently obey . . . being careful to do all His commandments." That is why the New Covenant tells us, "For whoever keeps the whole law and yet stumbles in one point, he has become guilty of all" (James 2:10). This is not invented in the New

Covenant; it is a direct reminder of what is written in the book of Deuteronomy. "If you . . . do **all** His commandments, then these blessings will come upon you and overtake you." Why? Because you will do them all. That's what happens when you keep all the commandments. If we break even one commandment, or commit even just one sin, then we have not kept them all, and we will not receive the blessings. That is why receiving these promises required such effort on our part.

In actual fact, man is not able to observe the entire Law. It is written, "none of you carries out the Law" (John 7:19). The giving of these promises on condition of "all" means that we have no choice but to rest in the grace of God to keep the Law as required, and to receive the promises.

A Better Covenant

So then, when we look at the promises in the Sinai Covenant, which were given by messengers, we see that they were given to the people as a whole. Furthermore, we see that they require impossible efforts, since it is impossible to observe all the commandments and conditions of the covenant, and retain the promises of the covenant. As we know, only a small remnant of the people of Israel really knew God personally. When there is no personal relationship with God, then it is much more difficult to observe the laws and commandments, or to honor the conditions of the covenant. If my boss is good, and I have close relationship with him, then it's much easier to do what he tells me. The relationship between us motivates me to do my job well, even if I don't understand why he wants things a certain way, or if I find them difficult to do. In the Sinai Covenant, and throughout the history of the people of Israel, only a small part of the people of Israel feared God and truly loved Him. Only a remnant of the people had a true relationship with God, so it was much more difficult for the people to meet the conditions, and thus receive the promises. The relationship with God for most of the people of Israel was like the relationship between a master and his servant instead of that of a brother, a lover, or father and son.

To help us keep the conditions given us, we have been given – under the New Covenant – the Holy Spirit. In the framework of the Sinai Covenant, the Holy Spirit was given to very few people. When seventy elders of the people were called to the Tabernacle to stand with Moses,[3] two of them, Eldad and Medad, stayed in the camp and began to prophesy there. Joshua, the son of Nun, complained about this to Moses, but Moses answered him, "Would that all the Lord's people were prophets" (Num. 11:29). Here we see that the Holy Spirit only fell on the seventy elders. In the Old Testament we are told that the Spirit of God fell on the prophets, on kings, and others, but not on all Israel.

In the New Covenant the situation is different. All the promises were given directly by the Messiah to the partakers of the covenant. As written in Hebrews 1:1-2, God spoke to us by the Messiah. Jesus is God in the flesh, the *mimra-de ya*, the word of God, Immanuel, and He himself came and gave us the promises whilst He was among us "as a shepherd cares for his herd in the day when he is among his scattered sheep"[4] (Eze. 34:12). As God said through the prophets, "I will dwell among you"[5] so that you would know that I am your God. God came Himself to bring what He had promised. Not by means of a messenger, and not by an angel.

The promises of the New Covenant are for the most part promises to individuals. Even the promise quoted from Numbers 28 in Hebrews 13:5, "I will never desert you nor will I ever forsake you," is given to the individual and not to a group. Neither is it only for the people of Israel, but for all those who belong to God and follow Him, as he writes, "for He Himself has said, 'I will never desert you, nor will I ever forsake you,' so that we confidently say, 'The Lord is my helper, I will not be afraid. What will man do to me?' (Heb. 13:5-6). The writer speaks here of individuals: what will man do to me? The promises are given here to each of us personally and individually.

In John 14:1-6 we read:

"Do not let your heart be troubled; believe in God, believe also in Me. In My Father's house are many dwelling places; if it were not so, I would have told you; for I go to prepare a place for you. If I go and prepare a place for you, I will come again and receive you to Myself, that where I am, there you may be also. And you know the way where I am going." Thomas said to Him, "Lord, we do not know where You are going, how do we know the way?" Jesus said to him, "I am the way, and the truth, and the life; no one comes to the Father but through Me".

These promises are not speaking to a people or a group that would then influence the individual, but rather to the individual who in his turn influences the people. The promises here are not given to the nation as a nation, or a group of people as a group, or to a church as a church, but to individuals that make up the group. In the New Covenant the direction is turned. In the Mosaic Covenant the promises were directed at the people, and thus affected the individual. Here the promises and the covenant are for the individual who then affects the group, the church, or the nation.

Even the promises to the believers who will reign over the earth, given in Revelation 5:10, are to individuals, "You have made them to be a kingdom and priests to our God; and they will reign upon the earth." In Matthew 25:14-30, Jesus describes the Kingdom of Heaven with the example of a king who travels abroad and leaves his servants talents of silver to trade with. In this parable, the king treats each one in a different way. Each one receives a different gift and a different reward. Every reference made here is not to a group, but to individuals, and the gift of the kingdom is to individuals. Even the prize, the reward for keeping the commandments and using what God has given us, is individual and personal. If you are in an unhealthy church, a congregation, or a home group, that is not an excuse to claim, "If that's the way they act, I am going to act like that too." God expects you, personally, to act in a worthy manner before Him, and to live according to His will. Never mind what those around you are doing.

Promises That Require No Effort

The promises of the New Covenant do not depend on our own efforts. As written in Ezekiel 36:22-27, it is God who brings us to Him, who gives us a new heart, who writes His Law in our hearts, who gives us the Spirit, and who gives us the necessary power to walk in His ways and keep His commandments. We cannot keep all the commandments, which is why He took on flesh and became a sacrifice offered for us and in our place, in order to atone for our sins and bring forgiveness. In order for the promises given us to be fulfilled, there is no need of a great effort on our part, but to receive what He has done for us. And that is still so difficult for us! It is hard for us to accept something we haven't earned, something we did nothing to obtain. If someone approaches you on the street and gives you $100, I am sure you wouldn't jump at the chance to take it immediately. Each one of us would first ask, "Why? What do you want in exchange?" No "normal" person would just come up to you on the street and give you something valuable without knowing you, or without you doing something to earn it. That is why it is so difficult for so many to receive the Gospel of the New Covenant. It requires them to accept things they do not deserve, and without them having done anything to earn them. In fact, in order to accept the promises of the New Covenant, I have to first confess that I do not deserve anything. I have to be ready to take an honest look at myself, to confess I do not deserve it, and to accept what He is giving me anyway. That includes forgiveness of sins, the Holy Spirit, and the Covenant. That is why so many refuse. In our pride, people insist on doing things their way, and not God's way. If you live your life your own way, as you see fit, then you will get to hell in your way, because there is only one way to God, and that is His way. If you want to be with Him, you have to do it His way. There are only two ways in the world: His way, and all the other ways that are all alike, even if they may seem to be different.

In order to go His way I have to humble myself. I have to admit to myself that I cannot make it on my own, in my own way, and I have to ask His help. For us to ask is begging, and that puts our pride to the test. To receive something we have not earned is what the Scriptures call "grace." Grace means that man cannot earn something by his own efforts but instead he receives it for free. Many of us are not willing to accept it. Many want to be found worthy, to feel we deserve it. But if we ask for and receive grace, God will change our hearts, He will write His Law on our hearts, and He will give us the Holy Spirit and the power that changes us from the inside. Many of us are not willing to accept these conditions. Many say, "Give everything to me, but do not change me!" But it does not work that way!

Promises Based on a Relationship

The New Covenant means a personal relationship with God. The promise of the New Covenant in Jeremiah 31 from verse 30 on, and especially verse 34 is, "'for they will all know Me, from the least of them to the greatest of them,' declares the LORD, 'for I will forgive their iniquity, and their sin I will remember no more.'" Whoever receives the covenant with God; whoever God has given a heart of flesh, and cut out the heart of stone; whoever has God's Law written on his heart; whoever has the Holy Spirit in his heart – knows God. If you only know about Him but do not know Him in a personal way, then you have no part in the New Covenant, because it is written, "for they will all know me, from the least of them to the greatest of them." Age or knowledge is not important. Whoever receives the covenant of God knows God. Of course, the more time a person spends with Him, the better he will come to know Him. The more a person relies on Him, the better he will come to trust Him.

God created us to have an intimate relationship with us. In order to restore us to this relationship, Jesus came, was crucified, and rose again. When we have an intimate relationship with God as our Father and we want to please Him, so the emphasis is not on effort anymore, but on love. Since I love Him so much, I delight in pleasing Him. When I love someone, I want what is good for Him. When we do things for someone out of love, it's heart-warming. Because of our relationship with God we do things for Him, not because we have to. God does not stand there with a whip just waiting for us to make a mistake so He can whip us. The things I do are out of my love for Him, because we have an intimate relationship.

The Holy Spirit as a Deposit

The Holy Spirit has been given to everyone with this kind of relationship. Whoever comes into covenant with God receives the Holy Spirit, as we are told in Jeremiah and in Ezekiel, "I will put my Spirit within you" (Jer 31:33; Eze. 36:27). The Holy Spirit is given to all believers. Ephesians 1:14 tells us that the Holy Spirit "is a deposit guaranteeing our inheritance until the redemption of those who are God's possession" (NIV). In Israel when you want to rent or buy a house, and you find a place you like, you speak with the owner, write up a temporary agreement, and pay a deposit. You pay a small part of the total amount in order to ensure that the owner will keep the house for you until the deal is closed, and when the entire sum is paid up, the property is possessed by you. We are told that the Holy Spirit is given us as a deposit until we receive what God has promised us. The deposit is just a small part of what God has prepared for us. Everything God has prepared for us is much more than the Holy Spirit! By giving us the Holy Spirit God proves that His promises are serious. He gives us the Holy Spirit until the time of restoration, when all things will be in its proper place and we will receive all He has prepared for us. Usually things happen the other way. I, who am interested in obtaining His promises, should be the one to place a deposit, just like the one who wants to buy a house has to place a deposit, not the owner. But God has done even this, in our place.

What is that deposit we have already received?

> But I tell you the truth; it is better for you that I go away, for if I may not go away, the Comforter will not come unto you, and if I go on, I will send Him unto you; and having come, He will convict the world concerning sin, and concerning righteousness, and concerning judgment; concerning sin indeed, because they do not believe in me; and concerning righteousness, because unto my Father I go away, and no more do ye behold me (John 16:7-10, YLT).

The promised deposit is called the Comforter. In rabbinical writings, one of the names of the Messiah is "comforter."[6] In Midrash Eicha Raba parasha 1:51[7] we are told that the Messiah, the Comforter, was born when the temple was destroyed. The Messiah actually came before then, but the comforter is the Holy Spirit, because that is one of His roles. Every believer in Jesus who has gone through difficult times in his life knows personally the comfort the Holy Spirit brings us. The Holy Spirit comforts us in our troubles. When we read the Scriptures, the Spirit makes a verse come alive and jump off the page at us, speaking to us and comforting us. The Spirit also shows us the love of God, encourages and strengthens us; and not only in difficult times.

The above verses indicate that the Holy Spirit convicts us (verse 8). When we fail or sin, the Holy Spirit convicts us and shows us where we went wrong. We usually prefer to interpret these verses as saying that the Holy Spirit convicts the unbelievers of sin, but in actual fact these verses are specifically speaking about believers. The verse tells us of three kinds of conviction: conviction of sin, conviction of righteousness, and conviction of judgment. Does this same comforter who dwells within us cause us to go out to the world and reprove the sin of others? Is that what is written here? What is written here is that the Holy Spirit convicts of sin, which begins first of all with me.

We have spoken about speaking the truth at all times. It is important to keep in mind that telling the truth must be done in love. "If I have the gift of prophecy, and know all mysteries and all knowledge; and if I have all faith, so as to remove mountains, but do not have love, I am nothing" (1 Cor. 13:2). Many times we claim that when we tell the truth, it is love. But often, if I do not know how to say something in love, it is better not to say anything at all. Many times we think it our duty to go and reprove others for sin. That is not our job; our job is to love them. The Holy Spirit is the one who comforts and also reproves us.

In Hebrew, which was the language that Jesus spoke, the word that is translated as "righteousness" also means "justice." The Holy Spirit comforts and convicts us of justice also. There is a large movement in the world that stresses the need to fight for justice. But usually, while chasing after justice, they do harm. For example: many people require justice from the state of Israel. They claim that the Jews took the land of the Arabs and have to give it back, including Jaffa, Haifa and so on. They hold demonstrations for this justice, and demand that Israel restore to the refugees the property that was taken from them. It is true that throughout the years of war Israel impounded Arab property and also exiled some from their lands. But if those same people were truly seeking justice, they would demand justice from all sides involved, including the Arab countries, and require that they restore the property of the Jews they expelled. The property taken from hundreds of thousands of Jewish refugees is much greater than the property the State of Israel impounded from the

Arabs. So those who demand justice usually demand justice only for one side, and thus bring about injustice.

There is no justice in the world! With all the pain of those who have been hurt, justice cannot be had on earth as long as the prince of this world rules over it. Justice will be done only when the Messiah returns. The Holy Spirit does not come to dwell within us so that we can demand justice from others. The role of the Spirit is to help us to walk in God's ways, convicting us of the injustice we do, not the injustice of others. It is very easy to see injustice in others, but the Holy Spirit does not come so that I can reprove others and try to make them do right. Justice begins with me, and influences those around me. Justice begins with me doing justice by God's grace.

The Holy Spirit dwells within me, and His purpose is to convict *me* of sin, of unrighteousness, and of justice. That is why we must not point an accusing finger at our neighbor. We have to examine and see where we have failed. We have to listen to the Holy Spirit who shows us the unrighteousness in our own lives. The Holy Spirit gives us strength. John tells us, "But as many as received Him, to them He gave the right to become children of God, even to those who believe in His name" (John 1:12).

The meaning of the Greek word John uses translates as, "he gave authority, or power." The deposit we have received (the Holy Spirit) comforts, convicts, and gives us power to become the sons of God. There is a lot of misunderstanding regarding how the Holy Spirit gives us power. Some think that the gifts of the Spirit are given us today, and there are those who deny that. There are some who think that miracles do not happen anymore. They say that miracles took place in the past, but not anymore, and maybe they will come back in the future. We will not expand on this subject, but let's have a look at what the Scriptures say about the relationship between the Holy Spirit and us. That will help us to understand how He gives us power.

In John 14:17 we read, "[T]hat is the Spirit of truth, whom the world cannot receive, because it does not see Him or know Him, but you know Him because He abides with you and will be in you." This verse gives us two prepositions regarding the Holy Spirit. Jesus was speaking to His disciples before the Spirit fell on them in the event that is described in the book of Acts. We see that He speaks of their relationship with the Spirit in two different ways: when the Holy Spirit is with you but not yet within you, and in the future, when He will be in you.

In John 20:22 it is written, "And when He had said this, He breathed on them and said to them, 'Receive the Holy Spirit.'" At this time Jesus has risen from the dead, but the Holy Spirit has not yet come upon the disciples. This would happen at the Feast of Weeks, or Shavuot. The Spirit was with them but not in them. Now Jesus tells them, "Receive the Holy Spirit." Now the Holy Spirit is in them. Later on we read of the event in Acts 1:8, which Jesus had promised to the disciples, "[B]ut you will receive power when the Holy Spirit has come upon you; and you shall be My witnesses both in Jerusalem." Jesus promised them that something was yet to happen: The Holy Spirit will come upon you and you will receive power to be My witnesses. He continues here with what was written at the beginning of the Gospel of John, that He will give them power to become the sons of God. He says this will happen when the Holy Spirit falls upon you.

The same preposition "upon" is used in the Old Testament, when speaking of the Holy Spirit falling upon people like David and the prophets. In Acts 2:3-4 we read, "And there appeared to them tongues as of fire distributing themselves, and they rested on each one of them. And they were all filled with the Holy Spirit and began to speak with other tongues, as the Spirit was giving them utterance." Here the author, Luke, uses the verb "filled with." They were filled with the Holy Spirit when He fell upon them.[8] We see three prepositions used with regard to the Holy Spirit: "with you," "in you," and "upon you." The Holy Spirit, the deposit, is given to us in three ways. The first promise to the disciples was: now He is with you, and He will be in you. Jesus gave them the Holy Spirit when He breathed on them and said, "Receive the Holy Spirit." But at that time the Holy Spirit had not yet fallen upon them. Later Jesus promised them that the Holy Spirit would come upon them, and then they would receive the promised power. This was fulfilled in the Feast of Shavuot.

In our lives as well, before we came to faith, before we were sealed by the Spirit of promise,[9] the Holy Spirit was with us, and worked in us to bring us to Messiah. When each one of us looks back at the time we were not yet followers of Jesus, we see the involvement of the Holy Spirit in our lives trying to guide us to faith in Jesus as Messiah and Lord. We did not see it then, during the whole process, but later we are able to see that God had already been at work in our lives through His Holy Spirit, before we believed and received Him, in order to convict us of sin and lead us to Him. When we believed and received Jesus into our hearts, He came and dwelt within us by the Holy Spirit. Whoever believes has received the Holy Spirit, and is sealed with the Spirit of Promises. The moment we received Jesus He placed His Spirit within us and wrote His Law on our hearts.

But there is something else He promised that we can receive: the power to be witnesses. When the Holy

Spirit comes upon you (not just with you or in you) you will receive power. Whoever has become a disciple of Jesus knows that the Holy Spirit is given to him and dwells within him. Without the Holy Spirit it is impossible have intimacy with God. We also need the Holy Spirit to give us power. If you do not know whether the Holy Spirit has come upon you and given you power, that is a sign the Holy Spirit has not fallen upon you. When we came to faith we knew that something special had happened in our lives because the Holy Spirit, who was with us before we came to faith, came and dwelt with us. In the same way we know when the Holy Spirit falls on us and gives us power to be the sons of God. This is the promise given by the Prophet Joel[10] and quoted in Acts 2:17-18, "'And it shall be in the last days,' God says, 'that I will pour forth my Spirit on all mankind; and your sons and your daughters shall prophesy, and your young men will see visions, and your old men shall dream dreams; even on my bond-slaves, both men and women, I will in those days pour forth my Spirit and they shall prophesy'".

It says, "I will pour forth of my spirit on all mankind" and as a result, supernatural things would happen. Your sons and daughters will prophesy, your young men will see visions, your old men will dream dreams. Even on my bond-slaves, both men and women I will in those days pour forth of my spirit and they shall prophesy. When the Holy Spirit fell (or was poured out) on them, supernatural things happened. They spoke in tongues, other languages, they prophesied, they began to heal the sick, they laid hands on people and the sick were healed; many things happened.

The Holy Spirit is only a deposit, just a little bit of what the Lord God has prepared for those who love Him. "But just as it is written, 'Things which eye has not seen and ear has not heard, and which have not entered the heart of man, all that God has prepared for those who love Him'" (1 Cor. 2:9). Even the great and wonderful things the Holy Spirit has done and continues to do in this world are just a taste, just a deposit, of all we will receive when we receive the fullness of what is promised.

Supernatural Power

Not all that is claimed to be done by the Holy Spirit really is by the Holy Spirit. There are people who have done many things in the name of the Holy Spirit, but have nothing to do with the Holy Spirit. Jesus said, "By their fruit you will know them" (Matt. 7:16). We have to always examine the fruit in their lives. Is glory given to God, or taken for themselves? Does money and material goods take a central place in their work, or does God receive all the glory He deserves? And, is the emphasis on spiritual health and a relationship with him? Do they stress the way in which God will bless us, or the way we have been called to bless God? A quick check like that will make a lot of things clearer. God does do miracles, but God is not like some of the people we see on television who claim to represent God. The purpose of the Holy Spirit is to exalt Jesus, not the one through whom the Spirit works. Moses, who was the greatest of all prophets, was also the most humble of all men[11], he did not seek to promote himself.

God is above nature. God is super-natural. He created all things but he is not a part of nature. Those who have received Him, whom God has come to dwell in by the Holy Spirit, have received power to become the sons of God. When the Holy Spirit falls upon them, He gives them power to be His sons and His witnesses. That is a different experience, – something different from receiving Jesus into our hearts – and is part of the deposit God has given us. If the Holy Spirit has not yet fallen on you, bring this matter to God. Ask other brothers or sisters to pray for you, and God will do it in His way and His time. You only have to ask.[12] Sometimes this happens the moment we receive Jesus as our Savior, and sometimes not. Sometimes it is accompanied by supernatural signs, as happened with the disciples of Jesus, sometimes not. But this is part of the deposit ensuring the fulfillment of all His promises. God is Lord of heaven and earth. He determines what He will do, and when He will do it. It is He who gives us power through the anointing of the Holy Spirit.

Dwight Moody, who was a famous evangelist, and founder of the Moody Institute in Chicago, required of his believing students to request the baptism of the Spirit. He knew that beyond receiving Jesus as Lord and Savior, and His coming to dwell within us, there is a further experience with the Holy Spirit.[13] Thousands of people around the world came to the Lord through him. He could not do that by his own strength, but only through the power of the Holy Spirit who fell upon him. That happened without being accompanied by supernatural signs. Billy Graham did not belong to the charismatic movement, but hundreds of thousands began to believe in Jesus through him. He did not do these things by his own power, but by the power of the Holy Spirit.

Some claim that if someone doesn't speak in tongues, he has not been filled with the Holy Spirit. That is absolutely not true. Dwight Moody and Billy Graham did not speak in tongues. Nowhere do the Scriptures tell us that speaking in tongues is a condition of being filled by the Holy Spirit. Sometimes the baptism by the Holy Spirit is evidenced by the speaking of tongues, and sometimes it is not. What is clear from Scripture is that when the Holy Spirit falls upon us, we have power. God does things in you and through you that you could not do before. The Holy Spirit also gives us words of knowledge to see and understand things we did not before. He gives us wisdom.

There are different gifts of the Spirit given by God. He chooses which gift to give to whom, and when to give them. But each and every one of us not only needs to receive Jesus as Lord and Savior, but also to have the Holy Spirit comes upon us and give us power to become a son of God.

The promises of the New Covenant are greater than those of the Old Covenant because they are directed at each one of us personally, and are not dependent on our own efforts. They are by the power of the living God, who dwells within us and works through us. It is the power from God given us as a deposit until we receive the fullness of the promises.

------

[1] www.merriam-webster.com/dictionary/promise

[2] Acts 7:53, Gal. 3:19, Heb. 2:2

[3] Num. 11

[4] Eze. 34:12

[5] 1 Kings 6:13, Eze. 43:9, Zech. 2:14

[6] Talmud Bavli, Masechet Sanhedrin 98:b: " Rab said: The world was created only on David's account . Samuel said: On Moses account; R. Johanan said: For the sake of the Messiah. What is his [the Messiah's] name?—The School of R. Shila said: His name is Shiloh, for it is written, until Shiloh come (Gen. 49:10, Psa. 72:17). The School of R. Yannai said: His name is Yinnon, for it is written, His name shall endure for ever: e'er the sun was, his name is Yinnon.(Jer. 16:13). The School of R. Haninah maintained: His name is Haninah, as it is written, Where I will not give you Haninah. Others say: His name is Menahem the son of Hezekiah, for it is written, Because Menahem ['the comforter'],

that would relieve my soul (Lam. 4)….The Rabbis said: His name is 'the leper scholar,' as it is written, Surely he hath borne our griefs, and carried our sorrows: yet we did esteem him a leper, smitten of God, and afflicted." According to the sages, one of the Messiah's names is 'comforter'. It is interesting that here they relate Isaiah 53 to the Messiah.

[7] Midrash Rabbah, Eicha I:51 tells the following story: A Jew was plowing with his ox. Suddenly the ox let out a huge bellow. An Arab who was passing by said to him, "From which people are you?" He answered, "I am a Jew". They Arab said to him, "You can leave your plowing because the Jewish Temple has just now been destroyed." "How do you know?" the Jew asked him. "From the ox's bellow." As they were speaking, the ox gave out another huge bellow. The Arab said, "Now you can resume your plowing, the Jewish Savior has just been born." "What's his name?" the Jew asked him. "Menachem" (Comforter).

[8] Simon Peter uses this word to describe the anointing of the Holy Spirit upon the Gentiles: "And as I began to speak, the Holy Spirit fell upon them just as *He did* upon us at the beginning" (Acts 11:15).

[9] Eph. 1:13 "In Him, you also, after listening to the message of truth, the gospel of your salvation—having also believed, you were sealed in Him with the Holy Spirit of promise"

[10] Joel 3:1-2

[11] Num. 12:3

[12] Luke 11:10-13: "For everyone who asks, receives; and he who seeks, finds; and to him who knocks, it will be opened. Now suppose one of you fathers is asked by his son for a fish; he will not give him a snake instead of a fish, will he? Or *if* he is asked for an egg, he will not give him a scorpion, will he? If you then, being evil, know how to give good gifts to your children, how much more will *your* heavenly Father give the Holy Spirit to those who ask Him?"

[13] Why God Used D. L. Moody, by R. A. Torrey, The Moody Bible Institute, 1923

Chapter 14

Jesus Gave a Better Hope

In Heb. 7:19 we read, "[F]or the Law made nothing perfect, and on the other hand there is a bringing in of a better hope, through which we draw near to God." It is written here that the Law does not make anything perfect. On the other hand, Jesus brought us a better hope through which we draw near to God. Jesus gave us a better hope so that through it we can do what we previously were unable to do: come close to God.

What Is Hope?
Hope is the expectation for the fulfilment of the promise: anticipation, aspiration, assumption, belief, confidence, dependence, desire, endurance, expectancy, expectation, anticipation, faith, confidence, chance, trust, and reliance .¹ The Merriam-Webster dictionary defines hope as "desire accompanied by expectation of or belief in fulfilment". Wiktionary calls it, "[t]he belief or expectation that something wished for can or will happen," or "the virtuous desire for future good."² Most people would define hope as looking forward to something you are not sure will come. You want it, but you are not banking on it. "I hope things will get better" means, "I really want things to be better, but I am not

sure whether they will or not." In Biblical Hebrew, the word means to expect something that you are sure will come.

In fact, the essential difference is not in the expectation, but on what, or on whom, the expectation is founded. Hope in the Scriptures is founded on the faithfulness of the one who promises. Modern hope has nothing to do with the character of the one who promises, or even the existence of someone who promises. Hope in modern language means to wish something would be better without any sense of expectation or promise. Hope in modern language depends on the hoper himself and not on the one who promises. It simply means I blindly wish for the situation to improve, if I just wait, if I just try harder, or if I just do not give up hope. The "future good" depends only on the one holding on to hope. In Scripture, the source of hope is the one who promises, not the one who hopes. The strength of hope depends on the faithfulness of the one who promises, and not on the one who holds on the hope no matter what. The "future good" depends only on the one who promised, not the one who holds onto hope.

I like comparing the modern view of hope to the expectation for a train in Israel, and biblical hope to the expectation for a train in Switzerland. In both places the train is supposed to arrive at 10:12. In Israel, you hope the train will arrive at some point in time. In Switzerland, the train arrives to the station at exactly 10:12 or even a bit before. The difference is in the one who promised, whether the Israeli railroad company, or the Swiss railroad company.

In Isaiah 40:31 we read, "[B]ut those who hope in the Lord will renew their strength. They will soar on wings like eagles; they will run and not grow weary, they will walk and not be faint" (NIV). God upholds the weary, but only those who hope in Him, and only those who base their hope on His character and His promises. God strengthens those who hope in Him to fulfil His promises, to do His work, without trying to solve their difficulties on their own. Those who hope in the Lord will gain new strength. In contrast to them, those who place their hope on themselves, on others, or on the chance that the situation will somehow change for the better, do not gain new strength.

We Have Been Saved in Hope

Romans 8:24-25 tells us, "For in hope we have been saved, but hope that is seen is not hope; for who hopes for what he already sees? But if we hope for what we do not see, with perseverance we wait eagerly for it." We read here that hope is in something unseen. It is not hope if you are expecting something you already see or have. Real hope is a hope built on a promise that has not yet been fulfilled, founded on confidence in the one who promised. These verses tell us something very interesting: that we have been saved in hope. Were we not saved by grace or by faith?[3] How can it be that we are told now that we were saved in hope?

Hope is connected to faith. In effect the definition of faith in the New Covenant, "the assurance of things hoped for, the conviction of things not seen" (Heb. 11:1) tells us that there were things we hoped for, things we anticipated. When we began to trust in the things we hoped for, that hope turned to faith, through which we were saved.

When we heard the Gospel, it awoke hope in us that perhaps there was something better to life. When we began to learn more about God and His promises, we began to think that perhaps we can truly trust in God, and His promises are real. As a result, faith was born in our hearts. That is to say, when we began to trust the things we hoped for, we were saved. Hope in God, and in His promises, gave birth to a saving faith.

Same Hope – Different Way

Acts 24:14-16 tells us:

> But this I admit to you, that according to the Way which they call a sect I do serve the God of our fathers, believing everything that is in accordance with the Law and that is written in the Prophets; having a hope in God, which these men cherish themselves, that there shall certainly be a resurrection of both the righteous and the wicked. In view of this, I also do my best to maintain always a blameless conscience both before God and before men.

Paul is speaking to Felix at the trial in Caesarea and telling him that part of believing the Scriptures is a hope for the resurrection of the righteous and of the wicked that will all stand before God's judgment throne. This hope (which is an expectation of something God has promised) caused Paul to do his best to keep a clear conscience before God and before man. Paul also claims here that his accusers, who were Pharisees and Sadducees – members of the Sanhedrin – shared the same hope, and also seek to live before God in such a way that when they stand before His throne of judgment, they will be found righteous. The difference between Paul and his accusers is not in the principles of their faith. Their hope to be found righteous by God is also similar, but their understanding of the way they can obtain the promises of righteous in the judgment of life and death before God is completely different. Paul confesses that the way he worships God and seeks to keep a clear conscience before Him, and before men, is a different way from the way the people of the Sanhedrin worship God. They call his way of worshipping God, in which he hopes and seeks to live, a "sect." Whereas, the way they live they call keeping the Law and the commandments. Everyone's hope is to be found righteous at the final judgment before God, but the way they hope to be found righteous before God is different.

Paul himself had previously hoped to obtain righteousness in God's sight in the same way his accusers continued to hope, but something happened to Paul on the way to Damascus. Something happened to him that changed not only his hope and faith, but the way he sought to maintain a clear conscience; the way he received righteousness in the judgment we will all be judged in before God.

But the way Paul sought to maintain a clear conscience before God and man was not the only difference between Paul (and all believers) and those who shared the faith of the Sanhedrin. In Colossians 1:27 we are told, "[T]o whom God willed to make known what is the riches of the glory of this mystery among the Gentiles, which is Christ in you, the hope of glory." The hope of the members of the Sanhedrin was founded on their understanding and interpretation of the Scriptures. The promises of God are written down, but not all of them are clear, and different interpretations affect what people hope for and what they expect. We see this in Acts 1:6 when the apostles hoped that Jesus would restore sovereignty to Israel. That is how they understood the promises of God, so that is what they hoped for. God's purpose was much greater: His purpose was that the Gospel be preached to all the nations, and people would enter the kingdom of God from all nations. The emphasis of God's promise was not restoration of Israel's sovereignty, but to increase and widen the kingdom to include all the nations. Their hope was founded, like the hope of the rest of the people of Israel, on an intellectual understanding of the Scriptures.

Believers in Jesus are given something else – the Messiah within them, who is the hope of glory. The Messiah who came and dwelt in us by His Holy Spirit. We do not have only the Scriptures, the written word of God, we have the Messiah Himself dwelling within us. The intimacy of our relationship with Him is deep. He not only dwells with us, walks with us, and watches over us as He did with the people of Israel; He also lives within us, in a deeper relationship than that of a man and wife. As believers, we are not limited to our intellectual understanding of Him. We know Him in the most personal way. This combination of close relations, and the light of the Holy Spirit, helps us to understand the hope that is in Him more deeply and more clearly. Since true hope is founded on the faithfulness of the one who promises, and our ability to trust the one who promises, God's promises are not only given us in written words, but we have received the Messiah within us by the Holy Spirit as a deposit until we receive the fulfilment of the promises. Our hope is not founded only on knowing the promises, but on an intimate acquaintance with the promise-giver Himself, who lives within us and has changed our lives. That is why our hope is better. That is why the hope that Jesus gave is better. It is founded on our personal relationship with the One who has promised and on our intimacy with Him. It is not founded on our own efforts or the strength of our hope.

A Continuing, Transforming Hope

But if the ministry of death, in letters engraved on stones, came with glory, so that the sons of Israel could not look intently at the face of Moses because of the glory of his face, fading as it was, how will the ministry of the Spirit fail to be even more with glory? For if the ministry of condemnation has glory, much more does the ministry of righteousness abound in glory. For indeed what had glory, in this case has no glory because of the glory that surpasses it. For if that which fades away was with glory, much more that which remains is in glory. Therefore having such a hope, we use greatboldness in our speech, and are not like Moses, who used to put a veil over his face so that the sons of Israel would not look intently at the end of what was fading away. But their minds were hardened; for until this very day at the reading of the old covenant the same veil remains unlifted, because it is removed in Christ. But to this day whenever Moses is read, a veil lies over their heart; but whenever a person turns to the Lord, the veil is taken away. Now the Lord is the Spirit, and where the Spirit of the Lord is, there is liberty. But we all, with unveiled face, beholding as in a mirror the glory of the Lord, are being transformed into the same image from glory to glory, just as from the Lord, the Spirit (2 Cor. 3:7-18).

In the presence of God, Moses was transformed and wore glory. This change was so great that his face shone in a way that the people of Israel dared not look at him. Moses was obliged to put a veil over his face.[4]

Paul tells us here that the ministry of Moses was the ministry of death engraved on stone, because the Torah brought judgment. His ministry is also called the ministry of condemnation in these verses because whoever broke one of the commandments was judged as if he had broken the entire Torah.[5] The Torah brought a responsibility with it. One could not tell the judge, "I didn't know." The Torah condemned man and revealed sin in all its seriousness. Moses, whose ministry was to bring the Torah that was given by God, was so transformed that he frightened those around him. His face shone, and in the light that shone from him the people of Israel saw all their sins and guilt, and they feared. The glory that flowed from him showed them all their sin clearly. That is why Moses had to put a veil over his face, to prevent the glory of God from shining through him and causing the people to feel guilt and fear. Because Moses did not want the people to be afraid of him, he hid the glory of God. The problem was that the glory he received faded away, but the veil still exists in the hearts of men. The transformation was only temporary. The glory of this ministry passed away and because of the veil, the hearts of our people, and anyone else who receives the ministry of condemnation, is prevented from seeing the true glory of God. Therefore, the ministry that was given to Moses was temporary, and its glory has passed away.

We received from God the ministry of the Spirit, the ministry of righteousness, which is far exalted beyond the ministry of Moses. Our ministry is to bring and present the Messiah within us to man. We were called to show our people, and the world, the righteousness of God, which is for eternity. This ministry also changes, us and fills us with glory, but this glory does not pass away as Moses' glory did. The promises is that the more we look upon Him without the veil, the more we will see ourselves in His light, with no fear of seeing our sins. The more we minister His righteousness through the Spirit, the more we will be transformed to His image. Then His glory in us will never fade, but will grow and increase from glory to glory.

Because we know God, and because the Messiah lives within us by the Holy Spirit, we know that the light that shows us our sins does not show them in order to condemn us, but in order to bring us to repentance. Our hope, and its fulfilment, is founded on our knowledge of the promise-giver who lives within us. So we dare to let His light shine in our lives and change us more and more into His image, from glory to glory. Our hope helps us move beyond the fear that is in guilt (which caused the people of Israel to flee from Moses), to receive his atonement and His life, and to be changed into His image. The Messiah dwells within us, which gives us the hope of a glory that will never pass away, but instead will increase for eternity from glory to glory.

We read in Hebrews 6:18-20:

[S]o that by two unchangeable things in which it is impossible for God to lie, we who have taken refuge would have strong encouragement to take hold of the hope set before us. This hope we have as an anchor of the soul, a hope both sure and steadfast and one which enters within the veil, where Jesus has entered as a fore-runner for us, having become a High Priest for-ever according to the order of Melchizedek.

This hope is an anchor to our souls. This Jesus, the hope within us, has entered into the Holy of Holies and become the High Priest forever for us. Our hearts are anchored in hope to the deepest place in God, to

Jesus Himself, and we are called to cling to this anchor throughout all the storms of life. The anchor is strong and steadfast for our souls, and we must hold tightly to it in order to escape the filth and corruption of this world. If we do not hold tightly to this anchor of hope that is within us, the storms of life will drown us. If we hold onto it, we will pass through the storms of life and come through the veil into the Holy of Holies, the place of God's presence, the *shechina*; to the place where we see Him face to face, where we will be like Him, and where we will remain in His presence for eternity.

On this, the author of Hebrews tells us, "For, on the one hand, there is a setting aside of a former commandment because of its weakness and uselessness (for the Law made nothing perfect), and on the other hand there is a bringing in of a better hope, through which we draw near to God" (Heb. 7:18-19).

In the past, our hope lay in observing the commandments. But the Torah did not help us to draw close to God. It was unable to change us and to make us like Him so that we would be able to stand in His presence. The commandments were unable to purify our hearts and our conscience. They could only reveal our sins to us, and the distance that separates us from God; thus causing us to fear judgment. Jesus, on the other hand, is a better hope because He forgives our sins, takes away the fear, and changes us into His image. Through Him we draw near to God. Our hope is not founded on ourselves who hope on our ability to keep the commandments. It is founded on the One who has not only promised but has also given us a deposit, which is a pledge that He will keep His promises. He is the anchor of our lives, the better hope.

[1] http://en.wiktionary.org/wiki/hope

[2] http://www.merriam-webster.com/dictionary/hope

[3] Eph. 2:8

[4] The story is from Ex. 34:29-35: "It came about when Moses was coming down from Mount Sinai (and the two tablets of the testimony *were* in Moses' hand as he was coming down from the mountain), that Moses did not know that the skin of his face shone because of his speaking with Him. So when Aaron and all the sons of Israel saw Moses, behold, the skin of his face shone, and they were afraid to come near him. Then Moses called to them, and Aaron and all the rulers in the congregation returned to him; and Moses spoke to them. Afterward all the sons of Israel came near, and he commanded them *to do* everything that the Lord had spoken to him on Mount Sinai. When Moses had finished speaking with them, he put a veil over his face. But whenever Moses went in before the Lord to speak with Him, he would take off the veil until he came out; and whenever he came out and spoke to the sons of Israel what he had been commanded, the sons of Israel would see the face of Moses, that the skin of Moses' face shone. So Moses would replace the veil over his face until he went in to speak with Him."

[5] James 2:10

CHAPTER 15

Jesus Gave a Better Sacrifice

Accordingly both gifts and sacrifices are offered which cannot make the worshiper perfect in conscience, since they relate only to food and drink and various washings, regulations for the body imposed until a time of reformation. But when Christ appeared as a High Priest of the good things to come, He entered through the greater and more perfect Tabernacle, not made with hands, that is to say, not of this creation; and not through the blood of goats and calves, but through His own blood, He entered the Holy Place once for all, having obtained eternal redemption. For if the blood of goats and bulls and the ashes of a heifer sprinkling those who have been defiled sanctify for the cleansing of the flesh, how much more will the blood of Christ, who through the eternal Spirit offered Himself without blemish to God, cleanse your conscience from dead works to serve the living God? (Heb. 9:9-14)

The Sacrifices of the Sinai Covenant

In order to understand why the sacrifice of Jesus is better, let's have a look at the sacrificial system, which played a crucial role in the Sinai covenant (the Mosaic covenant). Since the temple no longer exists, and the sacrificial system has ceased, whoever says he believes and observes the Mosaic covenant is not speaking the truth. The sacrifices in the temple constituted the lion's share of the Mosaic covenant. The detailed sacrificial laws are central to the Torah. Without sacrifices, the Sinai covenant cannot be observed.

The Torah speaks of various types of sacrifices, both main and secondary. The first five chapters of Leviticus detail the main sacrifices. There were two main types of sin sacrifices: the sin offering (for sins committed unintentionally, or unwittingly); and the guilt offering (for intentional sins committed knowingly, or on purpose). We often think or say that we did not mean to sin. How many times do we commit sin knowingly? The answer is simple: too many times. But God in His grace provided in the Mosaic Covenant – and how much more in the New Covenant – sacrifices to atone not only for unintentional sins, but also for sins committed on purpose. It is difficult for us to admit that we sin intentionally. We say, "Believers in Jesus don't sin intentionally," but in actual fact we fail in that all too often. If someone is supposed to work until four in the afternoon and leaves the office five minutes before the hour, he has stolen five minutes from his workplace and sins intentionally. If I let my eyes linger a bit longer on a woman's body, that is intentional sin. If I know that something is forbidden and still do it, that is intentional sin. In the Mosaic Covenant God provided the people with sacrifices for intentional sins, and for non-intentional sins. In order to receive atonement and forgiveness they had to offer up these sacrifices at the temple. The sacrifices could not be offered just anywhere.

The second type of sacrifice was the burnt offering.

There are about fourteen different types of these burnt offerings. These are offerings given entirely to God, without any part of them going to the priests. They were burnt up entirely, which is why we call them "burnt" offerings. For instance, every morning and evening the priests sacrificed a burnt offering, burnt it up entirely on the altar as a sweet savor to God, and at the same time renewed the fire on the altar. They did this on the Sabbath as well. That is to say, the priests that served in the Temple desecrated the Sabbath.[1] Some of the sages argue that this did not really happen. The sacrifices are a "perpetual" sacrifice.[2] So every morning and every evening, including the night and morning of the Sabbath, the sacrifices were offered up to God. The burnt offering was sacrificed on the Day of Atonement, as an atoning sacrifice.

The third main type was the thanksgiving offerings. With these also there are two categories: the peace offerings (given in gratitude to God), and the grain offerings (flour, bread, rye, honey, wine, etc.). The word that is translated as "peace" in the English is *shlemim* in Hebrew, and comes from the word "whole," which in turn comes the word *shalom*, meaning peace, paid in full, finished, or completed. When Jesus cried out on the cross, "It is finished" (John 19:20), all these words were included in His saying. There is wordplay in Hebrew of the root *shalem* where all the words come from that would be translated as: "When the perfect One said 'it is finished,' the bill has been paid in full, and the peace between us and God has been completed or perfected. In this offering He perfected and completed all the requirements – He paid the price, He brought peace, and He made us whole.". Nothing we can do will add to or subtract from what Jesus has done.

The various sacrifices were offered in the central

place God had designated for them in the Temple in Jerusalem. People came from all over the country to offer up sacrifices. Everyone gathered together, millions of people, in this one place for the offering up of sacrifices. There were many sacrifices, because a sacrifice was required for everything, and they involved a great deal of work. For every sacrifice brought to the temple, a priest had to take it, lay his hands upon it, slaughter it, and then sprinkle the blood on certain places as called for. Then he cut out certain parts that had to be placed on the altar, laid them on the altar in the courtyard of the temple, or in some cases, even entered in the Holy Place. There were a great many sacrifices, a lot of work, and many priests, so there was a lot of gore and blood. Some pictures portray the temple as a clean, pure place. They show a lamb with an innocent smile sitting comfortably on the altar from which rises up white, clear smoke. In actual fact a lot of sacrifices were offered up at the same time on the altar and there was a lot of blood and mess around the altar. The altar was about two by two meters, and the priests hustled and bustled around it. There were bloody corpses strewn about, and pieces of the sacrificed animals – oxen, sheep, and doves – all over the altar. The priests were constantly throwing new pieces of meat on the altar, of all kinds. Jerusalem was full of the smell of burnt meat and fat. The works of sacrifices were not something clean and sterile.

Priests and Sacrifices

One thing the sacrificial system needed was the priesthood. Not everyone was permitted to offer up sacrifices, only a group of people from the house of Levi, from the family of Aaron. Over time they achieved aristocratic status, or that of rulers. The High Priest and the priests were most important personages in the nation of Israel, religiously speaking, and this fact created different classes within society. Even today the synagogue treats the Priests (that many times hold Cohen, or other variety of that name, as a family name) differently and honors them specially. The class of priests was created as part of the covenant made by God with the people of Israel.

Only the priests ate from the sacrifices. There were guilt offerings that the priest was ordered to eat in order to figuratively take the sin into himself. This is an important point when thinking of atonement and the fact that Jesus took our sins on Himself. The sacrifices did bring atonement. If a person sinned in any way he had to take a lamb, or an ox, or a dove if he was poor, and come to the temple. The Law determined that for every sin, the person had to come to the temple to offer up a sacrifice.

The sacrifice gave atonement for sin. It taught the principle that someone else had to bear the punishment of the sin and die in your place. The sacrifice gave forgiveness. The person knew that he had received forgiveness even if the sacrifice did not give him a clear conscience. The sacrifice was a way to express submission and thankfulness to God, and of course was also an admission of sin.

Sin Was Not Removed

For the Law, since it has only a shadow of the good things to come and not the very form of things, can never, by the same sacrifices which they offer continually year by year, make perfect those who draw near. Otherwise, would they not have ceased to be offered, because the worshipers, having once been cleansed, would no longer have had consciousness of sins? But in those sacrifices there is a reminder of sins year by year (Heb. 10:1-3).

The sacrifices were not given only in order for us to obtain temporary forgiveness until the time of Messiah (who atones once and for all). They were also intended to remind us and the people of Israel that we are sinners. We always try to get out of acknowledging the fact that we are sinners. "It's not my fault! He made me mad," "She made me act that way," "It's the government's fault," "I am not a murderer, I didn't kill anyone," "I am not a thief," "It doesn't hurt anyone for me to take little things from the office or if I leave a little early" – all these are just a few of the excuses we use to excuse inacceptable behavior. We avoid the thought that we are sinners, which in itself is sinful, and the sacrifices were intended to remind us of that fact.

The sacrifices provided atonement only for the sin they were offered up for. The sacrifice atoned for the sin I confessed while the sacrifice was offered up. If a guilt offering was offered up (a sacrifice for things done unintentionally), but not for sin (which is the sacrifice for sins done intentionally), then atonement was received for the one and not for the other. When an offering was made for sin, it was required to lay hands on it and confess the sin. If I did not confess something, it was not covered by the sacrifice. By confession the sin was ceremoniously transferred to the victim, and when it was slaughtered, forgiveness and atonement were received. But the sin itself was not taken away. As we read in chapter 10:3-4, "But in those sacrifices there is a reminder of sins year by year. For it is impossible for the blood of bulls and goats to take away sins."

What Is Sin?

In order to understand why the sacrifices could not remove sin, we have to first understand what sin is. The word "sin" is often used without being fully understood. If we ask "what is sin?" most people will answer that sin is when we do something we are not supposed to, or something we do not do what we are supposed to. If we ask further, the answer we get will be something like, "Sin is something we do, say, or think that we are not supposed to do, say or think; or it is something we do not do, say, or think that we are supposed to, and therefore we miss God's purpose by not doing will." This answer is inexact. If it were correct, then if we did/said/ thought what we are supposed to, and did not do, say or think what is forbidden, then we would not sin. The problem is that we just cannot do that. The problem is much deeper. Sin is deeper than all the things I do or say or think. Those are just a symptom of sin, the result of sin, and not the sin itself.

When I place myself in the center of my life, instead of God, I am sinning. To place myself as the most important person in the universe instead of God, that is sin. This sin wears all kinds of shapes and forms and can even wear the form of good deeds, even work done in God's service. When the ministry becomes *my* ministry, it has become sin. Everything where "me, myself and I" play a central role in how I see things is sin. "Me in the center" – that's sin. All the rest: theft, murder, lies and so on, are only symptoms of that sin. They are behavior that flows out of sin and expresses it. They are a result of thinking that I am the center of the universe. *I* kill you because you hurt *me*. *I* steal because *I* want what you have. *I* commit adultery because *I* want to satisfy *my* lust. *I* lie because want you to think *I am* better than I really am. "Me, myself, for me, mine," are expressions of sin.

We were created so that God would be at the center of our being, in the most important part of our lives. When we sinned, we removed God from his throne in our lives, and placed ourselves there instead. Among the believers in Jesus, sin is often cloaked in spirituality. Many times sin reveals itself in competitive behavior among believers, where we try to outdo each other spiritually. I once heard a believer talking about a congregation that was not accustomed to lifting up their hands during worship and prayer. He said, "If I go there, I will lift up my hands, I will wave a flag, I will show them what true worship is." In actual fact he was saying, "Just look how much more spiritual I am than them." That is sin. It is good to lift up your hands to God. Lifting up your hands in praise expresses submission to God, but if it is done in order to show others how spiritual you are, then that is sin. Every good thing done out of competition is sin. To get down on your knees before God is good, but if it is done to impress others, it is sin. When someone serves in the congregation so that others will notice what a good servant he is, that is sin. Such an attitude indicates that in my heart I am more important to myself than God is to me, and I exalt God only in order to exalt myself. Sin is thinking what you can do is better than what God can do.

A Guilty Conscience

That is why the sacrifices in the temple did not take away sin. They did not change the heart, which places one's self in the center of one's heart. The sacrifices only provided a covering, or atonement. The word "atonement" first appears in the Bible when Noah covered the ark with pitch.[3] This was a complete cover so that nothing could be seen through it. The sacrifices covered sin but did not take it away. The sacrifices provided forgiveness but did not provide a clear conscience because they didn't deal with sin itself. We have seen that in chapter 9, which we read at the beginning of this chapter, "sacrifices are offered which cannot make the worshiper perfect in conscience" (vs. 9).

We are told here that the gifts and offerings do not cleanse the conscience or perfect it. The feelings of guilt remain. Gifts and offerings do not bring perfection of conscience. Chapter 10:1 tells us, "For the Law, since it has only a shadow of the good things to come and not the very form of things, can never, by the same sacrifices which they offer continually year by year, make perfect those who draw near."

The Torah is just a shadow of the real thing, and does not perfect. There are many people who place the Torah on a very high level of importance: the Torah is holy, the Torah is eternal. That is what the Rabbis teach, but this is not what the Scriptures teach us. We read that the law of Sinai is a shadow, and not the real thing. Just as my shadow is a bit like me, but not the real me, so the Torah is a shadow and does not bring about perfection. The sacrifices offered in the temple do not bring us into perfection.

A Perfect Sacrifice

The sacrifice of Jesus is better because the single sacrifice of Messiah replaces all the sacrifices, work, dirt, and blood and gore that were constantly in the courtyard of the temple. The author of Hebrews tells us:

[N]or was it that He would offer Himself often, as the High Priest enters the Holy Place year by year with blood that is not his own. Otherwise, He would have needed to sufferoften since the foundation of the world; but now once at the consummation of the agesHe has been manifested to put away sin by the sacrifice of Himself. And inasmuch as it is appointed for men to die once and after this comes judgment, so Christ also, having been offered once to bear the sins of many, will appear a second time for salvation without reference to sin, to those who eagerly await Him (Heb. 9:25-28).

So we are told that the Messiah was offered up once for all. The Messiah, who gave Himself up for us, fulfilled and replaced all the sin offerings that had been until then. We still offer up thank offerings, "Therefore I urge you, brethren, by the mercies of God, to present your bodies a living and holy sacrifice, acceptable to God, which is your spiritual service of worship. And do not be conformed to this world, but be transformed by the renewing of your mind, so that you may prove what the will of God is, that which is good and acceptable and perfect." (Rom. 12:1-2).

Our lives and our bodies are our offerings of thanks to God, but every sacrifice covering sin and atonement is included under the perfect sacrifice, that was offered once for all time – Jesus the son of God who gave Himself up once and for all to bear the iniquities of many. There is no more need for all the rites, there is no more need to come to the temple, no need for the blood, the fat, and the gore. The sacrifice of the Messiah is once for all time.

The sacrifice of Jesus also made us all into priests. In the ceremonial "Lord's Supper" we all eat of the bread and drink of the wine, just as in the days of the two temples the priests ate of the sacrifices. Jesus cancelled the different classes among the people. He rendered the priestly class obsolete. People in the world struggle for equal rights, and often that is achieved by bringing everyone down to the same level (as happened in communist Russia, China and other places). The Messiah made us all equal in the right way: He raised us all up to the same status. The sacrifice of Messiah made us into priests, and we all eat of the sacrifice.

The sacrifice of Jesus atones for our sins, "and not through the blood of goats and calves, but through His own blood, He entered the Holy Place once for all, having obtained eternal redemption." (Heb. 9:12). Eternal redemption means everlasting liberty, atonement forever. The atoning sacrifice of Jesus atones not only for the sins you did in the past, but also for the sins you commit now, and the sins you will commit in the future. The sacrifice of Jesus atoned for all sins forever, for eternity. There is no need to fear anymore what will happen if you sin in the future. The sacrifice of Jesus includes atonement for the sins of the future. There is nothing I can do to surprise God, or which the sacrifice of Messiah will not cover. The enemy of our souls does not wish us to receive forgiveness and atonement from God, which is why we have to respond to each sin by turning immediately to God in order to obtain atonement.

We do not need to go far to receive the atonement of the sacrifice because the temple, the house of God, is within us, in our hearts. Jesus placed his Tabernacle within us. There is no need to go up to Jerusalem to obtain forgiveness, because the sacrifice has already been made. We have to enter into the temple, where the presence of God dwells in our hearts, to place our hands on the sacrifice (on Jesus), to confess our sins and receive forgiveness. Some say, "I don't deserve to be forgiven," and the answer to that is "You are right.

You don't deserve it. You never will. Receiving forgiveness is not founded on worthiness, but on what Jesus has done for sinners." If you do not come to receive forgiveness, you will not have it. I can try my best to give you something, but if you don't put out your hand to take it, you won't have it. That is how it is with the Messiah. Jesus came and gave Himself up for the world, but He gave strength and the power to become the sons of God only to those who received Him. That is how it is with forgiveness of sins. When I have sinned I need to come to Him and receive forgiveness. If I try to ignore it, if I do not acknowledge my sin and confess it, I cannot receive forgiveness and atonement. If I ignore my conscience, which is moving me to acknowledge my sin, I will not receive the forgiveness and atonement that Jesus offers.

A Clean Conscience

There is another difference between the temple sacrifices and the sacrifice of Jesus: the sacrifice of Jesus purifies our conscience. What is conscience? I will tell you a story to explain: in Germany there are highways that have no speed limit (I once drove at over 100 miles per hour, and there were still cars that overtook me!). Suppose a man bought himself a brilliant red Porsche. He left the car dealership happy and content, and took the car out to the highway to try it out. He drove at over 150 miles per hour and enjoyed every moment. Suddenly a red light went on in the dashboard. He kept trying to concentrate on the road and enjoy himself, but the flashing light disturbed him. "What should I do about that troublesome light?" he asked himself. Suddenly he had an idea, he took a hammer out from under his seat and smashed the flashing red light. Now the light did not trouble him anymore. Then another red light began to flash. "Now I know what to do," he said to himself, and without thinking too much about it, he took the hammer and broke that light too. He continued driving and another red light went on, and he broke that one too, and this time he did not even give too much thought to what he was doing. After a short time, to his surprise, the engine blew, there was a lot of smoke, and the car ended up stuck on the side of the road. Then he sat in the car and thought, "What's wrong? It's a new car. They must have sold me a lemon. That's the assembly-line's fault for sure!"

This story may sound familiar because that is how most of us relate to our lives. Our conscience is a red warning light that God put into our lives. When we do something wrong, our conscience begins to flash. Many treat their conscience as something troublesome and try to silence it. Every time we silence it and ignore it, its voice gets weaker, its flashing gets dimmer, until we cannot hear it any longer. Later, when our lives are ruined, we sit in the rubble and blame God, "Why did you do this to me? I don't deserve this!" We sit among the remains of a broken relationship, a broken life, and blame everyone but ourselves because we silenced the voice of our conscience. The conscience is a flashing warning light that God placed in our lives, which warns us when something is not right. When your conscience starts flashing, what do you do? Do you ignore it and try to go on with your life as if everything is all right, or do you immediately go to the one you sinned against, whether man or God, to ask forgiveness?

The warning lights go on in order to help us stop, check what's wrong, and fix it. When we come to Jesus and confess our sins, He forgives us on the basis of the sacrifice He Himself offered up for us, and He cleanses our conscience.[4] The sacrifice of Jesus not only covers the sin, it not only atones for it, it also cleanses our conscience completely: "how much more will the blood of Christ, who through the eternal Spirit offered Himself without blemish to God, cleanse your conscience from dead works to serve the living God?" (Heb. 9:14)

An accusing conscience weighs us down with guilt and prevents us from worshiping the living God. We flee from him, we hide behind the bushes, like Adam and Eve, we try everything but we cannot worship Him. The sacrifice of Jesus gives us forgiveness and cleanses and purifies our conscience. The sacrifice of Messiah not only covers the sin, it also fixes what is broken so that we can continue in His way, because the sacrifice of Messiah removes the sin itself.

When I read Hebrews 9:26 and first understood what was written there, I was very moved. "Otherwise, He would have needed to suffer often since the foundation of the world; but now once at the consummation of the ages He has been manifested to put away sin by the sacrifice of Himself." To "put away" means to take something off me so that it is no longer on me. When you put away the dishes off the table, they are no longer on the table. To put away means to take away and it no longer exists in the place it was before. The sacrifices in the temple did not deal with sin itself, they atoned for it and covered it. The sacrifice of Messiah takes away the sin itself.

We clarified earlier that placing myself in the center of my life is sin. I rule over my own life, I am the most important one in my life. This verse tells us that when I come to Jesus and give him the reins of control over my life, He replaces me as the king in my life. He puts sin (myself) away. That has to be my choice. I have to say to Him, "You are the most important One in my life, You are the King!"

When I sin, I do not throw Him out of my life, I take Him off the throne and put Him on the side. I say to Him, in effect, "You are still a part of my life but I am in control of this area. I don't want to give this area of my life to you. Let me keep it, let me run things here. This area gives me a lot of pleasure. I am the boss here, leave this area of my life to me." Jesus is still in my life, but he no longer controls this particular area of my life, I do. Sin rules because putting myself in the center again is sin.

If there are areas of your life that you have not yet given over to Jesus to rule over, then sin rules there. But the moment you receive the sacrifice of Messiah, the moment you repent, ask forgiveness, and receive His sacrifice for this area, you give Him the reins of control over this area. He takes the sin away from the throne and sits on it Himself. This is an issue of utmost importance! Sadly, not many of us live in the knowledge that the sacrifice of Messiah not only deals with the consequence of sin, but also takes away the sin completely. We can cease striving to "be better" because Jesus has already done everything we need to enjoy God.

If there is an area of life you still have no victory over, that means that Jesus does not rule there. It means that you still live in this area of your life, the way people lived in the time of the Sinai covenant when a sacrifice dealt with the consequences of sin, but not with the source of sin. You ask for forgiveness, but still put yourself in the center, instead of God. The sacrifice of Messiah penetrates deep and deals not only with the consequences but also with the root. That is very joyful news for whoever wishes to receive it, for whoever is prepared to give up and receive His rule. He takes away the sin once and for all, for all eternity.

It Is For Freedom That Jesus Has Set Us Free

In an American native village, some children caught a baby eaglet. "He is so cute," they said, "Let's keep him as our pet." In order to prevent him from escaping, they stuck a big stake in the middle of the village, tied a long rope to it, and tied the end of the rope to the eaglet's foot. They played with it and fed it every day. After a while, the eaglet grew into an eagle. He began to sprout feathers, to flutter his wings, and learn to fly. But because he was tied to the stake he could only fly in circles. So life went on and the eagle continued to grow, and the children continued to play with it, and he kept on flying around in circles. One day the elder of the village came over, looked at the eagle and said to the children, "The eagle was born to fly great distances, to be free. An eagle was not born to be tied to a stake in the ground. If you really love the eagle, you have to let it go." And so they did. They let the eagle go so that he could fly into the horizon, high in the air. To their surprise, because he had been tied up for so long, he continued to fly in circles even after he was freed.

This is how it is with us, very often. Because of certain sins that have kept us in bondage for so many years, we are accustomed to being all tied up, so when Jesus frees us and deals with the root of sin, we still fly in circles and act as if we were still under bondage to sin. It seems as if we don't understand the most important point of all – that when Jesus forgives us, we are free. "So if the Son makes you **free**, you will be **free indeed**" (John 8:36). The Messiah stresses this: You will be free indeed. We tend to think, "No, sin is still binding me". But Galatians 5:1 tells us, "It was for freedom that Christ set us free; therefore keep standing firm and do not be subject again to a yoke of slavery." The sacrifice of Messiah frees us from sin itself. Hallelujah!

The sacrifice of Messiah takes away sin, but not only that, it also brings us to perfection, as written in Hebrews 10:1,14, "For the Law, since it has only a shadow of the good things to come and not the very form of things, can never, by the same sacrifices which they offer continually year by year, make perfect those who draw near... [f]or by one offering He has perfected for all time those who are sanctified." Jesus did it all, there is no need for us to do anything more. We have entered into the Sabbath rest. It is finished; He has perfected us. Every time I sin and receive His forgiveness, every time I allow the sacrifice to take away the sin completely (not only the consequence of what I have done), that is one more step that brings me closer to perfection. When God looks at us He sees as perfect, pure, fully sanctified before Him, as we are told in chapter 10:10, "By this will we have been sanctified through the offering of the body of Jesus Christ once for all."

He not only cleanses the body, He cleanses the spirit and the soul. When we spoke of the covenant we saw that He took out the heart of stone and replaced it with a heart of flesh. He put His spirit within us, He perfected us, He sanctified us by His blood, as is written, "For both He who sanctifies and those who are sanctified are all from one Father; for which reason He is not ashamed to call them brethren" (Heb.2:11). This is beyond our understanding. I think our perception is limited and warped because of sin, and we cannot fully understand this. Sometimes we have a flash of the truth, just a glimpse. As Paul the apostle said "[f]or now we see in a mirror dimly" (1 Cor. 13:12), we see only a little bit.

Jesus made us complete. He dealt with the sin, removing it entirely. He atones for all the sins, He sanctifies, and He cleanses the conscience. If there are still things in your life that give you a guilty conscience, than probably it is pride that prevents you from clearing your conscience because pride causes us to see ourselves as the center of everything instead of submitting to God. Jesus gave us freedom so that we would be free, as we read earlier: the disease that claims the most victims in the world today is guilt! The global suicide rate rises every year.[5] People harm themselves, destroy relationships, use drugs and alcohol, or become addicted to all kinds of things because of their guilt and their inability to cope with the burden of it. People were not created with the ability to bear guilt. Guilt entered the world when Adam and Eve sinned and it destroys us and tears us apart. Guilt is like several tons of weight that we carry around on our backs throughout life, unless we allow Jesus to take it away. The good news is that Jesus came to bear our guilt, take away and remove sin. I don't have to carry around all that guilt. He carries it for me and I am free and happy. I can live my life without feelings of guilt. I can rest in Jesus.

There are two kinds of guilt. One is from God, who seeks to awaken in us an awareness to sin by the guilt so that we repent. The other is from Satan who seeks to harm us, paralyze us, and extinguish our joy and our life by condemning us. When God rebukes and reproves us for something, He does so in a very clear way. We know that this specific thing we did was not right, or certain things should not have been said. God shows them to us clearly in order to bring us to repentance and be released from the guilt. But when Satan makes us feel guilty, he gives us condemnation when we just have a general sense that something is not right. We do not know exactly what it is, and in the end break down under the burden of these feelings. Satan is not interested in our repentance, he just wants to burden us with a load of guilt in order to extinguish our spirit. I suggest you memorize Romans 8:1 by heart. The answer to Satan is there, when you feel heavy and guilty and don't know exactly why, "Therefore there is now no condemnation for those who are in Christ Jesus." There is no guilt, no condemnation, for those who are in Messiah Jesus. If the feeling of guilt comes from God, He points at something specific. In such a case, ask forgiveness immediately from the person you have hurt and ask forgiveness from God. Ask for and receive forgiveness, because God's forgiveness is always overflowing, given in the sacrifice of Jesus.

Do not carry around a guilty conscience; there is no reason to continue to do so. The sacrifice of Messiah gives us life with a clear conscience. The sacrifice of Jesus is better than the sacrifices of the Sinai Covenant because one sacrifice was offered up once to atone for all sins. It cleanses our conscience completely, and takes away the sin itself. He is the One to bring us to perfection, not we ourselves. His sacrifice is the one that sanctifies us and makes us holy, completely belonging to God, the priests receiving the sacrifice within us.

---

[1] Matt. 12:5

[2] Ex. 29:38-42

[3] Gen. 6:14 Make for yourself an ark of gopher wood; you shall make the ark with rooms, and shall cover it inside and out with pitch.

[4] 1 John 1:9: "If we confess our sins, he is faithful and righteous to forgive us our sins, and to cleanse us from all unrighteousness.

[5] www.who.int/mental_health/prevention/suicide/evolution/en/index.html

CHAPTER 16

Jesus Prepared a Better Place

"And all these, having gained approval through their faith, did not receive what was promised, because God had provided something better for us, so that apart from us they would not be made perfect" (Heb. 11:39-40). Throughout this book, we have been building to this point: we have seen the superiority of the person of Jesus, the sufficiency of His work, and now we will finally see the reason why He has done so much for us. This is His "master plan", if you will. The entire epistle aims towards the something better spoken of here. This is the very heart and purpose of the letter to the Hebrews. This is the purpose God has for us, and this is the place God wants us to enter into. This is the place where we find the most satisfaction in God: the Sabbath.

Hebrews 3:17 – 4:11 reminds us of this place and expands on it further:

> And with whom was He angry for forty years? Was it not with those who sinned, whose bodies fell in the wilderness? And to whom did He swear that they would not enter Hisrest, but to those who were disobedient? So we see that

259

they were not able to enter because of unbelief.

Therefore, let us fear if, while a promise remains of entering His rest, any one of you may seem to have come short of it. For indeed we have had good news preached to us, just as they also; but the word they heard did not profit them, because it was not united by faith in those who heard. For we who have believed enter that rest, just as He has said, "As I swore in my wrath, they shall not enter my rest," although His works were finished from the foundation of the world. For He has said somewhere concerning the seventh day: "and God rested on the seventh day from all His works"; and again in this passage, "They shall not enter my rest." Therefore, since it remains for some to enter it, and those who formerly had good news preached to them failed to enter because of disobedience, He again fixes a certain day, "Today", saying through David after so long a time just as has been said before, "Today if you hear His voice, do not harden your hearts." For if Joshua had given them rest, He would not have spoken of another day after that. So there remains a Sabbath rest for the people of God. For the one who has entered His rest has himself also rested from his works, as God did from His. Therefore let us be diligent to enter that rest, so that no one will fall, through following the same example of disobedience.

This speaks of God's place of rest, the Sabbath that God has prepared for us. It is interesting that he refers to the Sabbath not as a period of time, but as a place we are to live in. He tells us, the believers, to enter the rest. In order to understand better what He meant, we have to first understand what the Sabbath is. I believe that the Sabbath is one of the least understood words in the Scriptures. Most people think of it as a day, and in the end observe the Sabbath in a manner completely contrary to what the Scriptures intended.

What Is the Sabbath?

The Sabbath in first mentioned in Genesis 2:1-3, "Thus the heavens and the earth were completed, and all their hosts. By the seventh day God completed His work which He had done, and He rested on the seventh day from all His work which He had done. Then God blessed the seventh day and sanctified it, because in it He rested from all His work which God had created and made." Many of us are familiar with this passage from the Sabbath eve blessings. God finished creating the heavens and the earth and all that is in them. Then He rested from His work, blessed the seventh day, and sanctified it. Did God rest because He needed to? Did He get tired? The answer, of course, is no! It is written, "Behold, He who keeps Israel will neither slumber nor sleep" (Ps. 121:4). God never gets tired, so the Sabbath was not created for God. As is written, Jesus told the disciples, "The Sabbath was made for man, and not man for the Sabbath" (Mark 2:27). The Sabbath is God's gift to mankind. We read here that God finished all his work. He created everything – the heavens, the earth and all that is in them. God blessed this day and set it apart for a special purpose.

Let's have a look at man for whom the Sabbath was created. What was man's first day on earth? We know Adam was the last thing to be created, so evidently he was created on Friday afternoon towards evening. We know that the biblical day begins at nightfall because it is written, "And there was evening and there was morning, one day" (Gen. 1:5). That means that Adam's first day was actually the Sabbath. When God created the world He had already prepared everything and there was no work for Adam to do. The first thing he had to do was rest. We think that first we have to work and get tired, and then we deserve to rest. But when Adam was created, the first thing he did before he began to work in the garden was to rest. He had not done anything to deserve the right to rest. He had not done anything to earn the Garden of Eden. He hadn't done anything to deserve life in this wonderful creation, or the position of the one in charge of the world. All he had to do was to receive what God had done, and rest. He received it all by grace, not by right or works.

If so, the Sabbath was given in order to teach men that God has already done it all. God has prepared everything and given the world to man by grace. Man has not earned this privilege. On the contrary, he was first of all to learn to rest.

The Week as a Parable

In the Talmud, Tractate Sanhedrine 97, we read, "Just as the seventh year is one year of release in seven, so is the world: one thousand years out of seven shall be fallow, as it is written, 'And the Lord alone shall be exalted in that day,' and it is further said, 'A Psalm and song for the Sabbath day', meaning the day that is altogether Sabbath—and it is also said, 'For a thousand years in thy sight are but as yesterday when it is past'. The Tanna debe Eliyyahu teaches: 'The world is to exist six thousand years. In the first two thousand there was desolation; two thousand years the Torah flourished; and the next two thousand years is the Messianic era.'"

The verse, "For a thousand years in thy sight are but as yesterday when it is past" is a quote from Psalms

90:4. Rabbi Eliahu said that the world would exist for six thousand years, and then the Sabbath would come. Two thousand years of desolation without the Law, two thousand years of Torah Law, and two thousand years of the Messiah. After that would be ushered in a thousand years of Sabbath. We know that according to the Jewish calendar we are at the end of the sixth millennium or even at the beginning of the seventh. So of course the question is raised in Jewish literature, "If he was supposed to come two thousand years ago, why hasn't he come?"[1] They have tried to solve the mystery. Various theories have been broached in order to answer the question, and the answer our spiritual leaders reached was that he did not come because of our sins. If we had been righteous, he would have come at the beginning of the two thousand years. If we had been just slightly sinful, he would have come in the middle. But if we are great sinners, he will only come at the end. In any case we know that the Messiah did come two thousand years ago. Even according to the Jewish understanding of the days of the world, at the end the Sabbath come, a time of rest and a time where there is no more stress or distress.

The Sabbath was the first day of man's existence, and will also be the last period. In effect this kind of understanding is not unfamiliar to the New Covenant:

> Then I saw an angel coming down from heaven, holding the key of the abyss and a great chain in his hand. And he laid hold of the dragon, the serpent of old, who is the devil and Satan, and bound him for a thousand years; and he threw him into the abyss, and shut it and sealed it over him, so that he would not deceive the nations any longer, until the thousand years

were completed; after these things he must be released for a short time.

Then I saw thrones, and they sat on them, and judgment was given to them. And I saw the souls of those who had been beheaded because of their testimony of Jesus andbecause of the word of God, and those who had not worshiped the beast or his image, and had not received the mark on their forehead and on their hand; and they came to life and reigned with Christ for a thousand years. The rest of the dead did not come to life until the thousand years were completed. This is the first resurrection. Blessed and holy is the one who has a part in the first resurrection; over these the second death has no power, but they will be priests of God and of Christ and will reign with Him for a thousand years (Rev. 20:1-6).

Some Christians believe this passage speaks of the Millennium, the thousand years of peace and rest that will come before the end of days and the resurrection. The Sabbath points at the first day, at the past, and at the future.

The Sabbath in the Ten Commandments
Let's go on and have a look at the Sabbath in the Ten Commandments (Ex. 20 and Deut. 5). The commandment concerning the Sabbath takes up most space among the commandments. The commandment is very detailed. I believe that God does not waste words. He is God, and the world was created by His word, as is written, "By the word of the Lord the heavens were made" (Ps. 33:6). Nevertheless, most believers consider the Sabbath commandment to be the least important.

"Do not commit adultery, do not murder, do not bear false witness, do not use the name of the Lord your God in vain" and others are considered very important commandments, but we ignore the Sabbath, or simply do not fully understand the essence of what it is. Some of us become extreme in observing the Sabbath according to rabbinical laws or other laws that, in the end, cause us to observe the Sabbath in a manner contrary to its real purpose and meaning. Others completely ignore the commandments and find excuses why they are no longer valid today. No believer in Jesus would claim that it is all right to murder or to lie because we are under grace, and therefore at liberty from the laws and free to lie or commit adultery as we like – but there are believers who claim that observing the Sabbath means to live under the Law, and we are after all free from the Law.

The Ten Commandments are quoted twice in the Bible, once in Exodus and once in Deuteronomy. There is a difference between both passages. Besides the commandment to honor our parents, which is the only commandment with a promise, the commandment regarding the Sabbath is the only one that explains why it must be observed, and this explanation in itself is very important.

In Exodus 20:8-11 we read:

> Remember the Sabbath day, to keep it holy. Six days you shall labor and do all your work, but the seventh day is a Sabbath of the LORD your God; in it you shall not do any work, you or your son or your daughter, your male or your female servant or your cattle or your sojourner who stays with you. For in six days the LORD

made the heavens and the earth, the sea and all that is in them, and rested on the seventh day; therefore the LORD blessed the Sabbath day and made it holy.

Here it is written: Remember the Sabbath day. We are commanded to remember it. The reason given here is that in six days God created the sea, the heavens and the earth and all that is in them. He created the world, resting on the seventh day and making it holy.

In Deuteronomy 5:12-15 we find:

Observe the Sabbath day to keep it holy, as the LORD your God commanded you. Six days you shall labor and do all your work, but the seventh day is a Sabbath of the LORD your God; in it you shall not do any work, you or your son or your daughter or your male servant or your female servant or your ox or your donkey or any of your cattle or your sojourner who stays with you, so that your male servant and your female servant may rest as well as you. You shall remember that you were a slave in the land of Egypt, and the LORD your God brought you out of there by a mighty hand and by an outstretched arm; therefore the LORD your God commanded you to observe the Sabbath day.

Here, instead of the commandment to "remember" the Sabbath day, we have the commandment to "observe" the seventh day. When the rabbis discussed why the wording is different, the accepted answer was that God said both "remember" and "observe" so we are to "remember-observe" or "observe-remember". Neither remember nor observe are mentioned by mistake – they are both important. In fact, the commandment we received regarding the seventh day was "observe in order to remember." But the reason for the commandment is also different. Exodus tells us that the reason is that God created the world in six days and rested on the seventh. Deuteronomy tells us that the reason is that God brought us out of Egypt, from slavery into freedom, and He is our Savior.

Past, Present and Future

We are commanded to observe in order to remember because we tend to forget the important things about the Sabbath. What are we supposed to remember? What was, what is, and what is to come.

Let's first look at what was. We have to remember, as is written in Exodus, that God was the one who created the world, not us. The world does not exist because of us nor was it created because of us. God created everything. There is no work He did not finish. We have to remember that we received all that God had done by grace, not because we deserved it. What He did was not dependent on us. We have to remember where we came from, and we have to remember that we were but dust. Sometimes we think that we are quite good, quite successful, and forget what we were without God. We were slaves – in bondage to our lusts, to our desires, to our own will, to other people, to all kinds of things. God is the One who freed us. He is the One who redeemed us. We were not made free by our own efforts and our own deeds.

As believers in Jesus we say that we have been saved by grace and faith. As is written in Ephesians 2:8-9, "For by grace you have been saved through faith; and that not of yourselves, it is the gift of God; not as a result of works, so that no one may boast." We all recite these verses with no problem, but still tend to think that God saved us because He found something special in us. We do not like to admit it, but many times when we wonder why God saved us and not someone else, we tell ourselves, "Because he found something special in me that others didn't have." Scriptures tell a different story: God saved us because He loved us, not because we are special, not because He wanted to use us, and not because He has some special job for us to do.

Many times I have heard believers in Jesus try to encourage others by saying, "God saved you because He needs you. He has a special job for you that only you can do, and if you don't do it, it won't get done properly." It is true that God has a task for each one of us, but the Sabbath teaches us first and foremost that God manages very well without us. He created the entire world without us, and He will continue to manage without us. God doesn't need us, God loves us. There is a big difference. God did not save us in order to use us, like servants. God saved us so that we would have a close relationship with Him, not so that we would do something for Him. That is why He said, "No longer do I call you slaves . . . but I have called you friends" (John 15:15).

There is only one reason God saved us: His love! Not because He needed us, and not because He couldn't manage without us. He saved us with a mighty hand and an outstretched arm. The image brought up by this description that is used to describe the way God redeemed us from Egypt is that of Jesus on the cross with his arms stretched out to the sides, hanging on nails. We have to remember that He is in control. When we stop everything to rest on the Sabbath, everything is still standing at the end of the day. The sun is still shining, the stars are still in the sky, the flowers still bloom, and the rain still falls. The world has not fallen apart just because we did not do any work, or expend great efforts; we did not earn our rest. Our rest is given to us by grace. God is the one who rules over the world. He will rule in the future, He rules now. That is what we have to remember by keeping the Sabbath. It is written in the book of Acts that God created the borders of the nations and their times.[2] That is to say, God rules over history and over our boundaries. We do not have to worry or be afraid of Ahmadinejad or Abu Mazen or any other leader who changes our borders. "The Lord has looked down from heaven upon the sons of men" (Ps. 14:2), and "[h]e who sits in the heavens laughs, the Lord scoffs at them" (Ps. 2:4). God is in control, not the politicians, not the kings, and not me either. God is the One who controls all in all. We will do well to remember that. We should keep in mind that God does not need us. He does us a favor when He uses us and allows us to do something for Him or for others. We have to also remember that God did not create us in order to serve Him. He created us to love Him. God did not create us because He has a special job in mind for us. He created us first and foremost in order to love Him and be with Him in an intimate way. The concept of the Sabbath stands in complete contrast to our human nature, which wants to achieve things in its own strength and to earn what we receive. So we are called to observe the Sabbath regularly, to remind us of where God wants us to be.

The Sabbath as a Way of Life

The best time for fellowship with someone you really love is not when you are doing something together – it's when you are simply together. I remember the years I lived in the United Sates. The easiest way to get people together was to initiate a project, something to work on together. Whereas in Israel, the neighbor will pop over for a cup of coffee with no special need to do anything at all. My wife is originally from Switzerland, and she was taught that a woman has to work at home, cleaning, cooking and so on. When we moved to live in the Galilee area many years ago we had a neighbor who knocked on our door every morning and stayed drinking coffee with my wife for several hours. My wife could not understand what was going on. "She should go work, she has a home and family, and she is keeping me from doing my own work," she told me. I explained the cultural differences to her, and told her to give time to the neighbor because it was not the waste of time it may seem to her. At the same time, my wife did not speak Hebrew very well, but that did not make a difference to our talkative neighbor. From all that endless chatter, from all that "wasted time," several important things happened. First of all, my wife learned Hebrew (which is very important). But the more important things were that this young woman began to believe in Jesus, and even brought her husband and children to faith, along with another friend. That same friend brought others to faith. Today that woman and her children are part of our congregation. So this "wasted time" of just sitting together over coffee was not a waste of time in the eyes of God. God did not create us to work, He created us to be together. The best times a man and his wife have are often when they simply are together in the living-room or in bed. She is reading a book and he is reading something else. She is doing one thing and he is doing something else. Sometimes they may talk and sometimes they may not, but they simply enjoy being together. This "togetherness" with God is what He has created us for. That is what the Sabbath reminds us of.

We have to remember what He is doing in our lives. Just as we do not need to make an effort to receive what He has done, we also do not need to strive to receive what He is doing and what He will do. Many will say, "Yes, we were saved by faith, but now I have to change myself. I have to work hard, I have to do this or that. I have to pray. I have to read the Bible." It is true that these are necessary and profitable things, but you do not have to do them. I can either do things because I love God, or because I think that is the way to please Him. Even as believers in Jesus, many of us believe that we began in grace, but now everything depends on what I say, how I dress, what music I listen to, or a long list of other things. It is true that when someone comes in faith and gives His life to Jesus, his life and behavior change. But that happens as a consequence of what God has done, not because of our own efforts.

We do not need to make tremendous efforts to receive what He has done. There is no need to strive to receive what He is doing or what He is going to do. That is what the Sabbath reminds us of. He is the One who changes us, not we ourselves. True, we have to cooperate. But he is the One who changes us. Many of us think we have to work at changing ourselves into being more spiritual and more like Jesus. The truth is that we cannot do it. What we do have to do is the exact opposite of effort – we have to rest and obey.

During the years of wandering through the desert, the people of Israel did not have to worry about finding their own way to the Promised Land, or be concerned for food and clothing. What they did have to do was to obey God, and follow wherever the pillar of cloud and the pillar of fire led them. This is what we have to do, too. Our job is not to change ourselves, but to trust rest in God, and to obey Him. He is the One who changes. He is the One who sanctifies. He sanctified the Sabbath, the Sabbath did not sanctify itself. He is the One who sanctifies us. It is not up to us or dependent on how may chapters we know by heart, or how many hours we pray. That is not what sanctifies us. God is the One who changes our hearts when we rest in Him and obey Him.

In the desert it was God who provided the manna. The people had to collect it, and only on the Sabbath, when did the manna not go bad, did the people not have to collect it. God provided all the needs of the people in the desert. That is also something we are called to remember on the Sabbath. God provides all our needs so that we don't have to worry about what we are going to eat or drink or wear. Again, we have to observe the Sabbath in order to remind ourselves of all this because we tend to forget easily.

When the car breaks down and we need a new one, or when there's an accident, or pressure at work, we immediately begin worrying about whether God will provide for us this time. This worry begins to eat away at us and our hearts begin to panic. Worry comes from a lack of faith, because we forget the Sabbath. We forget that God prepared everything and gave us all our needs – not because of things we did or did not do, but by grace.

We must continue to remind ourselves of what was in the past, and what is needed now, as King David reminded his soul again and again, "Return to your rest, O my soul"(Ps. 116:7), and, "Bless the Lord O my soul" (Ps. 103:1, 2, 22). David reminded himself of what God had done for him because David, as we all are, was forgetful.

We must remember, in the context of the Sabbath, what is to come. Many times the thought of what is yet to come in the future helps us to get through what is going on right now. In the future we shall at long last enter into perfection, into the inheritance that God has prepared for those who love Him. We will enter into peace. Creation itself will be healed and changed, and once again there will be perfection. There will be a place with no death, no pain and no tears. It is hard for us to understand such a place when we are sickly and always in pain (as all of us past the age of 40 know all too well). But God has prepared a perfect place for us. We cannot comprehend a place where we will be in perfect fellowship with God with no sin, no pain, no suffering, and no Satan to disturb us. We will see God face to face. It is written in 1 Corinthians 13:12, "For now we see in a mirror dimly, but then face to face; now I know in part, but then I will know fully just as I also have been fully known."

The Scriptures give us a glimpse of what the future will be like. So do things that happen in our lives. In 1 Cor. 2:9 we read, "[B]ut just as it is written, 'Things which eye has not seen and ear has not heard, and which have not entered the heart of man, all that God has prepared for those who love Him" (This is a quote from Isaiah 64:3). It's difficult for us to imagine perfection. We were born in sin, and we live in sin. We were born in pain and through pain. Our mother suffered in childbirth, and we ourselves experienced pain in coming into the world. We weep over and over, both outwardly and inwardly, but God has prepared a perfect place for us. This is a place where we will see Him face to face. This is the final rest. We will be in His presence, and nothing can cast a shadow over that. It will be a place with no pain and no tears, a perfect place. We will at long last enter into the rest He has prepared for us.

273

The Sabbaths as a Sign

Most of us think of the Sabbath as a day, the seventh day. Exodus 31:12-17 tells us:

> The LORD spoke to Moses, saying, "But as for you, speak to the sons of Israel, You shall surely observe My Sabbaths; for this is a sign between Me and you throughout your generations, that you may know that I am the LORD who sanctifies you. Therefore you are to observe the Sabbath, for it is holy to you. Everyone who profanes it shall surely be put to death; for whoever does any work on it, that person shall be cut off from among his people. For six days work may be done, but on the seventh day there is a Sabbath of complete rest, holy to the LORD; whoever does any work on the Sabbath day shall surely be put to death. So the sons of Israel shall observe the Sabbath, to celebrate the Sabbath throughout their generations as a perpetual covenant. It is a sign between Me and the sons of Israel forever; for in six days the LORD made heaven and earth, but on the seventh day He ceased from labor, and was refreshed."

Several important things are said here. First of all, the Sabbath is a sign given for something specific to teach us and to remind us, as is written in Isaiah 7:14, "Therefore the Lord Himself will give you a sign: Behold, a virgin will be with child and bear a son, and she will call His name Immanuel."

We read here that the Sabbath is an everlasting covenant, a perpetual sign. It doesn't pass away some time. Its importance is eternal. Another interesting thing is said here, "You shall surely observe My Sabbaths." This is Sabbaths, in the plural. The Sabbaths are a sign, an everlasting covenant, intended to teach us and remind us of all the things God has done, who He is, and the quality of relationship between us. But what Sabbaths is the text speaking of?

God established a Sabbath in every cycle of time. It begins with the cycle of a day, which according to Scripture begins in the evening. "And there was morning and there was evening, one day." The first thing we do in a biblical day is rest. God created us so that we need sleep, but in His plan rest comes before work. We have to understand this order of things because we tend to see things in the opposite order: work comes first, and only then "the worker is worthy of rest," and, "the hired man is worthy of his wages." God gave us rest (the Sabbath) in the everyday cycle in order to remind us that everything is given to us by His grace. The first half of every day (a 24-hour cycle) is given to rest, yet when we get up in the morning, the sun is shining, the flowers are blooming, and the birds are singing without us having done anything to deserve that.

God gave us a day every week also, and that is what we usually consider to be the Sabbath. Every week, we are commanded to stop and remember that God loves us but does not need us. The world won't fall apart if we stop doing things for God. The Kingdom of Heaven will not crumble to pieces if we take a break. God does us a favor when He uses us, but He does not need us.

In the annual cycle we have the feasts of the Lord. In Leviticus 23 each one of these is called a Sabbath to God.[3] I have heard believers in Jesus teach that there are seven feasts in a year. They try to organize the five feasts into seven, maybe because the number seven is considered a perfect number that represents God. There are some who divide Passover into at least two feasts, the Feast of Passover and the Feast of Unleavened Bread. Sometimes they add the Omer (lifting up of the sheaves) as well. Some divide the Feast of Pentecost (Weeks) into two – the Feast of Weeks and the Feast of the First-Fruits. Others divide the Feast of Tabernacles into two, considering the Feast of Harvest as a separate feast. If you divide each of the Feasts into their various names or by different events during the feast, the result will be much more than seven feasts. Therefore, the people who teach of seven Feasts usually create a patchwork of feasts that make up seven, but whose patches are up to the individual choice of the teacher.

There are five feasts of the Lord: Passover (which is also called the feast of unleavened bread and includes the day of waving the *omer*); Pentecost/Shavuot (which is also called the Feast of First-Fruits); the Day of Trumpets (which we know as New Year); the Day of Atonement; and the Feast of Tabernacles (which is also called the Feast of the Ingathering, or Harvest, and includes *shemini atzeret*, the day of gathering). I have heard that the number five expresses grace, and it is true that it is the grace of God that makes the year go round.

Once every seven years there is a sabbatical year, the *shmita*, which in Hebrew means "letting go" or "dropping something." This Sabbath is not for us, it is for the land.

> Speak to the sons of Israel and say to them, "When you come into the land which I shall give you, then the land shall have a Sabbath to the LORD. Six years you shall sow your field, and six years you shall prune your vineyard and gather in its crop, but during the seventh year the land shall have a Sabbath rest, a Sabbath

to the LORD; you shall not sow your field nor prune your vineyard. Your harvest's after-growth you shall not reap, and your grapes of untrimmed vines you shall not gather; the land shall have a sabbatical year. All of you shall have the Sabbath products of the land for food; yourself, and your male and female slaves, and your hired man and your foreign resident, those who live as aliens with you" (Lev. 25:2-6).

In the year of *shmita* the ground is not ploughed. Just as God did in the desert on a Sabbath, God provides enough food in the sixth year to last through the seventh year as well, and even through the eighth year until the fruit of the land can be eaten again. This is how He provided the manna in the desert. The world will not fall apart if we stop working, even if we stop for an entire year!

Every fiftieth year was a Jubilee.

You are also to count off seven Sabbaths of years for yourself, seven times seven years, so that you have the time of the seven Sabbaths of years, namely, forty-nine years. You shall then sound a ram's horn abroad on the tenth day of the seventh month; on the Day of Atonement you shall sound a horn all through your land. You shall thus consecrate the fiftieth year and proclaim a release through the land to all its inhabitants. It shall be a jubilee for you, and each of you shall return to his own property, and each of you shall return to his family. You shall have the fiftieth year as a jubilee; you shall not sow, nor reap its after-growth, nor gather in from its untrimmed vines. For it is a jubilee; it shall be holy to you. You shall eat its crops out of the field. On this year of jubilee each of you shall return to his own property (Lev. 25:8-13).

The year of Jubilee involves everything the Sabbath reminds us of. During the Jubilee the ground was not worked, God provided all our needs and looked after us, releasing the slaves and cancelling debts. What a clear picture of God's grace and salvation, when the slaves are released and return home, and debts are wiped out. All of this was in order to remind us that we have no control over the times. We cannot even control what happens to us. That reminds us that we are not that important, and God can certainly manage without us. The reason God chose us is His love and His grace, not our importance. We can rest, since God and the world can manage just fine without us.

The Sabbath as a Place

Now that we have understood a little of what the Sabbath is. and what it teaches us by returning to the epistle to the Hebrews 3:11-18 and digging a little deeper.

"As I swore in my wrath, they shall not enter my rest." Take care, brethren, that there not be in any one of you an evil, unbelieving heart that falls away from the living God. But encourage one another day after day, as long as it is still called "Today," so that none of you will be hardened by the deceitfulness of sin. For we have become partakers of Christ, if we hold fast the beginning of our assurance firm until the end, while it is said, "Today if you hear His voice, do not harden your hearts, as when they provoked me."

For who provoked Him when they had

heard? Indeed, did not all those who came out of Egypt led by Moses? And with whom was He angry for forty years? Was it not with those who sinned, whose bodies fell in the wilderness? And to whom did He swear that they would not enter His rest, but to those who were disobedient?

God promised those who believed in Him that we would enter His rest. The rest mentioned here is a place, not a time. It is mentioned here as the Promised Land God wants us to enter into as conquerors. He warns us to guard our hearts, to keep our faith, to encourage each other, to hold on, and to not sin or harden our hearts, so that we will enter the rest. When He mentions those who are unable to enter in, He details why. One thing in particular is mentioned in chapter 3:19, "So we see that they were not able to enter because of unbelief." Again, in Heb. 4:2, "For indeed we have had good news preached to us, just as they also; but the word they heard did not profit them, because it was not united by faith in those who heard." We read that those who did not believe – those who heard the word but it was met with unbelief – did not enter into the rest.

What Is Faith?
One of the best known passages in Hebrews is chapter 11, the chapter of faith, which says, "Now faith is the assurance of things hoped for, the conviction of things not seen" (11:1), and "without faith it is impossible to please Him, for he who comes to God must believe that He is and that He is a rewarder of those who seek Him" (11:6). These are just two of the pearls in this chapter, which deals entirely with faith. The concept of faith, and the need to have faith in order to enter into the rest, is an important, central concept in the epistle to

the Hebrews. This concept is returned to over and over. That is why this epistle has an entire chapter dedicated to faith, and to people of faith who, on one hand, did wonderful things for God by faith. On the other hand they suffered terrible things for God by faith, because without faith it is impossible to enter into the place of rest that God has promised to us.

Faith is a term that many believers in Jesus use a lot without fully understanding. Some speak of faith as if it were a kind of feeling, or guided imagery that we have to strive to create in our mind, clinging to that picture with all our strength until God gives us according to our faith. The problem with this description of faith is that it is the opposite of what faith really is, because faith is first of all assurance, as we read in Heb. 11:1. Assurance is not created by effort. The best example of faith is how you trust the chair you are sitting on right now. No one came into the room, looked at the chair, checked it out, and wondered whether the chair will hold him up or not. You simply placed all your weight on the chair without thinking about it. When you sit on the chair you do not try to help the chair support you. You sit down with all your weight in complete confidence. What would happen if we were to try and help the chair? A stretched muscle and pain. I am sorry to say this, but many of us live our lives in Messiah like that. We are not completely sure that He can hold us up so we try to help Him a little. Then we wonder why the life of faith seems so difficult. The reason is that we do not know how to rest in God. Each of you readers is sitting, reclining, or laying down right now, and that is the clearest picture of faith. When we do not believe that God can hold us up, we do not rest nor enter His rest. Instead, we try to help Him, and then our muscles strain under the effort, which keeps us from resting.

In the passage we have read we saw that those who do not enter the rest are called disobedient and rebellious against God. It says that if I try to make an effort to believe instead of entering the rest – if I try to do all kinds of things for God in order to make Him pleased with me, in order to change, in order to be sanctified, or in anyway disallow Him do the work and simply accept what He does – then I am disobedient. I am resisting what He says, and I do not enter the rest.

Chapter 3:18 and 4:6-7 speaks to the disobedient:

> And to whom did He swear that they would not enter His rest, but to those who were disobedient? . . . Therefore, since it remains for some to enter it, and those who formerly had good news preached to them failed to enter because of disobedience, He again fixes a certain day, "Today," saying through David after so long a time just as has been said before, "Today if you hear His voice, do not harden your hearts."

It is written here that the disobedient did not enter into the rest because of rebellion and hardness of heart. Whoever rebels says, "I am the king, not You! I will do it, not You! I will do it my way, not Your way." It also talks of hardness of heart.[4] The word used in Hebrew refers to a muscle. When a muscle is at rest, it is soft and pliable. When it makes an effort it becomes hard. It is written here that people do not enter the rest if they harden their hearts.

They did not enter in because they did not believe. They did not believe that the work has already been completed since the foundation of the world. They tried to enter the Kingdom of God by their works. It is important to understand that we are not only saved by grace, but that we live in grace. This means that we are justified by grace, we are sanctified by grace, and we are transformed by the grace of God. Justification, sanctification and transformation do not come about through our own efforts. Our efforts bring the opposite result of hardness of heart and rebellion. There is only one way to obtain justification, sanctification and transformation. That is by entering His rest, trusting Him, receiving the rest, and giving ourselves to God. As it is written, "[N]ot by works lest anyone should boast" (Eph. 2:8).

Enter into the Sabbath

So now the question is, who does enter into the rest? The answer is, whoever is numbered among the people of God enters in (Heb. 4:9). Even though entering into the rest is against our nature, God's people are those who believe the promise that God has done it all and completed His work. Believe the promise in His call to enter into the rest, and stop all the works knowing that the world will not fall apart. Our spiritual world will not fall apart if we rest, if we stop striving to please God to earn points with Him.

Chapter 11 speaks of faith, and of those who did various things through faith. A synonym to faith is rest in God, because confidence makes us rest without effort. If I have no confidence in someone, I am always worried. If my wife did not trust me, then every time I was away from her she would be worrying. She would be anxious. "Is he going to remain faithful to me?" But since she trusts me she can be at peace and rest. If we trust God we have no need to worry that He will not provide. We have no need to worry that He does not know what is going on. The fact that we are not completely able to understand God does not change the fact that we can trust Him, because He rules over all things and loves us.

Faith is first and foremost expressed in rest – rest in Him. It is written that ceasing from our own efforts and the "muscle" of our hearts, and instead receiving from God all that He has without rebellion, and without objecting to what He gives express our obedience. The ones who make a great effort and do not rest are hardening their hearts and disobeying God's word.

Heb. 4:10 tell us, "For the one who has entered His rest has himself also rested from his works, as God did from His." We are told that the people of God enter His rest, and then that whoever enters His rest has ceased from works. The result of entering the rest of God is that we also rest from all our efforts and activities and work.

Heb. 4:1 tells us, "Therefore, let us fear if, while a promise remains of entering His rest, any one of you may seem to have come short of it." The author is speaking here of the believing Jews (and the non-Jews), not to unbelievers, and says, "I am worried that some of you may come short of the rest of God." This shows us that there are believers in Jesus who do not live in God's rest. They do not live in the Promised Land. They are still living in the desert because the Promised Land is a place of rest where we enjoy our inheritance, the place of the Sabbath where God rests from all His works, and the place where we too are called to rest from all our works and receive all that He has prepared for us. The author of the epistle warns the believers in Jesus not to work hard any longer, but to simply enter into the rest.

We are taught a lot these days that if we do not do this thing or another, or make an effort here, or do not stand firm there, then we are not doing God's will. That is not true. We are doing God's will only when we let go and allow Him to do it. Just when we cooperate with Him and do not harden our hearts to oppose Him, then all the glory goes to Him and not to us!

Many Christian television shows are full of advertisements from organizations or "the ministry" of this or that person, and requests for financial support. That often causes me to shudder because there's a lot of "me, mine, we, and ours." People go around the world talking very much about their ministry, and very little about the ministry of God. To build "my ministry" – that is the goal of many. I knew a believer in Jesus who was still very young in faith, had not lived long with God, but had chosen a name for his ministry very quickly. He even had a nice logo. His priorities were upside down. He didn't have a lot to do in the Lord's service yet, but he had a logo already. If we serve God, the organizations and ministries we run are not ours, they are His. He will use us to the glory of His name. Bob Dylan once wrote a song saying that we either serve God, or we serve the devil. Part of our problem is that we think God needs us, so we are the ones to do things – "serve" – and take away from God the glory He deserves, when He is the one that works through us. So how do we really keep the Sabbath? Chapter 4:11 tell us, "Therefore let us be diligent to enter that rest." We are called to be diligent, but only in one thing: to enter that rest. The effort required of us is the effort to stop making an effort! That is the most difficult thing to do, which is why the writer uses the words "be diligent." When you strive to enter something, you push forward in the effort to get in. In the story of the four friends[5] who brought their sick friend to Jesus, we read that they did not strive to heal their friend; they strove to bring the sick man to Jesus' feet. We are to strive, to be diligent, and to do the same thing by coming to the feet of Jesus. God created us so that we would be intimate with Him and become more like Him. Our effort has to be focused on being with Him, in His presence, in order to be close to Him.

Let Go and Know That I Am God

When my eldest son came for a surprise visit after we had not seen him for a year and a half, my wife could not believe her eyes. She had just woken up, so she was surprised when she saw him. She called his name softly and hesitantly, and then broke out into shouts of joy and excitement, calling his name in a loud voice. She hugged him, sat next to him, touched him, and looked at him over and over to make sure it really was him. That was so touching that she cried, and I cried too. She did not say, "Daniel, let's do something together, let's work together, let's clean up, let's wash the dishes, let's go evangelize." She simply came to him and hugged him, to be with him, to touch him.

Very few congregations in the Western world have people who just come together for no special reason except the enjoyment of each other's company. In Israel things are different. Our culture is such that people get together just to enjoy each other, as we saw earlier in the story of our neighbor. God simply loves to be with us. That is love.

God created us so that we would have intimacy, which is possible for us only if we stop running around doing all kinds of things for him, and come to sit on his lap, so to speak. One thing I did when our son paid us a surprise visit was to ask him to come and sit on my knees. He was not a little boy any longer; in fact he isn't far off thirty years old. But he came and sat on my knees, and I enjoyed it and hugged him and held on to him. That is a wonderful picture of the Sabbath!

One of the commandments I think is the hardest for us is in Psalms 46:10. "Cease *striving* and know that I am God; I will be exalted among the nations, I will be exalted in the earth." The King James Translation, "be still" misses what is actually written. It sounds as if saying, be still, calm down. But the Hebrew word *leharpot*, means much more than to be calm, although that is part of it. The Hebrew word means, "You are hanging on to something, now let go, release it!" We are told here that the only way we will know that He is the God exalted among the nations, exalted in the earth, is by letting go.

"Let go and know," or, "Cease striving and know." What does the word "know" mean? Today the word "know" is used in the sense of intellectual knowledge and information, but in the Scriptures the word is something much deeper. "Now Adam knew Eve his wife, and she conceived and bore Cain, and said, 'I have acquired a man from the Lord'. . . And Cain knew his wife, and she conceived and bore Enoch" (Gen. 4:1, 17 NKJV). To "know" in the Bible means to have intimate relations, not just to know about someone, but to really know someone. I am glad that I do not only know about my wife, I also *know* my wife (and that's why we have three sons!). The difference between the way the word is used in the Bible and its modern meaning is huge. This verse tells us, "You want to know? You want an intimate relationship with Me? You want to see me high and lifted up among the nations, exalted in the earth? Let go. Stop striving and hanging onto to things. Let go and allow Me. Stop and relax your grip, for that is how you will get to where there is no need to work so hard". To live by letting go of everything but the effort to come and sit at Jesus' feet – that is where God wants us to be. That is the place God wants us to "be diligent" and "strive" to enter. That is the Promised Land. This is how we are to live every day, all day. That is the Sabbath. Sabbath was not given just for the Sabbath day or for the Feasts or for the night. Sabbath is the place God wants us to live our lives in all the time. Let go and know God.

This commandment was not a new invention of the New Covenant. "Let go and know" is written in the psalms. Zechariah 4:6 also tell us, "'Not by might nor by power, but by My Spirit,' says the LORD of hosts." Often, as believers in Jesus, we say that "we need to let go in order to come to faith and receive Jesus, but now that we are believers, both might and power is needed and the Spirit will help **us** and strengthen **us**." We are taught that, "Now that you are believers, come and do great things for God!" We see the Spirit of God as Someone who helps **us** do great things for Him. We see Him as Someone who helps **us** serve Him through **our** organizations and ministries. God becomes my helper so that I can have fame, wealth, authority, and power.

"Not by might nor by power, but by My Spirit" – that is how we are to draw near to God and repent, and that is how we must live our daily lives in God. That is how we must rest in Him and follow Him: following the pillar of fire and the pillar of cloud. When He says, "Get up!" we have to get up. When He tells us to strike the stone with a stick so that water will come out, we will strike the stone with a stick. When He says to speak to the stone, we will not strike it with a stick, we will speak to it. That is what is called letting go, resting in Him. That is the Promised Land. That is the place God wants us to enter into. That is the place the letter to the Hebrews is talking about. The people of Israel are striving to enter the Promised Land, and are doing so in exactly the opposite way from what God has commanded. Instead of letting go, we add more laws and strive harder.

How should the Sabbath be observed today? By observing more and more commandments and avoiding a lot of things? There are so many rules of the Sabbath we are supposed to strive to keep and observe – or avoid doing – that in the end, the Sabbath becomes the opposite of what a Sabbath really is. The Sabbath was made for us as a sign. The Sabbath reminds us of the place of rest, the place of letting go and trusting God. The place where we allow Him to do His work in us and through us.

We have seen that Jesus has prepared a better place for us. We have seen that the epistle to the Hebrews speaks of the Sabbath as a place rather than a time. We have seen that God created all things. The Sabbath was Adam's first day of life, and he did not have to make any effort to obtain anything – everything was received by grace. God does not need to rest. The world was not created because of what Adam did, and its existence does not depend on the work of Adam (or the children of Adam). The first thing Adam had to do was learn to rest. We have seen that, in both Jewish tradition and Christian understanding, the world enters into a Sabbath when the Millennium of rest and peace is ushered in. We have seen that the Sabbath speaks of the past, as well as the future and the present. We have seen that the Ten Commandments instruct us to keep the Sabbath in order to remember that God is the One who created the world, not us. He rested on the seventh day and sanctified it. He is the One who delivered us from Egypt, and from bondage into freedom. It is He who saved us, not we ourselves. We have seen that we are to remember that God created all things and there is no work left unfinished. It is not necessary, nor can we strive to be found worthy to receive what God has done. We must remember where we come from, to remember that we were slaves, separated from God by sin. Remember that God is the One who delivered us, not we ourselves by virtue of our works. He delivered us with a mighty hand and an outstretched arm.

We have to remember that now He is in control. He does not need us, but He loves us. We tend to forget that and think that God cannot manage without us. God does not need you, nor does He need me. But He loves us, and that makes all the difference. We need to remember that even now there is no need to strive to receive what He has done, what He does, or what He will do. It is God who transforms and sanctifies us. We have to cooperate with Him by receiving, but we cannot change or purify ourselves. A drowning man cannot save himself. A defiled man cannot purify himself. A man can change himself to a certain degree, but cannot change himself substantially.

We have to remember that it is God who provides all our needs. He always has and always will provide. God works in our lives. He saved us, and He will not leave us alone. He has promised, "I will never desert you, nor will I ever forsake you" (Heb. 13:5).

We have to remember what is going to be in the future, that same perfect place, the place of perfection, the rest and inheritance we all seek. "Eye has not seen and ear has not heard all that God has prepared for those who love Him" (1 Cor. 2:9). We find it hard to understand how there could be a place with no pain and no tears, a place where the world is perfect. and there is no death. There are no dangerous animals, and there is no decay; a place where we will be together with God in perfect intimacy. We feel a tiny bit of that sometimes during worship, when we approach God in prayer, or when God pours His love upon us. Such intimacy is disturbed today by sin, thoughts, and troubles, but in the future we will be in His presence for eternity and will see Him face to face. The Sabbath helps us to remember everything that our pride and human nature try to forget.

The Sabbath is a situation and place where God

wants us to be every day, not just on the Sabbath. It is where we let go of our own efforts. A place where we trust and rest in Him, and allow Him to live His life through us; contrary to our human sinful nature.

Jesus Is the Sabbath

More than anything else the letter to the Hebrews talks of Jesus being all in all. The epistle was written to the Hebrews. That is – to Jews. Neither the temple, nor angels, nor prophets; neither Moses nor Abraham, nor the High Priests; neither the Torah, the Sinai covenant, nor the promises given in the Sinai Covenant; nor are sacrifices the purpose of life with God. The Sabbath is. The purpose of our life with God is that same place of rest He prepared for us. He prepared us a better place, an inheritance. He prepared a better thing, which is Himself, and He calls us to live in Him.

In Ephesians chapters one and two, the words "in Him" and "in" are repeated many times:

Blessed be the God and Father of our Lord Jesus Christ, who has blessed us with every spiritual blessing **in** the heavenly places **in** Christ, just as He chose us **in Him** before the foundation of the world, that we would be holy and blameless before Him. **In** love He predestined us to adoption as sons through Jesus Christ to Himself, according to the kind intention of His will, to the praise of the glory of His grace, which He freely bestowed on us **in** the Beloved. **In Him** we have redemption through His blood, the forgiveness of our trespasses, according to the riches of His grace which He lavished on us. **In** all wisdom and insight He made known to us the mystery of His will, according to His kind intention which

He purposed **in Him** with a view to an administration suitable to the fullness of the times, that is, the summing up of all things **in Christ**, things in the heavens and things on the earth. **In Him** also we have obtained an inheritance, having been predestined according to His purpose who works all things after the counsel of His will (Eph. 1:3-11).

In Him – in Christ – we find the place He has prepared for us. That is the Sabbath.

The Sabbath points to Jesus because it speaks to us of the beginning, the middle and the end: yesterday, today, and tomorrow: the past, the present, and the future. The Scriptures are very clear about this in several places. For instance, in Rom. 9:16 we read, "So then it does not depend on the man who wills or the man who runs, but on God who has mercy." It is so clearly written yet still as believers we forget the message over and over again. It is not in the hands of whoever tries and strives and insists – it is in the hands of God, the One who has already prepared everything. All that is left is for us to receive what He has done. "I, the Lord, am your God, Who brought you up from the land of Egypt; Open your mouth wide and I will fill it" (Ps. 81:10). What keeps God from filling us more is that we do not open our mouth wider. It is not up to man who wants to strive, but is given by God to whoever enters His rest. "I am the Alpha and the Omega, the first and the last, the beginning and the end" (Rev. 22:13). Jesus is God. The Messiah is the Alpha and the Omega, the first and the last.

The first thing Adam experienced on his creation was the rest of the Sabbath. The last thing we will receive is the Sabbath. Jesus is the Alpha and the

Omega, the beginning and the end. I love the word "end" because it not only means the end of something, it also means a purpose. Jesus is the purpose. We are told that when we see Him, we will be changed to be like Him. The more we are with Him, in His presence, the more we become like Him. We will not become like Him by doing a lot for Him, but because we are with Him, see Him and look to Him. When we see Him in the Scriptures, when we simply sit in his lap like children, put our heads on His chest and listen to His heart, we become more like Him. The Sabbath points us to Jesus. Jesus is the Sabbath.

The epistle to the Hebrews was written in order to help us make a very important transition: from work associated with the worship of God (and in Hebrew, "worship" is the same word as "work") – which requires effort and focuses on the temple and the sacrificial system – to the thinking that focuses on God's rest. He prepared it for us from the beginning, but we have not entered it. That is why today God has prepared another day. "Today if you hear His voice, do not harden your hearts" (Heb. 4:6-7) because "To Him be the glory in the church" (Eph. 3:21) forever and ever. To Him be the glory in us and in the church. To Him! We have no right to detract even slightly from His glory. There is nothing I can do for Him that He has not already done. There is nothing I can fill that He lacks, there is nothing in Him that needs me. There are things He allows me to participate in with Him by His grace, but not because He needs me. God did not choose me because He needed me. He chose me because He loves me! What a liberating Gospel this is. This is the Good News of the letter to the Hebrews. Jesus is the Sabbath and we must live in Him.

Jesus is all in all and all glory be to Him alone, forever and ever amen.

Let us trust in Him, and enter the rest. A peaceful Sabbath to us all!

---

[1] "at the conclusion of the septennate the son of David will come. R. Joseph demurred: But so many septennates have passed, yet has he not come! The Tanna debe Eliyyahu teaches: The world is to exist six thousand years. In the first two thousand there was desolation; two thousand years the Torah flourished; and the next two thousand years is the Messianic era, but through our many iniquities all these years have been lost. He should have come at the beginning of the last two thousand years; the delay is due to our sins." Sanhedrin 97

[2] Acts 17:26 "and He made from one man every nation of mankind to live on all the face of the earth, having determined their appointed times and the boundaries of their habitation..."

[3] The first and last day of Passover is a resting day (v. 7,8), the first day of Passover is called a Sabbath (v. 11,15), it is forbidden to work on the Feast of Weeks (Pentecost) (v. 21), The day of blowing of the Trumpets (modern Jewish New Year), is called a Sabbath (v. 24-25), Day of Atonement is called a Sabbath (v. 32), and is The Feast of Tabernacle, the first and last day are called a Sabbath (v.39)

[4] Psalms 81:12, "So I gave them over to the stubbornness of their heart, To walk in their own devices." Jer. 11:8, "Yet they did not obey or incline their ear, but walked, each one, in the stubbornness of his evil heart; therefore I brought on them all the words of this covenant, which I commanded *them* to do, but they did not." 2 Pet. 2:10 "...and especially those who indulge the flesh in *its* corrupt desires and despise authority. Daring, self-willed, they do not tremble when they revile angelic majesties..."

[5] Mark 2:3-12